NEW WORK SCHEDULES IN PRACTICE

Managing Time in a Changing Society

NEW WORK SCHEDULES IN PRACTICE
Managing Time in a Changing Society

Stanley D. Nollen, Ph.D.
Georgetown University
School of Business Administration

Van Nostrand Reinhold/Work in America Institute Series

VAN NOSTRAND REINHOLD COMPANY
NEW YORK CINCINNATI TORONTO LONDON MELBOURNE

Library of Congress Catalog Card Number: 81-7574
ISBN: 0-442-26899-8

Manufactured in the United States of America

Published by Van Nostrand Reinhold Company
135 West 50th Street, New York, N.Y. 10020

Van Nostrand Reinhold Limited
1410 Birchmount Road
Scarborough, Ontario M1P 2E7, Canada

Van Nostrand Reinhold Australia Pty. Ltd.
17 Queen Street
Mitcham, Victoria 3132, Australia

Van Nostrand Reinhold Company Limited
Molly Millars Lane
Wokingham, Berkshire, England

Published simultaneously in Canada by Van Nostrand Reinhold Ltd.

15   14   13   12   11   10   9   8   7   6   5   4   3   2   1

Library of Congress Cataloging in Publication Data

Nollen, Stanley D.
    New work schedules in practice.

    (Van Nostrand Reinhold/Work in America Institute
series)
    Includes index.
    1. Hours of labor, Flexible.   I. Title
II. Series
HD5109.N64   331.25′72   81-7574
ISBN 0-442-26899-8   AACR2

VNR/WORK IN AMERICA INSTITUTE SERIES

The VNR/Work in America Institute Series is designed to provide practical insight into new and better ways to advance productivity and the quality of working life. The objective is to create heightened awareness of the opportunities for an enriched work life that can exist in innovative organizations, and to reveal the benefits of linking people and production in a common goal, through clearer understanding of the key factors contributing to worker output and job satisfaction.

The Series will provide guidance on a number of concerns that influence work performance, not only in today's work environment, but also in the even more complex world of work that lies ahead. Titles in the World of Work Series will focus on five fundamental issues affecting the work community: (1) *The quality of working life,* exploring opportunity, recognition, participation, and rewards for employees to optimize their involvement in and contribution to the work organization; (2) *Productivity,* focusing on the human factors in the productivity equation, to increase both individual and organizational output through more effective use of human resources; (3) *Education and the world of work,* discussing ways to improve the match between the entry-level worker and the job, by building bridges from education to the world of work; (4) *Employee-management cooperation,* recognizing that employees contribute important know-how and ingenuity to increase output, reduce waste, maintain product quality, and improve morale; and (5) *National labor force policy,* examining policies of the United States and other industrialized nations as they affect productivity and the quality of working life.

Preface

New work schedules, when carefully chosen, designed, and executed, are among the best investments an employer can make. The cost is small, the risk is low, and the potential return is high. Best of all, they benefit all parties involved.

Although demographic, social, and economic conditions have altered drastically since 1940, when the eight-hour day and 40-hour week became the standard, the vast majority of American workers still work eight (or seven, or seven-and-a-half) hours a day and five days a week, with fixed times for starting and stopping. As a result, their work schedules conflict in many ways with their personal needs, often unnecessarily. In the 1970s, however, thousands of employers voluntarily adopted "new" schedules that departed from the norm: flexitime, compressed weeks, part time, job sharing, and work sharing. In 1977, 11.1 million people were voluntary part-time workers. As of May 1980 *7.6 million workers,* or 12 percent of those on full time, nonfarm wage and salary jobs, were on flexitime or other variable schedules.

These figures represent a good start, but Work in America Institute is persuaded that there are opportunities for many more millions of American workers to go on to new schedules which simultaneously advantage employers, employees, unions, and the general public. *New Work Schedules in Practice* is meant to inspire, encourage, and guide those who have thought about trying new schedules but have held off doing so because of uncertainty about either the techniques or the consequences.

For any manager or union official who has considered adopting new work schedules, *New Work Schedules in Practice* offers a mine of information and experience to answer such questions as: "What will work best in my organization? How should I go about gaining support? Where are the boobytraps? Is it worth the effort?"

It is eye opening to learn that informed estimates place the percentage of the work force currently on flexitime in West Germany at over 45 percent!

Some other eye openers:

• It is widely believed that unions oppose the introduction of new work schedules. The cases of the International Federation of Professional and Technical Engineers, Local 21, and the Service Employees International Union, Local 6, refute that. Unions not only favor but, indeed, sometimes demand new work schedules, provided that they (the unions) share with management the responsibility for selecting, designing, and implementing them. What unions oppose is having an employer unilaterally thrust a new work schedule on employees without the unions participating in the decision or, ultimately, sharing in the credit.

• It is also widely believed that new work schedules are for white-collar workers and are not really suited for blue-collar workers, least of all in manufacturing. Again, cases in the real world prove otherwise. Production workers in the Fa. Mey, Fa. Thomae, and J. Hengstler companies of West Germany are happily using flexitime. Assembly workers at the Sercel and Hewlett Packard companies on the West Coast of the United States enjoy flexitime. Continuous-process shift workers at Shell plants in Sarnia, Canada, and in the United Kingdom are on compressed-week schedules with a great deal of flexibility. And the Physio-Control Corporation, near Seattle, offers its employees three different kinds of compressed-work schedules as well as the conventional eight-hour day. Most of those on a compressed workweek are production workers.

• Those who have been wanting to raise voluntary part-time work to equal status with full-time work have long struggled with the problem of equitably apportioning fringe benefits. Practical solutions were found in the cases of the Port of Seattle and the State of Hawaii.

• One of the main reasons unions have been strongly opposed to flexitime with debit and credit hours and to compressed workweeks is that both schedules expose workers to the danger of overtime violations. The problem was solved to the satisfaction of unions, workers, and management in the cases of six public-sector organizations in California and the International Federation of Professional and Technical Engineers, Local 21; the Group Health Cooperative of Puget Sound and the Office and Professional Employees Union, Local 8; and the Municipality of Metropolitan Seattle's pollution-control plants and the Service Employees International Union, Local 6.

• Many employers have the impression that new work schedules complicate the job of management. In some ways they do, although, as a rule, the extra effort is amply repaid by improvements in attendance, punctuality, and morale. Furthermore, there are cases in which the work of management is actually simplified by new schedules. For example, at Shell Canada's Sarnia plant and at Pedigree Pet Foods, Shell Chemical, and Savalco, Ltd., in the United Kingdom, the workers relieved management almost entirely of the perennial headache of ensuring coverage on continuous-process shift work. Comparable responsibility was assumed by unionized workers on flexitime at the Group Health Cooperative of Puget Sound and by job sharers at the XYZ Company.

• Since most new work schedules stay in effect only as long as employees want them, it is a truism to say they are popular. Less well understood is the fact that new work schedules are good business for the employer. Almost without exception new schedules either maintain or improve productivity. They consistently reduce absenteeism, lateness, and overtime. By reducing conflicts between work and personal needs, they enable workers to devote more wholehearted effort to the job at hand. They encourage workers to take more responsibility for organizing their work. They enlarge the pool of talent from which the employer can recruit. They raise employees' approval of the enterprise.

• Lastly, as the cases of community-wide flexitime programs show, new work schedules serve the interests of the general public by facilitating urban transport and reducing the consumption of gasoline for commuting.

New Work Schedules in Practice is one of two books produced by an 18-month Work in America Institute policy study, jointly funded by The Commonwealth Fund and Carnegie Corporation of New York. The other book, *New Work Schedules for a Changing Society,* is a policy report. Our study focused not on the how-to's of new work schedules (which have been explored at length elsewhere), but on the policy issues that determine whether a new schedule is introduced at all, and, if so, how well it succeeds. In a sense, the two books are obverse and reverse. *New Work Schedules in Practice* emphasizes actual case descriptions (occasionally under a fictitious name) to illustrate major policy issues; *New Work Schedules in a Changing Society* emphasizes policy issues and recommendations, drawing on real cases for illustration.

Much of the information in the book is based on first-hand research by the principal author and his colleagues, some by telephone, but most through site visits, both in the United States and Europe. Before selecting cases for further investigation, Dr. Nollen conducted a broad survey of U.S. employers with new work schedules, and a survey of the literature (summarized in *Alternative Work Patterns*, a volume in the Highlights of the Literature series published by Work in America Institute). His associates contributed their specialized knowledge of job sharing, of area-wide flexitime programs, and of European advances.

The result is 35 detailed case studies and a large number of brief references. A wide spectrum has been covered: manufacturing and service industries; batch, assembly-line, and process industries; blue-collar and white-collar work; union and nonunion companies; successes and failures; high-technology and low-technology firms; private and public employers. In addition to the standard forms of flexitime, compressed workweeks, job sharing, work sharing, and part-time work, there are many variations of these forms. An open-minded reader cannot help but conclude that the only limit to the design of new work schedules is ingenuity.

The structure of the book is well suited to its intended use. Originally it had been conceived as a series of chapters, each treating a single category of work schedule (e.g., flexitime, compressed workweeks, and so on) and related policy issues. As the research proceeded, the principal author and Work in America Institute became increasingly aware that the categories were anything but static and that the possibilities for combination and permutation were innumerable. The cases, therefore, have been organized according to the policy issues they illuminate, paralleling the companion volume, *New Work Schedules for a Changing Society*.

The issues are as follows:

- Who can use new schedules?
- What are the costs and benefits?
- What role do unions play in changing work schedules?
- How do new schedules affect individuals and families?
- What is involved in managing new work schedules?
- Can new work schedules serve as alternatives to layoff?
- Do new work schedules help to save energy and increase transportation efficiency?
- Does government have a role in furthering new work schedules?

When a case touches more than one key issue, the main body of the case appears under the most appropriate issue heading, while supplementary material is reported in other chapters. This arrangement makes it clear that *New Work Schedules in Practice* is a handbook for decision makers rather than a textbook for students.

The principal author and Work in America Institute wish to acknowledge all those who helped assemble and produce the book:

- Robert Zager, vice-president of policy studies, for his professionalism and high standards in directing the policy study and working with the principal author and other contributors to produce this volume.
- Gretl Meier, pioneer writer and researcher in the field of job sharing; Virginia Hider Martin, consultant with Vail Associates; and William McEwan Young, University of Technology, Loughborough, England, for their invaluable research and contributions to this book.
- Those company managers, employees, and labor union officials, too numerous to name, who gave generously of their time, and on whose information the case studies are based.
- Members of the policy study's national advisory committee, and members of the board of directors of Work in America Institute, for suggesting case sites and contacts.
- Lisa Murphy for transcribing research notes, charts, and graphs.
- Beatrice Walfish for an outstanding job of editing.
- Frances Harte for managing the production of the book.
- Virginia Lentini for keeping the threads of the project unsnarled.
- Joyce Derian for her patient and serene supervision of a difficult publishing endeavor.

The statements made and views expressed in this book are those of the primary author and contributors and do not necessarily reflect the views of either The Commonwealth Fund or the Carnegie Corporation of New York.

Jerome M. Rosow
President
Work in America
Institute, Inc.

Contents

NEW WORK SCHEDULES IN PRACTICE

Managing Time in a Changing Society

1.
New Work Schedules

WHAT ARE NEW WORK SCHEDULES?

New work schedules are alternatives to the standard of eight fixed hours of work for five days a week. That this is the standard is not in doubt. Over 80 percent of all employees put in five days a week (not counting farmers). Nearly two-thirds of all employees work 40 hours in those five days. Work starting time is predominantly 8:00 A.M. and quitting time is usually 5:00 P.M., and less than one worker in ten has any choice about his or her work schedule. The standard fixed-hours, five-day, 40-hour workweek has been with us since the 1950s, more than a generation ago.[1]

New work schedules permit changes in the standard work schedule. The changes are of these kinds: (1) they let the length of work time change (e.g., 30 instead of 40 hours a week, or 1500 instead of 2080 hours a year, as in part-time employment); (2) they let the allocation of work time change (e.g., ten instead of eight hours a day, or four instead of five days a week, as in compressed workweeks); and (3) they let control over work time change (e.g., decisions by workers instead of managers, as in flexitime).

These changes appear to be simple enough. They are not complex, and they are not costly. And they offer some benefits to both companies and workers. However, new work patterns are not just minor changes in work schedules. They are an adjustment in the sociotechnical system of the company. They are an element of human-resource management. They usually require some changes in management practices and values.

What exactly are new work schedules? How do they work? What distinguishes one new work schedule from another? Here are brief definitions.

1

Part-Time Employment

Part-time employment is an umbrella term that includes all work less than full time. How many hours that is varies. In U.S. government statistics, people who work less than 35 hours a week have been counted as part-timers. For federal government employees, 32 hours a week is the dividing line between part-time and full-time hours (beginning in 1979). Many companies say you must work at least 20 hours a week to have part-time status. While neither the idea nor the use of part-time employment overall is new, several ways in which it is now used are.

The status of the part-time employee is more important than the hours worked. There are two key variables: permanence and choice. Based on these variables, there are several kinds of part-time employment:

- *Permanent Part-Time Employment.* The job and the worker are expected to be part time for a long time. Both are regular and stable.
- *Job Sharing.* A new version of permanent part-time employment in which two (or more) part-timers share one job. The workers are part time while the job is full time.
- *Work Sharing.* A temporary reduction in working hours chosen by a group of employees during economic hard times, usually as an alternative to layoffs.
- *Temporary Part-Time Employment.* The worker is expected to stay at a job only a short time, either because the job does not last or the worker does not have a long-term commitment to the labor force (temporary employment can also be full time, of course).
- *Phased Retirement.* Part-time employment chosen by employees who gradually change from full-time to retired status.
- *Workyear Contracts.* Annual agreements between a worker and his or her company about how much time will be put in and where. Usually these agreements, which are rare, involve part-time work distributed in blocks over the year.

Part-time employment is allocated as part day, part week (full day), or part year. Part-timers may or may not have a choice about their working times.

Some uses of permanent part-time employment and job sharing will be discussed in this book, but not all. Case study research on phased retirement is available in Jacobson (1980), information on work sharing in companies in a report by Best (1981), and an introduction to work-year contracts in Teriet (1977).[2]

Flexitime

Flexible work hours (flexitime for short) means that employees choose their starting and quitting times within limits set by management.[3] Flexitime schedules differ along three dimensions: (1) daily vs. periodic (e.g., weekly or monthly) choice of starting and quitting times; (2) variable vs. constant length of working day (whether credit and debit hours are allowed); and (3) core time—the hours of the day when all employees are required to be present. Here are the different types of flexitime, from the least to the most flexible:

- *Flexitour.* Flexitime that requires employees to choose a starting and quitting time, stick with that schedule for a period, and work eight hours every day.
- *Gliding Time.* Daily variation in starting and quitting times is permitted, but every day still must be eight hours (or another company-set length of day).
- *Variable Day.* Credit and debit hours are allowed (e.g., one can work ten hours one day and six hours another day), as long as the total hours worked come out even at the end of the week or month.
- *Maxiflex.* Credit and debit hours are allowed, and core time is not required on all days, such as Monday and Friday; workers can use maxiflex as they do a compressed workweek.

Flexitime can be used with part-time as well as full-time employment, but flexitime does not change the numbers of hours worked. The variable-day and maxiflex versions enable workers to reallocate their working time over the day or week.

Another new work pattern that looks like flexitime and is sometimes confused with it is *staggered hours*. Staggered hours is a work schedule in which groups of employees regularly arrive at and leave from work at different times established by management. For example, one department's employees may begin work at 8:00 A.M. and leave eight hours later, while another department's employees arrive at 8:30 A.M. and leave eight hours later. Staggered hours differ from the most conservative flexitime model (flexitour) in that management sets the schedule rather than employees and entire groups of workers follow the same schedule.

Compressed Workweeks

Compressed workweeks refer to full-time employment accomplished in less than five days per week. The schedules that are used include (1) four-day workweeks with ten-hour days, (2) three-day workweeks with twelve-hour days, (3) four-and-one-half-day workweeks with four nine-hour days and one four-hour day (usually Friday), and (4) the 5/4–9 plan of alternating five-day workweeks and four-day workweeks with nine-hour days throughout.

Compressed workweeks do not change the length of work time, nor do they give workers control over their working hours (unless the compressed workweek also explicitly has flexitime); they do reallocate work time over the week.

Why New Work Schedules?

If the standard five-day, 40-hour workweek has such wide and long-term usage, why bother with alternatives to it? Of course, wide usage need not mean wide favor—if there is no alternative, people will likely accept what they have. And we do not suggest that every company should use every new work schedule. We only suggest new work schedules as options to be picked up when and where they are useful. Flexitime still lets those people who want to work 8:00 A.M. to 5:00 P.M., Monday through Friday, do so. Part-time options still permit those people who need to work full time do so.

As options, new work schedules offer some economic gains to companies, and they offer some human gains to workers. Experiences from hundreds of companies demonstrate these possibilities.[4] New work schedules also bring some problems, but usually these are problems that can be solved. As work technology changes, and as workers' expectations change, we believe a look at alternative ways to organize work schedules is worth taking.

WHO USES NEW WORK SCHEDULES?

The question "Who uses new work schedules?" needs answers so that prospective first-time users will have some idea of how widespread these work schedules are. There are actually several questions: (1) How many employees are on these alternative work schedules? (2) How many companies use them? (3) What kinds of companies (industry, size) use them? (4) What kinds of employees (occupation, age, sex) have these work schedules? (5) What are the growth trends?

Part-Time Employment

In 1977, 22.1 percent of all wage and salary workers, or 17.6 million people, were part-time employees. This covers all people who worked less than 35 hours per week, including temporary, intermittent, and involuntary part-time workers. Permanent part-time employees (those who usually and voluntarily work part time) accounted for 13.9 percent of all those who worked, or 11.1 million people. Part-timers average about 20 hours per week. The time pattern is most often part day, but many part-time employees also work full days for part of a week (see table 1-1).

Table 1-1.   Part-Time Employment Models Used, 1977

A. Type	Total	Men	Women
All part-time employees			
percent of all wage and salary workers	22.1	14.5	32.6
number (millions)	17.6	6.7	10.9
Usual voluntary part-time employees			
percent of all who worked	13.9	7.6	22.7
number (millions)	11.1	3.5	7.6

B. Permanent Part-Time Employment Models	Percent of User Firms
Part day, full week, or part week	75
Full day, part week, or part month	49
Minishift	23
Job sharing	22

Note: Data in Panel A refer to nonagricultural industries. Part time means 1–34 hours per week. The total in Panel B exceeds 100 because the catagories are not mutually exclusive and some firms are more than one model.

Sources: William V. Deutermann and Scott Campbell Brown, "Voluntary Part-Time Workers: A Growing Part of the Labor Force," *Monthly Labor Review,* June 1978, pp. 3–10.

Stanley D. Nollen and Virginia H. Martin, *Alternative Work Schedules, Part 2: Permanent Part-Time Employment* (New York: AMACOM, a division of American Management Associations, 1978).

Bureau of Labor Statistics, *Work Experience of the Population in 1977,* Special Labor-Force Report No. 224 (Washington, D.C.: U.S. Government Printing Office, 1978).

Women outnumber men as part-time employees by a large margin; people who are young or old are especially likely to be permanent part-time workers (see table 1-2).

Permanent part-time employment is used much more in some industries and occupations than others. Both wholesale and retail trade as well as service industries use large numbers of permanent part-time workers, both absolutely and relative to their total employment. Mining and manufacturing are especially low-use industries (see table 1-3).

A large number of firms (over two-thirds of all companies) have permanent part-time employees, especially in office and clerical jobs; but they have only a few such employees—between 2 and 7 percent in most cases (see table 1-4).

Permanent part-time employment increased during the 1950s and 1960s, expanding roughly twice as fast as the overall labor force. But there has been no relative growth since then (see figure 1-1). This pattern holds for both women and men.

Flexitime

In 1980, 11.9 percent of all nonfarm wage and salary workers, or 7.6 million people, were on flexible schedules. If professionals, managers,

Table 1-2.   Characteristics of Voluntary Part-Time and Full-Time Workers

Characteristic	Voluntary part time (percent)	Full time (percent)
Marital status and sex—total	100	100
married men	26	55
single men	20	11
women with children ≤ 15 years old	27	12
other women	27	23
Age and sex—total	100	100
young men	21	10
prime-age men	17	39
older men	8	17
young women	19	7
prime-age women	23	19
older women	13	9

Note: Data refer to nonagricultural wage and salary workers in 1973. Young = age < 25; prime-age = 25–49; older = age ≥ 50.

Source: John Owen, "Why Part-Time Workers Tend To Be in Low-Wage Jobs," *Monthly Labor Review,* June 1978, pp. 11–14.

Table 1-3.   Part-Time Employment Usage by Industry and Occupation, 1977

Industry	Usual voluntary part-time number (thousands)	percent
All nonagricultural industries	10,433	13.3
Mining	17	2.2
Construction	225	5.0
Manufacturing	687	3.4
Transportation, public utilities	334	6.2
Wholesale, retail trade	4,168	25.4
Finance, insurance, real estate	410	9.1
Service industries	4,294	19.9
Public administration	257	5.2
Self-employed	972	16.4
Occupation		
All nonagricultural workers	10,665	13.5
White collar	5,427	13.5
professional, technical	1.341	10.9
managerial	328	3.3
sales	1,166	23.8
clerical	2,645	17.2
Blue collar	1,981	7.0
skilled	397	2.9
operatives, except transport	556	5.5
transport operatives	300	9.1
laborers	813	18.9
Service workers, except private household	3,255	31.0

Note: Data refer to wage and salary workers (except for self-employed).

Sources: William V. Deutermann and Scott Campbell Brown, "Voluntary Part-Time Workers: A Growing Part of the Labor Force," *Monthly Labor Review,* June 1978, pp. 3–10.

Stanley D. Nollen, Brenda B. Eddy, and Virginia H. Martin, *Permanent Part-Time Employment: The Manager's Perspective* (New York: Praeger, 1978).

and salespeople are excluded (many of whom have always set their own hours without calling it flexitime), the usage rate is still 8.1 percent. Flexitime is used in all major industry groups, but with a somewhat heavier concentration in finance and insurance and in the federal government than in manufacturing (see table 1-5). (The relatively heavy use of flexitime in the federal government may be partly due to the legislatively mandated experiments with new work schedules that com-

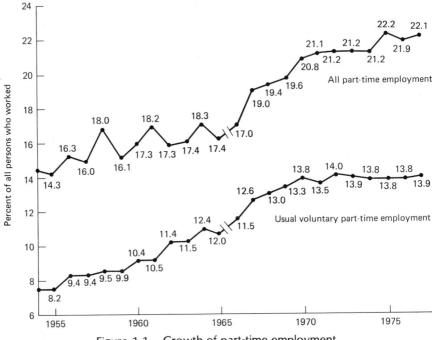

Figure 1-1.   Growth of part-time employment.

Note: Beginning in 1966, persons age 14–15 were excluded, thus making data noncomparable between the 1954–65 and 1966–77 periods; the trend lines have been roughly adjusted for comparability, although the numbers have not.

Source: William V. Deutermann and Scott Campbell Brown, "Voluntary Part-Time Workers: A Growing Part of the Labor Force," *Monthly Labor Review*, June 1978, pp. 3–10.

menced in 1979.) Neither sex, age, nor family status make much difference in flexitime usage, although union members are less likely to be on flexible schedules than nonunion employees (see table 1-6). Flexitime has grown steadily since its inception in the United States, in about 1971 (see figure 1-2). It is more common in Europe than in the United States, especially in Germany and Switzerland where one-third or more of the work force has flexible hours.

Compressed Workweeks

In 1980, 2.7 percent of all full-time nonfarm wage and salary workers, or 1.7 million people, were on compressed workweeks. Of this number,

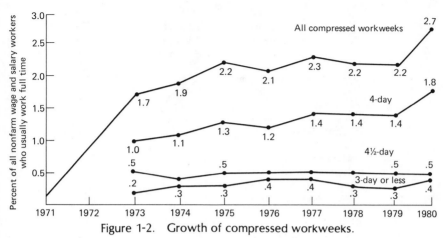

Figure 1-2.   Growth of compressed workweeks.

Sources: Janice Neipert Hedges, "How Many Days Make a Workweek?" *Monthly Labor Review*, April 1975, pp. 29–36. U. S. Bureau of Labor Statistics, News Release, February 24, 1981.

Table 1-4.   Number of Firms Using Part-Time Employment, by Occupation, 1974

Occupation	Percent
All companies	
Production workers	26
Office/Clerical workers	64
Professional/Technical workers	21
Sales workers	14
Manufacturing firms	
Production workers	30
Office/Clerical workers	42
Professional/Technical workers	13
Sales workers	9
Nonmanufacturing firms (retailers, banks, service and nonprofit organizations)	
Production workers	20
Office/Clerical workers	88
Professional/Technical workers	29
Sales workers	21

Source: Bureau of National Affairs, *Bulletin to Management: ASPA–BNA Survey No. 25—Part-Time and Temporary Employees* (Washington, D.C.: Bureau of National Affairs, 1974). Reprinted by special permission. © 1974 by the Bureau of National Affairs, Inc., Washington, D.C.

Table 1-5.   Usage of Flexitime in the U.S. by
Occupation and Industry, 1980 (Full-Time Nonfarm
Wage and Salary Workers)

Occupation and Industry	Number (thousands)	Percent
All occupations	7,638	11.9
professional and technical workers	1,914	15.8
managers and administrators	1,622	20.2
sales workers	878	26.5
clerical workers	1,296	9.8
craft workers	753	7.4
operatives, except transport equipment	387	4.4
transport equipment operatives	388	14.3
laborers	214	7.3
service workers	569	8.7
Occupations, excluding professional and technical workers, managers and administrators, and sales workers	3,608	8.1
All industries	7,922	11.9
mining	83	10.6
construction	439	10.1
manufacturing	1,516	7.9
transportation and public utilities	620	11.7
wholesale and retail trade	1,633	14.7
finance, insurance, and real estate	725	17.1
professional services	1,555	11.4
other services	696	16.9
federal public administration, except postal	404	24.9
postal service	47	7.6
state public administration	125	14.4
local public administration	148	8.9

Source: U.S. Bureau of Labor Statistics, news release, February 24, 1981.

two-thirds, or 1.2 million people, were working four-day weeks. Compressed workweeks were used more in some industries than others; their heaviest use was in local public administration (especially police departments), and in small manufacturing firms (see tables 1-7 and 1-8).

Compressed workweeks began in earnest in the United States in the early 1970s (there has never been noticeable usage in Europe), and increased to 2.2 percent of the full-time work force by 1975. There was little change in usage up to 1980, when an increase occurred. This may have been caused partly by the gasoline shortage in 1979 (see figure 1-3).

Table 1-6.   Usage Rate of Flexitime by Sex, Age, Family
Characteristics, Labor Union Membership, and Days
Worked, 1980

Item		Percent on Flexitime
Sex		
Men		13.2
Women		9.8
Age		
16 to 24 years		9.6
25 to 54 years		12.7
55 to 64 years		10.6
65 years and over		14.1
Marital status		
never married		10.9
married, spouse present	men	13.5
	women	9.5
other		12.1
Presence of children		
with children under 18 years	men	13.9
	women	10.1
without children under 18 years		11.3
Union status		
union member (includes employee association)		7.3
other		13.7
Days worked		
4 days per week or less	men	12.0
	women	16.0
5 days per week	men	12.0
	women	9.0

Note: All data refer to full-time nonfarm wage and salary workers who were at
work in the survey week in May 1980.

Source: U.S. Bureau of Labor Statistics, news release, February 24, 1981.

BENEFITS AND PROBLEMS OF NEW WORK SCHEDULES

Examining the experiences of hundreds of companies and thousands of
workers over the past several years provides some idea of what benefits
can be derived from new work schedules—and what problems may
arise. There are economic as well as social gains and losses, and they
affect both companies and workers. Both benefits and problems are
listed here as background for the case studies that follow and as a means
of judging the value of these case studies as models.

Table 1-7.   Compressed Workweek Usage in the U.S.
by Industry and Occupation in 1980

Industry	Employees on Workweeks Less Than Five Days Number (thousands)	Percent
Mining	17	2.0
Construction	148	3.4
Manufacturing	422	2.2
Transportation, public utilities	143	2.7
Wholesale, retail trade	267	2.4
Finance, insurance, real estate	76	1.8
Professional services	382	2.8
Other services	148	3.6
Federal public administration except postal service	34	2.1
State public administration	31	3.6
Local public administration	180	10.8
Occupation		
Professional and technical	303	2.5
Managers and administrators	88	1.1
Sales workers	63	1.9
Clerical workers	225	1.7
Craftworkers	244	2.4
Operatives	290	3.3
Laborers	73	2.5
Service workers	439	6.7

Note: All figures refer to nonfarm wage and salary workers who usually work full time.

Source: Janice Neipert Hedges, "The Workweek in 1979: Fewer but Longer Workdays," *Monthly Labor Review*, August 1980, pp. 31–33.

Flexitime

No one company's or worker's benefits or problems with flexitime will be quite the same as another's, and so generalizations are risky. The following list includes, therefore, only the largest and most frequent benefits that companies or workers derive from flexitime:

• Increased labor productivity and lower labor costs due to less paid absence and idle time, improved organization of work, accommodation to "biological clocks," and increased morale.

Table 1-8.   Usage Rate of Compressed Workweeks by Characteristics of Employees, 1980

Item	Percent of Compressed Workweeks
Sex	
Men	2.7
Women	2.8
Age	
16 to 24 years	3.0
25 to 54 years	2.7
55 to 64 years	2.0
Marital status	
Never married	2.8
Married, spouse present	2.7
Other	3.0
Union status	
Labor union member (includes employee associations)	2.2
Other	2.9

Note: See notes to Table 1-6.

Source: U.S. Bureau of Labor Statistics, news release, February 24, 1981.

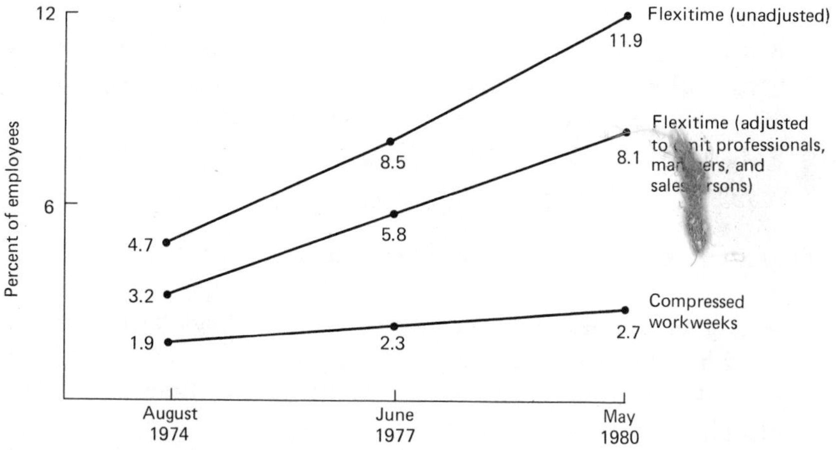

Note: Estimates are obtained from three different surveys whose methodology, coverage, and reliability differ.

Figure 1-3.   Growth in usage of flexitime and compressed workweeks in the U.S.

Source: For all compressed workweek data: U.S. Bureau of Labor Statistics, news release, February 24, 1981. For flexitime data, for 1980: U.S. Bureau of Labor Statistics, news release, February 24, 1981; for 1977: Stanley D. Nollen, and Virginia H. Martin, *Alternative Work Schedules, Part 1: Flexitime.* New York: AMACOM, 1978, and Work in America Institute; for 1974: calculated by Stanley D. Nollen from data by Virginia H. Martin, and Work in America Institute.

● Improved management practices due mainly to better and less supervision, with an emphasis on positive planning.
● Increased morale and job satisfaction due to the transfer to workers of choice and responsibility.

Other benefits that are reported, but which may not happen as often or be as consequential, include:

● Easier recruiting due to less turnover and the desire of many workers to have flexitime.
● Less overtime pay for the company.
● Better use of production facilities and greater flexibility in scheduling production operations, including opportunities to extend customer service.
● Easier, faster, and cheaper commuting due to off-peak travel and less need for single-driver commuting.
● More and higher-quality family and personal time.

The biggest problems that flexitime companies have run into and the major issues they have had to grapple with are these:

● Reluctant supervisors who have to change their methods and perhaps work harder at the outset, especially in scheduling production, insuring coverage of functions, and communicating.
● Knowing which employees, doing what kind of jobs, can or cannot use flexitime, and dealing with the equity consequences.

Other problems and issues that sometimes arise include:

● Higher utilities and overhead costs if buildings have to be open more hours to accommodate flexitime workers.
● Additional timekeeping costs or effort, if either time-accumulating machinery is used or honor systems are tried.
● Doubts about labor-union acceptance of versions of flexitime that permit debit and credit hours, thereby changing overtime pay practices.
● Conflict between variable-day/maxiflex versions of flexitime and labor law that requires overtime pay after eight hours a day for nonexempt workers on government contracts (see also tables 1-9 and 1-10 for more complete information).

Table 1-9.   Economic Effects of Flexitime on User Firms

	Direction of Effect	Frequency and Size of Effect
Labor Performance and Costs		
Productivity	positive	One-third to one-half of all users; 5 to 15 percent gain in output per worker[a]
Absence and lateness	positive	One-half to three-quarters of all users; 7 to 50 percent less absence; lateness virtually eliminated[b]
Turnover	positive	One-half of all users, degree or reduction unknown but likely small[c]
Overtime pay	positive	One-third to three-fifths of all users, degree of saving unknown, but can be large[d]
Capital and Production Operations		
Utilities and overhead	negative	Twenty to twenty-five percent of all users; size of cost increase estimated to be only a few percent[b]
Equipment and facilities utilization	positive	No systematic data; case studies suggest gains are frequent but small
Scheduling, coverage, communication	often negative, sometimes positive	Thirty-five to forty percent of all users report these outcomes to be worse under flexitime, but about 25 percent report them to be better; dollar impact indirect and unknown[d]
Management and Personnel Administration		
Supervision	negative	About 20 percent of all supervisors feel adversely affected in terms of control and scheduling, but translation into dollar costs unknown[e]
Timekeeping	negative	Thirteen percent of all firms use flexitime accumulators, costing minimum $50 per employee; for others, no change in timekeeping methods; cheating is infrequent (a problem for one in ten users)[e]
Recruiting	positive	Easier for 65 percent of all users; dollar impact unknown but probably small[d]
Training	negative	Cross-training occasionally done, but with little or no out-of-pocket costs

[a]The balance of the users, with few exceptions, reported "no change"; this result also holds for the other results reported below. Sources are 13 case studies, with 21 "hard" measurements of the size of the productivity increase measured as output per worker before and after flexitime, and eight surveys of user firms who subjectively reported the direction of productivity changes.

[b]Sources include some "hard" data and several subjective measures from case studies and surveys.

[c]Source is one survey.

[d]Source is a few surveys.

[e]Source is a few case studies.

Part-Time Employment

Considering all permanent part-time employment, including job sharing but not work sharing (and excluding all temporary employment), the main benefits from company and worker experiences are:

Table 1--10.   Social and Organizational Effects of Flexitime

	Effect
Employee morale, job satisfaction, and quality of work life	Improvements in morale reported by 85 percent or more of all workers, stemming from easier commuting (reduced time and stress reported by three-quarters of all workers) and more choice about work
Family life	Better family life reported by 20 to 69 percent of all workers; stress and work–home conflicts reduced; effects on role equality and time spent with spouse and children are mixed
Labor–management relations	Labor unions usually support flexitour and gliding time but object to variable days; less than 10 percent of flexitime workers are union members; it is seldom a bargaining issue
Management practices	Changes sometimes reported are toward less supervision, more self-management, and more short-term planning; companies with one alternative work schedule are likely to have other innovative human-resource programs
Labor-market conditions	No direct evidence of effects of flexitime on employment or unemployment; labor supply likely to increase (since recruiting is easier); no evidence of increases in moonlighting
Transportation and energy	Rush-hour peaks are spread out, with savings in commuting time and cost for many; building energy costs for utilities went up for one in four flexitime users

- Reduced labor cost, including less overtime, due to a better match between the size of the work load and the size of the labor input made possible by part-time staffing.
- Better balance for workers between work life and home life or other interests, due simply to more time spent outside the workplace.

Among other benefits of permanent part-time employment that are often, but not always, experienced are these:

- Higher productivity due to less absence and idle time, greater efficiency at either mentally stressful jobs or tedious routines, and higher morale.
- Job opportunities for people who are not able to work full time but who require some labor earnings, such as students, older people, and parents with young children or other dependents.

Table 1-11.   Economic Effects of Part-Time Employment on User Firms

	Direction of Effect	Frequency and Size of Effect
Labor Performance and Costs		
Productivity	positive	One-quarter to one-half of all users; size of effect is not documented
Absence and lateness	positive	Forty to fifty percent of all users; size of effect is unknown
Turnover	mixed	Twenty to forty percent of all users have reduced turnover, but one-third may have worse turnover; economic impact is small
Wages	positive	Wage rates paid to part-timers (compared to full-timers) are lower in 15 to 30 percent of user firms; gap is 8 to 30 percent, due to lower job levels
Overtime pay	positive	Seventy percent of all users have proportionately higher costs; 60 percent have lower costs because not all benefits are offered; size of effect is hypothetically $150 to $1500 per employee per year
Capital and Production Operations		
Scheduling, coverage, communication	mixed	One-half or more of all users solve scheduling problems of part-timers with large, but undocumented, cost savings; one-third of all users have more difficult production operations
Management and Personnel Administration		
Supervision	negative	Thirty-five to fifty percent of all supervisors have more difficult jobs due to part-time employment; cost impact is unknown
Record keeping	negative	One-third of all users; size of cost increase is not documented but is probably small
Recruiting	mixed	One-third of all users report each outcome; size of effect is unknown
Training	negative	Twenty to thirty percent of all users have marginally higher training costs

Note: Sources of quantitative data for most effects are one or two surveys supplemented by qualitative impressions of a small number of case studies. See notes to table 1-9.

There are several problems often encountered by companies and workers that use part-time schedules. These are the main ones:

- Fringe-benefit costs will be higher per labor hour if part-timers get the same fringe benefits as full-timers, since not all benefits can be prorated to the time actually worked; some sharing arrangement may need to be worked out.
- Labor unions are often opposed to increasing part-time employment, mainly because it might increase job competition.
- Career paths are hard to follow because of the stereotype that part-timers are not career employees, and because part-timers actually get less experience.

Two more, somewhat less critical, problems that sometimes occur with part-time employment are:

- Supervision can be more difficult because part-time employees are not always present and coverage and communication may take extra attention. However, this problem does not occur with job sharing.

Table 1-12.   Social and Organizational Effects of Permanent Part-Time Employment

	Effect
Family life	Improvements in balancing work life with family life and other interests are indirectly suggested by evidence that most part-timers are also caring for a household or pursuing education
Labor–management relations	Most labor unions are opposed to part-time employment except where it is necessary due to the nature of the work; it is seldom a bargaining issue; less than one in six part-timers is a union member
Labor-market conditions	Moonlighting is higher for part-timers, with a rate of 11 to 23 percent, as compared to full-timers, with a rate of 5 percent. Sizable numbers of currently full-time workers (perhaps 8 to 20 percent) say they would prefer to work less; labor-force entrance due to the availability of part-time employment is unknown; net labor-supply effect is unknown
Transportation and energy	Extra commuting trips are few in number since few part-time jobs result from conversion of full-time jobs, except for job sharing

● Training is more expensive per labor hour if it is provided by the company because part-timers do not work as many hours as full-timers (see tables 1-11 and 1-12 for more information).

Compressed Workweeks

The principal advantages of compressed workweeks, whether four-day or three-day or 5/4–9 schedules, in general, are:

Table 1-13. Economic Effects of Compressed Workweeks on User Firms

	Direction of Effect	Frequency and Size of Effect
Labor Performance and Costs		
Productivity	mixed	Gains for one-third to one-half of all continuing users; but losses for one-fourth of all one-time users; size of effects unknown[a]
Absence and lateness	positive	Absence reduced by a modest amount (perhaps 10 percent) for one-half or more of all users; lateness reduced less frequently[a]
Turnover	positive	One-third to one-half of all users; size of effect unknown[b]
Overtime pay	mixed	One-third of all users pay less, but one-fifth pay more; size of effects unknown but likely sizable[b]
Capital and Production Operations		
Utilities and overhead	positive	One-fourth to one-third of all users operate fewer days per week; size of effect not documented, may be partly offset by operating more hours per day[b]
Equipment and facilities utilization	positive	Gains for 10 to 20 percent of all users; size of effect unknown
Scheduling, coverage, communication	mixed	One-fourth of all continuing users report gains, but one-third report losses; dollar impact unknown but likely substantial[b]
Management and Personnel Administration		
Supervision	negative	One-third of all users report management job is more difficult; size of effect unknown
Recruiting	positive	Two-thirds of all users report better results; dollar impact unknown
Planning, coordination, control	negative	One-fifth of all users have coordination problems; effect on dollar costs unknown

[a]Sources are a few surveys and case studies.
[b]Source is basically two surveys.
See notes to table 1-9.

- Production operations can be rationalized, raising output and lowering costs, if there are fewer start-ups and shutdowns, or if facilities are utilized more fully.
- Personal time is redistributed into longer blocks, which many workers like; the unpleasant aspects of shift working can be partially alleviated.

Other benefits of compressed workweeks include:

- Commuting trips to work are reduced, saving time and money.
- Morale is sometimes higher and paid absence lower.

The most serious problems with compressed workweeks are partly problems that stand in the way of the use of this work pattern in the first place. They are:

Table 1-14.   Social and Organizational Effects of Compressed Workweeks

	Effect
Employee morale, job satisfaction and quality of work life	Higher morale experienced by over half of all compressed workweek workers on the average, but employee acceptance is highly variable; young workers and men favor compressed workweeks the most, while women with children and older workers often disapprove; greater fatigue reported by one-third to one-half of all compressed workweek employees
Family life	One-fourth of all workers report compressed workweeks upset family life; but some male workers spend more time in child care and household work
Labor–management relations	Labor unions usually oppose compressed workweeks; collective agreements often require overtime pay beyond eight hours in a day; compressed workweek workers are union-represented in only 16 percent of all user firms
Labor-market conditions	Moonlighting increases in some cases (e.g., from 5 percent to 17 percent moonlighters), thus aggravating unemployment; no other labor supply or demand effects
Transportation and energy	Reductions in building utilities costs reported by one-third of all user firms (other users do not reduce their days of operation); commuting trips reduced, but personal travel increased on the day off for 70 percent of workers in one study

• Work-technology requirements for successful use are stringent; interfacing and coverage problems often appear.

• Labor law and labor unions often prevent usage because of rules about paying overtime after eight hours a day; companies may have to ask the union to waive or renegotiate these rules.

• Family life and child care are more difficult for some workers because of the long days.

Another, less important, problem with compressed workweeks, which does not occur as often is:

• Fatigue at the end of longer days contributes to productivity declines and safety hazards in some jobs (see also tables 1-13 and 1-14 for more information).

A summary of the economic effects of new work patterns as they can be discerned from previous company experiences is available in table 1-15.

Table 1-15.   Summary of Economic Effects of New Work Schedules

	Flexitime	Permanent Part Time	Compressed Workweek
Labor Performance and Costs			
Productivity	+	+	±
Absence and lateness	+	+	+
Turnover	+	±	+
Wages	0	+	0
Overtime pay	+	+	±
Fringe benefits	0	−	0
Capital and Production Operations			
Utilities and overhead	−	0	+
Equipment and facilities utilization	+	+	+
Scheduling, coverage, communication	±	±	±
Management and Personnel Administration			
Supervision	−	−	−
Time- or record-keeping	−	−	0
Recruiting	+	±	+
Training	−	−	0
Planning, coordination, control	+	0	−

Note: +, −, 0 indicate gain, loss, and no effect, respectively.
Source: Tables 1-9 to 1-14.

NOTES

1. Most of these data and other statistics are from U.S. Bureau of Labor Statistics surveys, reported in sources such as *Employment and Training Report of the President, 1979,* and *Handbook of Labor Statistics,* annual issues.
2. Beverly Jacobson, *Young Programs for Older Workers.* Van Nostrand/Work in America Institute Series (New York: Van Nostrand Reinhold, 1980).

   Bernhard Teriet, "Flexiyear Schedules—Only a Matter of Time?" *Monthly Labor Review,* December 1977, pp. 62–65.

   Fred Best, *Work Sharing: Issues, Policy Options and Prospects* (Kalamazoo, Mich.: W.E. Upjohn Institute for Employment Research, 1981).
3. Many short names other than flexitime are in use, such as "flex-hours." The word "Flextime," however, should not be used to describe a work schedule, because it is a registered trademark applied to a specific time-accumulating machine.
4. See Stanley D. Nollen, *New Patterns of Work* (Scarsdale, N.Y.: Work in America Institute, 1979) for a review of some companies' experiences.

2.
Who Can Use New Work Schedules?

A. The Use of Flexitime in Manufacturing Operations

The use of flexitime in manufacturing operations is one of the big question marks about this work schedule. Although flexitime is widely used by many different kinds of companies, it is not often well suited to manufacturing firms. We know that the usage rate of flexitime is lower in manufacturing than in other industries. Where there is continuous-process work and moving assembly lines, and where there is shift working, it is surely not possible to have individual workers coming and going as they please. On the other hand, batch-process manufacturing systems do not have shifts, and the jobs permit workers to be somewhat independent. In these systems flexitime can be and is used successfully. The question of interest concerns the in-between cases. Most manufacturing operations are not purely in one or the other category. What are the features of the work technology in a manufacturing operation that determine the likely success or failure of flexitime? In what kind of work schedule can flexibility be implemented? For example, swapping systems might permit individual flexitime to work in some situations, or group flexitime might be used. Both systems are in effect in a few companies. But the "who can use flexitime" question goes beyond work technology. It is also a question of management philosophy and organizational structure. Unsuited management, even with a well-suited work technology, will likely spell doom for flexitime. And good management may be able to overcome work technology problems.

The question to be answered in these case studies is: What kind of manufacturing company can successfully use flexitime? What are the features of the work technology and the management that not only permit but also recommend flexitime?

23

SOCIOTECHNICAL CONDITIONS FOR FLEXITIME IN MANUFACTURING: THE CASE OF HEWLETT-PACKARD

The case of Hewlett-Packard Corporation is studied here, not only because it is a large manufacturing enterprise, but also because Hewlett-Packard has used flexitime for many years and because the company has an unusual management structure and style. This case study is about the sociotechnical conditions that favor the use of flexitime in manufacturing operations.

Flexitime at Hewlett-Packard

Every Hewlett-Packard employee, worldwide, has some degree of work schedule flexibility. The flexitime idea was imported from the company's German manufacturing division and was first put into practice in the United States in 1972 at the Waltham, Massachusetts, manufacturing location. Now most employees have the option of varying their working hours daily, with two-and-a-half-hour windows at both the beginning and the ending of the workday, during which an employee can arrive or leave. There are core hours when everyone must be present. No banking and borrowing of hours is allowed, however. This restriction is due to the company's policy of paying overtime for hours worked beyond eight in a day to each and every employee, whether covered by labor law or not (there is no union representation in the company), and to the company's concern about fatigue after long hours in precision assembly work. A small number of the company's manufacturing shift workers are limited to group flexitime.

Hewlett-Packard tried flexitime because "it sounded like a good idea," according to the general manager of the Waltham division. There was no urgent employee problem to solve, but "if it doesn't hurt operations, we'll go ahead," it was decided. The company president informally gave the go-ahead, and despite the lack of pilot project and hard data collection, flexitime was judged a success and spread thereafter throughout the company.

Social Conditions: Management Structure and Style

The way managers do their job—both the concrete tasks they do and the spirit they generate—are surely as important to the success of flexitime at Hewlett-Packard as the way the physical production operations are set up. Here are the key elements of management structure at Hewlett-Packard that dovetail with the use of flexitime.

1. The company is decentralized into 35 manufacturing divisions. Each is quasi-autonomous; all staff functions (e.g., personnel) are lodged within each division. The division is the decision unit and the profit center. Hewlett-Packard is actually 35 companies.
2. The span of control is short. The optimum is 10; the number never exceeds 15. A worker is never far in either time or space from a supervisor.
3. Jobs are designed to give workers maximum independence and responsibility. Workers rotate jobs regularly; cross-training is continual. These steps were not taken because of flexitime; they were a preexisting part of the management structure.
4. Personnel administration is not just a staff function. Every manager and every supervisor is a part-time personnel officer. Corporate personnel policies are scant; one thin notebook contains them all. In fact, they are not called policies at all, but rather, guidelines.
5. Productivity is a project- or job-based concept. It is not tied to an individual worker. Further, productivity is reckoned as variance from plan; it is not physical output per unit of labor input. These productivity concepts are favored because they encourage team spirit and planning. They succeed because the supervisors' short span of control permits them to know who is doing what informally (maintaining individual accountability), and because there are standard rates of output for each project.
6. Employee performance appraisal depends on output, not on time input. Here are the performance-appraisal criteria: work quantity, work quality, contribution to the workplace, teamwork, compatibility, judgment, initiative, and dependability. For supervisors, there are additional criteria, such as leadership, innovation, planning and organization, and employee development.
7. The physical plant at corporate headquarters is open and has no built-in status distinctions. Office workers and plant workers are intermingled. Managers and production workers sit side by side. The general manager of the division sits scarcely 10 feet distant from an assembly worker. The manager has a desk instead of a

workbench, probably wears a tie if he is male, and has his own telephone. Otherwise, you could not tell the two apart. Both have tile floors, neither has walnut paneling. The office–plant building is totally open and naturally lighted from an old-style factory saw-tooth roof. Yet the facility is quiet and warm, rather than noisy and cold. In sum, the physical plant reflects and encourages the human spirit.

8. The organizational climate is one of informality, trust, and equity. There is an air of growth and change.

9. There is an articulated "HP way." A 15-page company publication describes it as a "belief that men and women want to do a good job, a creative job, and that if they are provided the proper environment they will do so." It is "a system that places great responsibility on the individual concerned ... the dignity and worth of the individual is a very important part of the HP way." New young workers are mixed with senior workers in production lines, partly to socialize them into the HP way.

Flexible work hours figure prominently in the Hewlett-Packard management structure and style. Doing away with time clocks and introducing flexitime is part of the HP way because it contributes to the dignity and worth of the individual. Flexible hours are mentioned by the company's vice-president for human resources as one of the elements in the HP way, along with informality, small-company atmosphere, and knowing one another on a first-name basis.

Technical Conditions: How the Work Is Done

A look at an instrument-assembly work unit and a fabrication unit in the Stanford Park division, near Palo Alto, and a calculator-assembly unit at Corvallis, Oregon, can provide some insight into what kind of flexitime works in what kind of manufacturing operation.

Instrument Assembly. Assemblers can arrive at work and leave work any time they want to within the two-and-a-half hour window at the beginning and end of each day, but they must work eight hours every day. Assembly takes place at a workbench; the product moves from worker to worker, but there is no assembly line. The work is light and clean. The work unit is a low- to medium-volume operation. Parts used in assembly are small, permitting inventories or buffer stocks to be maintained. Because the assembly operation is labor intensive, employment policy is quite important.

Going beyond a simple description of the work operation, what are the key features that make flexitime succeed? There are eight:

1. Each worker does a "meaningful entity of work" by preflexitime design. Workers can be independent of each other for at least two or three hours, and perhaps as long as three days. This means that different time schedules adopted by different workers do not disrupt production.
2. In those places in the work unit where worker independence is insufficient to tolerate variable work schedules, group flexitime is used: the interdependent workers together choose a uniform work schedule for their group. To prevent any sense of loss on the part of workers with group flexitime, the company cultivates a spirit of teamwork among them.
3. Supervisors also have flexible schedules and need not be present all the time. "Why should anyone imagine such a need in the first place? On fixed schedules, supervisors are occasionally absent for meetings anyway," as the unit's manager put it.
4. It turns out that there is almost always at least one supervisor present on the floor as a natural outcome of workers' different schedule preferences. If a worker has an administrative problem, a supervisor is usually available.
5. Technical leaders (skill specialists) can also be called on to help if the worker has a technical problem. With both supervisors and skill specialists available to provide assistance, there will be little worker downtime.
6. No worker may work alone, according to company policy. There must always be at least two workers at a location for safety reasons. Of course, this policy also helps with coverage and supervision.
7. Workers rotate jobs every few months to insure that they are fully cross-trained and can do a broad range of tasks. This means, for example, that workers can fix their own tools, increasing their independence. Job rotation was not introduced because of flexitime; Hewlett Packard has always used job rotation to maintain workers' interest and speed, and to cover absences.
8. On-the-job training is continual, done by supervisors and skill specialists working with the employee. Each worker can do from 10

to 100 different kinds of jobs. The training cost amounts to about a 50 percent loss in output rate at the first performance of the new job, with full speed attained after three performances.

Calculator Assembly. Assemblers at the Corvallis location also have flexitime, but the assembly operation is somewhat different from the Stanford Park instrument assembly. Calculator assembly is high volume rather than low; the operation is a hybrid somewhere in between continuous process and batch process. Instead of a moving assembly line or a stationary workbench with buffer stocks, there is a large rotating carousel that carries elementary parts as well as partially assembled calculators. The carousel type of assembly offers some of the advantages of continuous flow (such as high-speed assembly), and yet it preserves some worker independence too, an advantage of the batch process.

Flexitime is suited to carousel assembly at Hewlett-Packard because (1) each operator is responsible for a certain level of assembly (not just one task), (2) there are always two or more people responsible for each assembly operation, and (3) operators are cross-trained in several operations.

Fabrication. The fabrication unit, comprising 270 production workers overall, has 45 people on a rotating three-shift schedule. The shift work is heavy and dirty, but it is skilled labor. Shift work is necessary because of the high value of machinery that, for economic reasons, must be utilized around the clock. In addition, the machinery must operate continuously to maintain critical operating temperatures.

In the case of continuous-process shift working, individual flexibility of work hours is quite clearly not possible. In these demanding technical conditions, Hewlett-Packard uses group flexitime. All the workers together decide what the shift changeover hours will be, subject only to the management's requirement of a 15-minute overlap between shifts. Each year the shift hours are reconsidered. (See pages 33 to 49 for case studies of flexitime in continuous-process shift working in Europe.)

FLEXITIME FAILURE AND FLEXITIME SUCCESS IN MANUFACTURING: THE CASE OF SERCEL INDUSTRIES

The case of Sercel Industries in Redmond, Washington, points out the interaction between work technology and management in the use of flexitime. This is a case in which flexitime initially failed both because it was poorly managed and because it was not suited to the manufacturing operations. It is also a case of the reimplementation of flexitime in conjunction with improved management and a changed production system. Flexitime reincarnated has succeeded.

The Company and the Work Schedule

Sercel Industries is a very small, new French-owned manufacturer of seismographic instruments. There were 40 employees in 1980 of whom 32 were production workers. Employment is increasing rapidly and is expected to exceed 100 by 1982. There is no labor-union representation. The plant is a semicontinuous shift-working operation using two shifts.

The first shift has flexible compressed hours. Starting times may vary between 6:00 A.M. and 8:00 A.M. Monday through Thursday; nine hours must be worked each of these days. Lunch and break times are also flexible. Friday morning hours are fixed at 6:00 A.M. to 10:00 A.M. by the workers' collective choice. The plant closes at 10:00 A.M. on Friday. One week a month workers may put in 10-hour days Monday through Thursday and have all of Friday off. About half of the workers use this option.

The second shift follows a fixed four-day, 10-hour-a-day schedule, 2:00 P.M. to 12:30 P.M. This is a four-day schedule so the plant can close Friday afternoons; the hours are fixed so the supervisor can lock up without delay each night. There is an overlap between the two shifts that can vary from one and one-half to three and one-half hours. The overlap is so far not a problem because second-shift workers do other jobs until first-shift workers leave; space and equipment are abundant.

The Old Production System and Flexitime Failure

Flexitime began when the company began in 1977. At that time the production system was a conventional assembly-line type of operation with the product being passed successively from worker to worker, each of whom did a single task. The flexitime program was very flexible, including debit and credit hours.

Neither the flexitime schedule nor the production system worked. There was lots of production downtime (when workers had neither parts nor equipment to work with) and a high rate of absence and turnover.

Many workers abused the flexible hours. Some debited hours without crediting them back. While they were, of course, not paid for the short hours, the company needed the work time more than the saved labor cost. Flexitime was soon abandoned; later, the production system was changed.

A New Production System and a New Flexitime Schedule

The production system was redesigned in 1979 to solve the company's serious productivity problem. Production remains an assembly operation, and the product goes from one worker in the plant to another during assembly. But the assembly is not continuous process and there is no moving assembly line. The redesigned production process is suited to flexitime.

The key features of the new production methods are:

- Advance production scheduling
- Buffer stocks
- Independence of one worker from another
- Multiple tasks and skills for each worker

Here is how production takes place: The assembly begins with a kit of parts. Each worker does several tasks with this kit—preparing parts, inserting parts in a board, soldering the board, and inspecting the partially completed product. These workers in the first stage of assembly comprise their own department. One kit or production job may take from an hour to a day to complete. The product then moves to a worker in the next department.

Buffer stocks are maintained, both of input parts for the first assembly operation and of partially completed products for the next assembly operation. Work loads are scheduled for each department more than a week in advance so that the size of buffer stocks is optimal.

When workers do several jobs and work out of buffer stocks, they are independent of other workers for at least the span of the flexitime window, if production planning is adequate. Thus the arrival and departure of workers over two-hour time slots does not disrupt production operations.

Flexitime was reimplemented in 1979 after the production system was changed, with the following conditions:

- A fixed day length of nine hours (four hours on Friday) was required rather than variable hours with debit and credit provisions. This change made production planning easier (especially for buffer stocks), and it prevented workers from working less than 40 hours (for less pay).
- Guidelines for employee privileges and responsibilities under flexitime were written down and used.
- A stiffer policy on absence was adopted.
- Time accumulators were installed to insure time accountability.
- Cross-training was undertaken to make sure that every worker could do every other worker's job. This was done mainly to help cover for absences, but it also helped to make flexitime work.
- The reimplementation was coincident with a wholly new work force (occasioned by a move to a new plant in a new location) that did not carry the burden of a previous failure of flexitime.

The Role of Flexitime

The role of flexitime at Sercel Industries is not to increase productivity in the conventional output/input sense. Productivity in this manufacturing operation is principally a matter of the design of production methods. The old poor productivity turned into the current good productivity (the output rate exactly doubled) when the production methods were changed. The relationship of flexitime to productivity at Sercel Industries is that the redesign of production methods to increase productivity also suited the use of flexitime—and then flexitime could fulfill its intended function. That function of flexitime is to aid the management of the work force.

Because of Sercel's location in the distant suburbs of Seattle and because most of the plant jobs are low-skill, yet light and clean, the company's work force is unusual. The average age is only 21, the education level of the workers is very low (many are high school dropouts), and a majority are women. This combination of characteristics makes for a very-low-wage labor force, but it also makes for trouble with absence, turnover, and training. Flexitime is regarded as almost a necessity by the company. These workers have strong outside interests. Flexitime, in combination with the four-and-one-half-day workweek, permits these workers to follow their outside interests whether they consist of weekend leisure or further education. The company has noticed that many of these workers are taking 4:00 P.M. classes at a local community college on their own time which, before flexitime was implemented, they could not do. While only part of this education is directly job related, it nevertheless produces a brighter and more adaptable young worker and indirectly reduces the company's on-the-job training time and costs.

The Interaction of Work Technology and Management Practices

The experience of Sercel Industries with both a failure and a success of flexitime in conjunction with two different kinds of work technologies offers several lessons in general applicability. First, it takes both good management practices and a suited work technology to insure flexitime's success. For Sercel Industries the suited work technologies included worker independence, multiple tasks for workers, a batch process with buffer stocks between workers and departments, and adequate space and equipment. The good management practices included fixed day lengths for flexitime, written guidelines of workers' responsibilities, cross-training, and time accumulators. For other companies, these characteristics may be somewhat different.

When management practices are bad and work technology is unsuited, flexitime will surely fail. At Sercel Industries, the chief errors in management practices were uncontrolled debit and credit hours in flexitime and the lack of clear responsibilities for workers. Other companies with a more mature and more highly skilled work force might not find these to be management errors. The most ill-suited work technologies were (1) single tasks for workers, and (2) an assembly-line operation.

If work technology is suitable but management practices remain bad, it is still likely that flexitime will fail. This conclusion was not tested at Sercel Industries because both factors were improved when flexitime was reintroduced. However, experiences at other companies suggest this outcome. If work technology is not suited but management practices are good, the prospects for flexitime are uncertain; they will depend on case-specific information (see figure 2-1).

Management practices	Work technology	
	Suited	Not suited
Good	Success	Uncertain
Bad	Failure	Failure

Figure 2-1. Effects of work technology and management practices on success of flexitime, based on Sercel Industries' experience.

B. Flexitime for Production Workers in Britain and Germany

by William McEwan Young

The question of how flexitime can be used for production workers as well as for office workers is being addressed in Europe in ways that should interest American companies. Already in the United States there is some, but not much, use of flexitime in manufacturing settings where the work is batch process and the workers are quite independent of each other. But is there any way that flexitime can be used in continuous-process shift-working operations? Is it possible to have widespread use of flexitime in production areas rather than only in isolated instances?

In Britain, flexitime in production areas is as unusual as in America, but there are a few cases of genuine flexitime in continuous-process shift-working operations. In Germany, flexitime in production areas is quite common, and so prospects for transference of these outcomes to the United States can be assessed.

BRITISH EXPERIENCE WITH FLEXITIME IN PRODUCTION AREAS

The overall use of flexitime in Britain appears to be of the same order of magnitude as in the United States. An informal estimate as of 1980 suggests that about one million workers, or roughly 8 percent of the work force, are on flexible-work-hours schemes (not counting those professionals and managers who have always had schedule flexibility). Of this total, however, perhaps only 3 percent are working in manufacturing operations. There is no evidence of much growth here, either.

In Britain the largest number of production applications of flexitime are in pharmaceutical manufacturing. Evans Medical at Speke, Liverpool, with 1500 employees, is probably the largest manufacturing installation in Britain. Outside of pharmaceuticals, there is only one major installation: Ilford, Ltd., in Essex, a company producing photographic film (about 1500 employees, but recently closed due to market changes in this field). While these are manufacturing installations, the nature of the work (involving as it does small teams of people working on batches of material as it is processed through the plant) lends itself to collective decisions among the team members as to how and when the work should be carried out. Thus, in Riker Laboratories at Loughborough, tablet production in one unit is carried out by three persons and a leading hand who acts as liaison with a supervisor. Provided this unit can maintain the input stocks to a packaging department, it is productively effective. In the packaging department itself, small groups of workers staff the flow lines which constitute packaging work stations and, by consulting among themselves as to how the lines are to be staffed throughout the band width (flexible period), production is maintained.

Similar arguments would hold in explaining how flexitime has been made to work at some seven or eight pharmaceutical companies, such as Electro-Mech Engineering in Northampton and Pye Unicam in Cambridge. Either the members of the work force have complete independence from one another, or small groups can work out their "own solutions" on a collective basis, in conjunction with supervisors. These findings correspond to the American experience.

Many companies have chosen to exclude their production workers from flexitime schemes, which cover clerical, administrative, and technical staff only. Metal Box, Ltd., a large multiplant company, states that although they have installed many flexitime schemes for white-collar staff, "such schemes are not feasible for production workers because of constraints imposed by machine-based operations." Pfizer, Ltd., part of the Glaxo group of companies, excludes not only production workers, but also categories of staff directly connected with production work, as for example, production-control clerks and materials-management clerks.

But there are a few notable examples where plant workers in companies with apparently unsuited work technologies have nevertheless asked for and designed a type of work-schedule flexibility for themselves. These cases are described below.

Flexible Work Schedules in Continuous-Shift Production: The Case of Pedigree Pet Foods Ltd.[1]

Flexibility in working hours in shift work is usually limited to individual arrangements between opposite numbers on other shifts. But Pedigree Pet Foods Ltd. has a flexible system that greatly extends the discretion accorded to operatives in their overall use of time. This case is unique because it shows how a version of flexitime can be implemented for continuous-process shift workers, and because the flexible system was requested and designed by the workers themselves.

Pedigree Pet Foods is a division of a privately held American multinational food manufacturer. The plant with flexitime is located in the Midlands of England and employs over 1,500 production workers. This plant has mixing, cooking, canning, and packaging functions that take place in several production lines. Production is continuous, with three shifts and four crews.

There is no trade union representation among production workers. Still, personnel policies are positive and progressive, although the management structure is hierarchical and the style somewhat autocratic. In the local labor market the company is seen as a good employer. Labor turnover is low, and there is always a waiting list of potential employees. In recent years a sophisticated and apparently highly effective internal employee council has been developed.

After flexitime was introduced for the white-collar office workers at this location, the shop-floor shift workers saw the gap between themselves and the office staff being widened, and so they asked for more work-schedule flexibility also. The company formed a working party with the employee council to explore ways of introducing a system of flexible working hours for plant workers. The objective was to "improve working conditions for shift-working employees by providing an opportunity to adjust scheduled working hours to meet personal requirements."

The Production System.   Production lines combine batch and continuous-flow modes of manufacture. They must be fully staffed around shift changeover times, although at other times they can operate at somewhat less than 100 percent staffing. Each production line has four work groups; each group performs a series of operations on a product. The jobs within a group call for different levels of skill and experience. The interchangeability of workers both within a group and between groups varies considerably—some workers can do any job in any group, but others with less experience and seniority are not even interchangeable within their own group.

The company employment policy stated that no person should work more than 12 hours at a stretch nor more than 60 hours in a calendar week nor more than eight calendar days in a row. These rules were unevenly enforced and caused controversy in the plant. An individual swap system was in operation, under which a worker could ask another worker on another shift for relief for either an early quit or a late start. The supervisor had to approve the swap, and the workers had to arrange a payback on their own.

The New Flexible Scheme.   The new work pattern that was designed and now operates successfully amounts to a large-scale expansion of the previous swap system. Of course, where there is continuous-process production, there cannot be completely free and individual flexibility in work schedules, but the Pedigree Pet Foods plan does give very lightly constrained individual flexibility. The key elements are a flexible time register and a new supervisory role.

The main principles that the working party adopted to guide a new work pattern were:

1. An operator wishing to make a time swap should be able to make an "offer" to all other "suitable" operators working, not only on other shifts, but also on other production lines and in other sections of the plant.
2. Supervisors should ensure that the proposed substitute (the worker accepting the offer) has the necessary skills, and that required staffing would be maintained; but otherwise the supervisor is not to deny the swap.
3. The existing rules about how long an employee can work per shift or per week are to be maintained.
4. A centrally located flexible time register is used to request and accept swaps. This register, a large board, eliminates the need for face-to-face negotiation to find a swap, and greatly eases and expands the chances of getting a swap offer accepted.
5. Each employee is to have a flexible time account, with debit or credit hours that were recorded on the employee's pay slip; there are no additional cash transactions. The maximum number of debit or credit hours is 12. There will be a settling-up period each year when net credits will be taken as time off in lieu of pay and net debits will be time worked without additional payment.

Experiences.   Utilization of the expanded swap system immediately increased to a high level. After six months of operation, the number of swaps was 300 per week on the average (among 1500 employees). This is about three times the rate of the old individual swap system. About 60 percent of the swaps were for four-hour time slots or half-shifts. Only 10 percent of the swaps were for periods of less than two hours. About half the swaps continued to be prearranged among friends (that is, an accepter had already been found by the offerer before the offer was made). But the other half of the swaps were speculative. The bulk of the swaps took place within a section of the plant rather than between similar work groups across sections. Supervisors unanimously felt their work load was eased because responsibility for arranging time off had shifted from them to the operators themselves. The quantity of leave-of-absence time taken decreased dramatically. Abuses in the form of substitutes failing to show up have been exceedingly rare.

The work-schedule flexibility enjoyed by production workers at Mars, similar to that available to office workers, is judged a success and has become a way of life in the plant. Part of the success is clearly due to the motivation that workers have, stemming from the design and implementation of the plan on the part of the joint labor–management working party and employee council.

WEST GERMAN EXPERIENCE WITH FLEXITIME IN PRODUCTION AREAS

Although the number of West German workers who are on flexitime is not precisely known, an informed guess is that it is more than 45 percent of the work force. Of this number, a large proportion—perhaps 30 percent—are production workers. Such a high level of usage makes it possible to compare a wide range of different companies.

Four case studies are reported here from the Schwabia area, which is a large upland territory south of Stuttgart. It is a prosperous industrialized area but not dependent on heavy industry. In each case study, several key company variables that affect work patterns are described. The resulting company profiles are then compared, permitting us to identify the variables that pose problems for flexitime as well as those that ease or solve flexitime usage problems.

The variables that make up each company's profile are:

1. Technology
    Interchangeability and interdependence of operators
    Criticality of output
    Work structure and flow

2. Wage payment system
     Frequency of payment
     Relationships of payment to output
     Overtime-payment rules and other premiums and allowances .
3. Social organization
     Management structure and style (for example, hierarchy,
       paternalism, autocratic vs. democratic)
     Employee benefits
     Promotion channels within the organization
     Consultation machinery
4. Labor relations
     Unionization—single vs. multiple unions, density of rep-
       resentation
     Industrial-relations climate
5. Employee attitudes: morale, job satisfaction, motivation
6. Operational factors
     Legal constraints
     Occupational exclusions

The Case of Fa. Mey[2]

Fa. Mey is a small knitwear firm producing a limited range of women's
and girls' underwear and beachwear. The company employs 120 persons of whom 98 are blue-collar workers. The work force is mainly
female. The work flow follows a pattern of: yarn intake, knitting, steam-
ing, cutting, sewing and finishing, packaging, and dispatch.

   At the initiative of management, which saw benefits for the work
force, flexitime was introduced in 1971 for all employees except the ten
knitters, who were on shifts. The flexitime configuration is shown in figure 2-2.

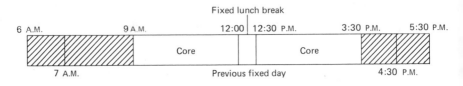

Figure 2-2

The key features of the flexitime program are:

- Debit and credit hours are allowed, with a maximum cumulative balance of plus or minus six hours and a settlement period of four weeks.
- Half-days off are not allowed.
- Overtime can only be paid after nine hours worked in one day and if authorized by a supervisor.
- Personal business commitments, such as doctor's visits, must be met out of flexible time.

In addition to flexitime, a few production workers are part-time employees. And 30 workers have flexiplace—they are called outworkers, and work in their own homes. Supervisors are responsible for the outworkers as well as in-plant workers, and physically handle raw materials and products between the factory and the outworker's home.

Technology. The work structure is essentially batch process, with individual operators repeating a work process on a batch of parts or components; the product moves through the factory, with buffer stocks held at various points. Production rates are sensitive to rapidly changing demand but are somewhat unpredictable with regard to seasonality. Production control schedules the work process and the load (for a particular customer or for stock) for specific machines and employees by means of a computer program. This sophisticated process controls operations from acceptance of customer orders to dispatch of finished goods.

Operators are highly interchangeable, with a low level of interdependence. For example, a sewing and finishing section comprises 20 work stations, and each garment requires work to be done on it at one or more stations. Operators, depending on their level of training, are interchangeable for tasks *at* the work station and interchangeable *between* work stations. The use of flexiplace illustrates the large degree of worker independence.

Wage Payment System. In addition to straight wages, all shop-floor employees are paid a bonus, determined by either individual or group performance, and depending on the task. A moderate level of overtime (about 10 percent of the average) has always been worked. This tends to be seasonal and can reach peaks of 20 to 25 percent for short periods. Managers, including supervisors, are paid a bonus related to the profitability of the company.

Social Organization.   Control is exercised directly by the two Mey brothers through a short line of control: two senior managers and seven supervisors. The management style is autocratic and paternal. Consultation machinery is nil, although it was claimed that the workers could have a council if they wanted one. Promotion prospects seemed to be extremely limited given the rather scanty hierarchical structure.

Labor Relations.   No union was recognized or negotiated with, and no employees were union members. No work stoppages had taken place in the previous ten years.

Employee Attitudes.   Physical conditions were extremely good since the factory was new and situated on a green site near the small town of Lautlingen. The workplaces were well lighted and provided with adequate ventilation. The level of automated handling was high. The general atmosphere was relaxed and friendly, and motivation to work appeared to be high. One could conclude that the wage system was correctly structured, and the work flow was organized to enable the employees to make money.

The supervisors appeared to be extremely competent and were obviously accorded high status by their seniors and subordinates. Within the existing work-flow structures, they did not feel that flexitime increased their work load in any way, nor did it lengthen their work hours. If they did not intend to come in at the start of the band width on any given day, they could arrange work for their subordinates and have a senior operator cover for them.

Operational Factors.   Federal legal constraints on maximum hours per day and per week applied. No employees were excluded from flexitime except the ten shift workers. Even security guards and telephone operators all participated in flexitime by operating an informal group system.

About half the employees lived in the immediate area, and many walked to work. The others traveled from surrounding small towns and villages (up to a radius of 20 kilometers), mostly by public transport.

The Case of Fa. Thomae

Fa. Thomae is a large pharmaceutical firm, with 3,000 employees engaged in the manufacture of chemicals, drugs, and cosmetics. There are 1,500 blue-collar employees in production departments, where the sequence of work begins with raw materials and ends with packaging.

At the suggestion of the works council, a flexitime scheme was first introduced in three white-collar departments in March 1972 and then quickly extended to cover all employees by October 1972. During the implementation, a working party was set up, consisting of three representatives from the works council and three from management. The flexitime schedule is shown in figure 2-3.

The three overlapping fixed lunch breaks are used by occupational groups. Debit and credit hours are allowed, but with only a small carryover of plus or minus three hours. However, one half-day per month (or one day per two months) may be taken, under debit hours, if the supervisor consents. Personal business normally is to be taken out of the worker's flexible time. Overtime is paid, if requested by the supervisor, for work done after the old fixed-hour finishing time of 4:30 P.M.

About 200 workers are part-timers, usually working either mornings or afternoons. They also have flexitime.

Technology. The work structure varied from the production of vaccines by small teams operating completely independently in sealed environments, through the batch production of basic chemicals and the manufacture of tablets, to balanced-flow line systems for packaging. The flow of work through the plant changed frequently in direction and magnitude. Large interdepartmental buffers were often held, but the buffers between work stations within a department were generally small. Output requirements could usually be predicted about three months in advance. There were fluctuations due to weather, catastro-

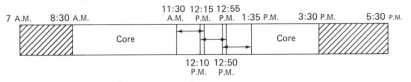

Figure 2-3

phes, and sales drives. For individual departments, supervisors were aware of output requirements for the week ahead.

Production control was very sophisticated, computer based, and employed 150 persons. Responsibility for all staffing problems associated with flexitime belonged to production-control people. This eased the burden on the supervisor, who appeared to work very closely and in an informed way with production control.

Within departments, the aim was to develop operators who were multiskilled. This had the overall effect of reducing the interdependence between one work station and the next. Where this could not be overcome by increasing the interchangeability of the operator, production-control techniques were used.

Wage-Payment Systems. A performance-related bonus scheme was superimposed on a base wage rate for all shop-floor workers. This scheme took into account a moving average of sales, output, and profit and could be related to group effort. There was no individual bonus paid. Overtime accounted for about 5 percent of the wage bill before flexitime. The company estimates that this level has changed very little.

Social Organization. The management hierarchy was complex, as expected in a large company with complex technological processes. There were large service departments and long lines of communication between the top and bottom of the structure. The management style was democratic. But although the works council was growing in importance, there was an impression that the Thomae family was closely overseeing the activities of the company at all levels.

Employee benefits were generous. The company had its own medical center, a deluxe canteen, and comprehensive recreational facilities. Promotion prospects were excellent in this large company, surely a major consideration for many workers. Training facilities could handle a throughput of 200 new supervisors each year. The works council was well established (as required by law) and appeared to be dominated by members of the trade union, although about one-quarter of that council were nonunion members. The council had played a very positive role in the implementation of flexitime. Relations between the personnel department and the council were good.

Labor Relations. About one-third of the total work force were members of IGCPK (the Chemical, Paper, and Ceramic Workers Union). There were no other unions in the plant. At the time of installation this union had very little experience with flexitime. Some initial problems arose when the management and the works council consulted together without previously informing the union. The disputes level at the factory was low, and the local union appeared to back the works council, often in defiance of the head office of IGCPK.

Employee Attitudes.   Sickness, injury, and labor turnover at Fa. Thomae were well below the national average after the introduction of flexitime. (No figures were available for the period prior to flexitime implementation.) The physical workplace environment was good—well lighted, air conditioned, and modern. The jobs themselves were often of a routine and repetitive nature, expecially in packaging, where 180 women were employed on 23 moving assembly lines. Morale seemed to be high. The morale of the supervisors appeared to be very high, and they obviously had high status.

Operational Factors.   The normal federal laws applied plus some special safety rules in certain departments working with chemicals. No occupational groups were excluded from flexitime. Four-fifths of the work force had to travel into Biberach where the plant was located. Two-thirds of those who did so traveled in company and public-bus transport.

The Case of H. Stoll u Co.

H. Stoll u Co. manufactures knitting machines in a factory located in Reutlingen. The work force numbers 1300, of whom 300 are white-collar workers.

The sequence of work flow following receipt of an order would normally be to produce parts (turn, bore, and mill), assemble parts (drawing additional parts from stock), build machines, test, and ship. The throughput time (in actual work terms) is from two to three weeks, but actual delivery times will vary greatly, depending upon the state of the market.

At the initiative of management, flexitime was proposed for white-collar employees in 1972 but rejected by the work force; six months later full agreement was reached with the works council, which demanded a full application to all employees. A series of trial schemes was introduced for administrative and production workers. The system produced so few problems that by January 1974 the scheme was operational for the whole factory. The flexitime day for all employees is shown in figure 2-4.

Debit and credit hours are allowed up to a maximum balance of plus or minus 10 hours. Workers' time accounts must be cleared each four weeks. Using debit and credit hours, one half-day per month may be taken off. Overtime is paid after eight hours per day, when attendance has been requested by a supervisor. Personal business commitments must be met out of flexible time.

Technology.   The work structure is essentially batch work in general engineering shops (turning, milling, boring), utilizing small teams of skilled workers. The batch size averages about one and one-half days of work per work station. Production is for stock or immediate assembly. Parts flow to the assembly bay from stores and engineering departments. The sequence of tasks varies, depending on the supply of parts and on the supervisor. Output requirements are predictable one to two weeks in advance.

Occupationally, a typical work unit, such as a milling shop with 70 employees, would have (1) five setters who are highly skilled and interchangeable inside and outside their group, (2) nine skilled craftsmen who are completely interchangeable and operate independently of each other, (3) 56 semiskilled operators with limited interchangeability in terms of skills but who normally operate independently of each other, and (4) a supervisor with a foreman as assistant. The main assembly department is staffed by 400 highly skilled workers. They are interchangeable within and between assembly teams; their dependence on each other's presence is low—for example, one assembler can start or continue work even if other members of the team are absent.

Wage Payment Systems.   All shop-floor employees are paid piece rates except setters in engineering departments, who are on fixed time rates, and assemblers, who operate an assembly-group bonus scheme. Over-

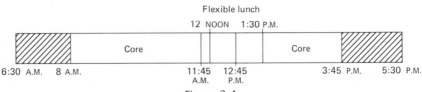

Figure 2-4

time has always been a major part of the wage reward in this company. Before flexitime was introduced, all employees worked at least one hour's overtime per day as part of their normal day. The union stipulated that these expected additional wages be retained under flexitime. This was built into the scheme but, due to a shortage of orders, was subsequently withdrawn and the standard day returned to eight hours.

Social Organization.   Stoll is a large public company in which the management hierarchy is complex. But the management style is very participative, with a professional management team that is committed to the principle of consultation. There is a powerful works council (all of its members are trade unionists), which management needs to consult at every stage.

Employee benefits are limited—these rank low in employees' perceptions of what constitutes a just reward system. Promotion prospects appear to be limited to skilled workers, with little mobility among departments.

Labor Relations.   About 95 percent of the members of the work force are unionized, most of them members of I.G. Metall (the metalworkers' union). The remainder belong to the white-collar union, DAG. The disputes level at the factory is not serious, but there have been a number of stoppages over the past few years. In the German context, the labor-relations climate is not the best.

As evidence of the hard bargaining over flexitime, I.G. Metall argued that if employees went into credit hours, they would in effect be lending money to the company free of interest. The outcome of the negotiations was that the company offered to make a prepayment to every employee of ten hours' pay (the maximum carryover) at a 25 percent premium. An adjustment is made when an employee leaves the company.

Employee Attitudes.   In the main assembly shop, where teams operate virtually as autonomous work groups, relationships with supervisors are relaxed, friendly, and informal. Morale, motivation, and job satisfaction are high, as expected among skilled craftsmen operating within a favorable work environment. In the engineering shops, morale is variable. The workers are noticeably more dependent on supervisors. Labor turnover is quite high, due partly to the demand for skilled labor in the area.

The supervisors, all I.G. Metall members, are given high status by the work force.

Operational Factors.   Normal federal laws apply; there are no special rules for engineering factories of this type. Certain occupational groups are excluded from flexitime—senior managers, warehouse workers, security guards, and telephone operators. The majority of the work force lives in the immediate area and most travel to work by bicycle or public transport. Parking problems preclude the use of private cars.

The Case of J. Hengstler K.G.

Hengstler is a large engineering company engaged in the manufacture of digital counting equipment (mechanical, electrical, and pneumatic). The main company is at Aldingen and has 1,200 employees. There are subsidiary companies at Trossingen (110 employees), Spaichingen (50 employees), Schramberg (80 employees), and Seitingen (50 employees). These companies are located within a 20-kilometer radius of Aldingen and manufacture subassemblies for the parent company.

There are 700 blue-collar production workers at the Aldingen factory, where the various shops are concerned with raw materials intake, guillotine and press work, plastic-component production, general machining, tooling, partial assembly, complete assembly, spraying, packaging, and shipping. There are 500 white-collar employees engaged in research and development, personnel, wages, finance, marketing, and production planning.

Flexible working hours were initially installed at Aldingen for 400 white-collar workers in 1969. In 1971 the works council asked for its extension to production areas. After a small trial, flexitime was implemented throughout the Aldingen factory and the satellite factories for both full-time and part-time employees. (A special version is used at Seitingen, in which there is no core time and employees are free to choose their hours between 7:00 A.M. and 7:00 P.M.) Five different flexitime configurations are in use. For production workers the scheme is shown in figure 2-5.

Debit and credit hours are allowed, and one half-day per month may be taken with the consent of the supervisor. Absence for private reasons (including medical appointments) during core time is allowed and cred-

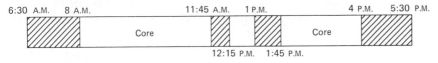

Figure 2-5

ited, subject to the consent of the supervisor. However, short breaks for private reasons (telephoning, receiving private visitors at the factory gate, etc.) are not credited, and keys must be removed from the recording machines. Overtime is only paid if requested by a supervisor and if the employee is less than ten hours in debit at that time.

A "flexitime authority," consisting of managers and shop-floor representatives, operates in each main department. This person looks after the operation of flexitime and arbitrates in the case of disputes. But this does not diminish the line authority of the supervisor, who has principal and primary responsibility for flexitime.

Technology.   Work structure varies considerably across the company. The range of products is wide, and production is usually for stock. The production method is batch process in the machine shop (with 180 employees) and in the plastics department (with 35 employees), with buffer stocks held between the work stations and between the various shops in the departments. But two very large departments, with a total of 285 employees, are involved in nonbalanced assembly work—operators moving about, among work stations, to perform various assembly tasks, with flow lines. The work flow, beginning with raw-materials stores, consists of three main departments (press, plastics, and machine shop) feeding a subassembly department, staffed by highly skilled personnel, which in turn feeds a final assembly shop, with less skilled personnel. Stocks were generally held at six weeks' level of demand, an amount which fluctuated somewhat. Long production runs were often possible, but it was not unusual to switch programs up to three or four times per day.

Within a department there appeared to be considerable flexibility in staffing work stations, constrained only by the skill level of the operator. Supervisors respected the desire among some operators to retain certain jobs as "their own property," but the deployment of staff to satisfy a production schedule took precedence over such wishes.

Wage-Payment Systems.   Payment for all production workers was based on rigourous work–study ratings and related to individual output. Jobs were graded on a complex scale and, where a transfer to a work station of lower grade was made, the higher grade was paid. Transfer to a higher-grade work station called for payment at the higher grade. Overtime was estimated at 8 percent and has been reduced slightly since flexitime was introduced.

Social Organization.   In this complex technological environment, lines of communication were extensive. As far as the shop-floor employee was concerned, the supervisor performed a key role in keeping him or her informed. Management style was paternal, yet the power of the works council was evident, and participation in decision making was an everyday occurrence. The chairman of the works council had his own office with a secretary and, although he was nominally employed on the telephone exchange, his works council duties appeared to occupy him full time. The works council covered the main factory and its four satellite factories and met with management every four weeks. Its ongoing function included trouble shooting; the council plays a very positive role in monitoring the performance of flexitime. Membership on the council is almost entirely made up of trade-union members.

  Employee benefits were generous, including canteen, medical benefits, and sports. Extensive development and training programs are operated for supervisors, and promotion to this grade is coveted. Supervisors have high status and are clearly regarded as career grades to which shop-floor employees aspire.

Labor Relations.   About half the total work force were members of trade unions, with 95 percent belonging to I.G. Metall and the remaining 5 percent to DAG (the white-collar union). There was no dichotomy of interest between the unions and the works council. Industrial relations in the factories were extremely good, and strikes were virtually unknown.

Employee Attitudes.   Morale was high, and supervisors reported that although flexitime meant slightly more work for them, it also gave them an opportunity to develop a better balance between their own private and work lives. For example, the supervisor and his assistant in the spraying shop found flexitime to be a personal benefit even when they had to arrange start and finish times to cover the wider band width. (They also claimed that because the longest possible spray-cycle time was now 10 hours instead of 8.2 hours as before, production schedules were more easily met and shop-floor employees were more flexible in their approach to staffing.) In the final assembly department, supervisors never had to refuse anyone a request for a half-day off. In any case, they explained, such a refusal might involve an explanation to the "flexitime authority," and that was to be avoided since it implied a breakdown in supervisor-subordinate relations.

Senior managers agreed that the company was as efficient as it had always been, pointing to employees' readiness to put production needs first when considering their usage of flexitime. Although sophisticated production-control systems (which sometimes updated shop-floor schedules four or five times per day) were helpful, managers all felt that the success of flexitime was due to the unique solutions worked out for every department and shop by the supervisors and their assistants.

Operational Factors.   Normal federal law applied with no special rules relating to this mode of production. There were no occupational exclusions although many senior managers confessed they could not benefit from the scheme because of work pressures. Only three-fifths of the work force lived in Aldingen. The remainder traveled in, mainly by private car.

WHAT DOES IT TAKE TO USE FLEXITIME IN PRODUCTION AREAS?

The two key questions to which the German case studies can give partial answers are: (1) What firm-level conditions permit or discourage the use of flexitime in production areas, and (2) can the German experiences be transferred to American companies? Let us begin by comparing the four German cases.

Comparing German Company Profiles

Technology.   All four of the German flexitime users studied had a substantial amount of batch-process production. However, all of them also had some continuous-process operations which, nevertheless, were under the control of workers and supervisors, rather than machine-governed. Workers in all companies had some, but not complete, inter-

changeability and independence. Problems of the latter sort were minimized by production-control systems that were themselves highly
flexible and responsive. They succeeded in reducing the disruptive
effects of individual absence during any part of the flexible band on any
given day. Fa. Thomae asked for one-day advance notification from
each worker of expected arrival and departure times, but Fa. Mey did
not do so.

The criticality of output in these companies was quite low. Much of
the production was for stock as compared to immediate delivery, and
output requirements that fluctuated could usually be predicted in
advance by a week or more. Buffer stocks between work stations and
reasonably long work tasks in most cases contributed to worker independence. None of the companies had to alter their existing work technologies to accommodate flexitime.

Wage Payment Systems.   Although a wide variety of wage-payment systems were in effect in the four companies, a common characteristic was
the existence of some type of production-related bonus system. This is
important to flexitime because it establishes that employees' performance is evaluated on the basis of output rather than on time input.
Overtime pay adjustments were made in all cases because the version
of flexitime implemented in all cases permitted debit and credit hours.
Although the redefinition of overtime hours varied across companies
(for example, different hours per day were the overtime triggers), a
common feature was that overtime was to be paid when supervisors
authorized long or unusual hours of work rather than when employees
chose it. There was little if any loss of overtime pay to workers. The
unusual advance payment of debit hours potential that Stoll agreed to
with I.G. Metall was not followed by other companies.

Social Organization.   The hierarchical structures of the companies differed widely in keeping with their diversity in size, technology, and
labor skill level. Management styles were also diverse, ranging from the
autocratic paternalism of Fa. Mey to the democratic consensual
approach of Stoll. The range of employee benefits was also wide. The
one commonality among three of the four companies was the highly
developed and effective works council (the very small Fa. Mey had no
such council). There was good labor–management communication and

participation in the planning and implementation of flexitime due to the active role played by the works councils.

Labor Relations.   Here we are confronted with company profiles ranging from the highly unionized and militant work force at Stoll to the non-union workers at Fa. Mey. Local unions, where present, supported the move to flexitime. When these implementations were taking place, the national unions were ambivalent, if not opposed, to flexitime. But the local union in each case appeared to be influenced by the works council (usually dominated by union-represented members) more so than by the remote national union office.

Employee Attitudes.   The regional work ethic was dominant in these four companies. This expressed itself in a commitment to work and high earnings. Workers were willing to see that the job was done on schedule. They were flexible about using their flexitime opportunities. They were ready to move to another work station if work was not available at a present work station. They wanted to become multiskilled so they could be more valuable to the company and, of course, to themselves. The existence of work groups in every case strengthened this cooperative spirit.

Supervisors were accorded high status in all these companies. Perhaps this was related to the quality of supervision or to an ethnic respect for authority. Clearly supervisors had a key role in production and staffing decisions. They were ultimately responsible for flexitime, and they favored it.

The proactive role of shop-floor workers in these cases was also demonstrated by the fact that flexitime was first implemented for white-collar office workers, after which blue-collar production workers asked for and helped design work-schedule flexibility for themselves. The production workers were aware of status gaps that were being widened by opportunities available to some workers but not to all, and they took action to obtain those same opportunities for themselves.

Transferring German Experiences to American Settings

It is clear that flexitime works in a variety of production operations in Germany. It is also clear that the four German manufacturing companies studied do not have a common profile of characteristics. But there are key commonalities that portend success with flexitime. What must now be examined is how well the West German profiles match profiles of potential American manufacturing companies. What are the similarities and differences?

There appear to be no outstanding differences between German and American companies with respect to technology, wage-payment systems, management style, labor-union representation, or employee benefits. That is, in both countries there are companies with batch-process and continuous-process production operations, production-related wage-payment systems, autocratic and democratic management styles, and high and low union representation. In all of these terms, an installer of flexitime is likely to encounter a similar range of environments, constraints, and choices.

There may be major differences, however, between German and American companies in terms of supervisors' skills and status, production-control systems, the role of works councils, and employees' attitudes. For example, in the German companies studied, the supervisors were accorded high status by superiors and subordinates alike. Supervisors were uniformly highly skilled in human-resources management and in production-control techniques, and their role was respected by work groups, trade unions, works councils, and senior managers. Do supervisors have the same status and roles in the United States? Similarly, do American companies usually have the same kind of advanced production-control systems that the German flexitime user companies had?

The German works council does not usually have an American counterpart; yet we saw how crucial the works council was in both the adoption and the management of flexitime in the German manufacturing companies. This suggests that perhaps new mechanisms for channeling workers' voices to management and for formalizing labor-management cooperation might encourage the use of flexitime in American companies. Overall, workers' attitudes in the German companies may also be somewhat different from those attitudes commonly found in American companies. Flexitime is not regarded by these German workers as their right, nor is it granted by the company as a privilege. Rather, flexitime is seen by workers principally as a way for them to improve their work life and their home life. Companies, in turn, do not require that flexitime yield productivity gains, but they do look for continued efficient operations.

C. Job Sharing: From Factory Workers to Professionals

Part-time employment is often stereotyped as low level clerical, sales, and service employment. Many business people think of it as a special purpose work schedule that cannot be widely used. Some jobs cannot be done on a part-time basis, these people claim.

Job sharing is a version of part-time employment that combines some of the advantages of both part-time and full-time employment: The job is full-time but the job holders are part-time. This feature should let job sharing succeed in a wide range of jobs. Yet even job sharing is often associated with low- to mid-level white collar jobs. And it is often an isolated work pattern—quite a few companies have just a handful of job sharers scattered about.

But it need not be so. In this section, we look at a case in which a large number of blue collar production workers in one company are job sharers. We also look at several instances of job sharers as high-level professionals and managerial employees. Then we ask: what does it take for successful job sharing for workers as diverse as factory operatives and physicians?

JOB SHARING ON A LARGE SCALE FOR PRODUCTION WORKERS: THE CASE OF THE XYZ COMPANY

At the XYZ Company a large number of manufacturing shift-work employees participate in a formal program of job sharing. This company uses job sharing because it solves a business problem for the company and improves job performance. The idea for job sharing came from workers; the company listened, and put the workers' idea into effect. This case is an example of both management skill and management trust—skill because the job-sharing program guidelines are clearly established, and trust because workers are left to manage their time schedules within the guidelines.

This case is also an example of an unusual and promising treatment of the extra fringe-benefit cost that job sharing can bring. It is also an example of the simultaneous use of both a compressed workweek and an unusual work-sharing arrangement, with job sharing.

The Work Schedule in the Plant

The XYZ Company is a medium-sized, family-owned manufacturing company in a small midwestern town, with an additional plant in Europe. About 1425 of its 1775 employees in the United States are production employees.

The plant normally runs a two-shift operation for four and one-half days a week, with a 40-hour workweek for each shift. This is a compressed workweek that was begun in the early 1970s. Here is the shift schedule:

First shift: 6:30 A.M.–4:00 P.M., Monday–Thursday
               6:30 A.M.–10:30 A.M., Friday
Second shift: 4:30 P.M.–2:00 A.M., Monday–Thursday
               12 noon–4:00 P.M., Friday

If overtime work is necessary the 40-hour workweek is extended to 45 hours for both shifts by having both shifts work the Monday–Thursday schedule also on Friday. If still more overtime is needed, these shifts are repeated on Saturday. A small third shift of 50 people is added only occasionally to work in bottleneck areas in times of extremely high demand.

There is no rotation across shifts; the company has little difficulty staffing the second shift, perhaps because there is usually no weekend work. Those workers who do want to go from the second shift to the first shift wait for openings based not on seniority but on their position on a waiting list. The wait-list position is determined on a "first request, first served" basis.

How Job Sharing Works

Perhaps this is a case of "out of adversity springs virtue." A woman employee with a high absenteeism record who was about to be discharged suggested via the "Speak Up" suggestion box in 1976 that she share her job with someone else—two people for one job, as she put it.

The plant personnel manager thought her idea was worth trying, and the company vice-president for operations approved a one-year experiment with this woman alone. She found a work partner (her sister-in-law) and the year's experiment succeeded—her absenteeism went way down.

In the next year an expanded number of job-sharing teams was permitted, and in the third year the number was increased to 30 teams of 60 job sharers, where the number stands currently. There are no limitations now, but the requests have settled down. Here are the key management-set rules that govern job sharing at XYZ.

- Job sharers are responsible for finding their own partner; the company only serves as a clearinghouse for requests.
- Previously full-time workers may cut back to job sharing; no new employees come in as job sharers.
- Job sharers work out their own work schedule—who works when—subject only to the two following requirements:

    - Each job sharer must work at least one day a week, and full days rather than part days are required.
    - Job sharers are responsible for covering their own absences; supervisors are relieved of this duty.

- All fringe benefits are paid, including the same coverage and company contributions for health and dental insurance that full-timers receive.
- Any plant worker in the lower three job classifications (covering 600 of the 1400 plant employees) may job share. Workers in the higher-skill jobs ordinarily may not job share.

The reasons the company offers for not permitting job sharing in higher-skill positions are: (1) the company wants to protect the interest of full-time workers who need good earnings, (2) the task of brokering one worker with another and the pair of workers with jobs would be more difficult at higher skill levels, and (3) new training would be substantial to make job sharing work in these classes. The higher-skill-class jobs are bid jobs. Bidding rights are conditional on an absenteeism record of less than 3 percent, or six or less incidents, and on satisfactory job performance; after that, seniority is the determinant. It would be hard to bid for half a job and find a job sharer to meet the requirements and skills necessary. Even if you went down a list of bidders in line to find a job sharer, you would still be taking a full-time job away from another high bidder who did not want to share jobs.

The company believes that restricting job sharing to lower-pay jobs is acceptable since the job sharers, who are willing to voluntarily reduce their earnings by half, must have less need for income than full-time workers. The median annual base wage for a class 3 job (the highest class eligible for job sharing) was $15,144 in 1980.

What Are the Results of Job Sharing for XYZ?

Absenteeism and Productivity.   The problem that gave rise to job sharing in the beginning has been solved completely. Absence among job sharers is 0.4 percent whereas the same people as full-timers, before they began job sharing, had a 7.6 percent absenteeism record. Previously, the company built in 5 percent overstaffing to allow for absence: overstaffing was eliminated where there was job sharing. These results demonstrate that when employees are given the responsibility and the flexibility to prevent absenteeism, they will do so. In turn, supervisors like job sharing because it relieves them of the task of scrambling to cover for absences. (Only two job sharers out of 60 in three years have had to cope with partners who asked them to fill in for absences too many times. These two workers quit the company.)

Productivity is believed to be higher for those jobs held by job sharers simply because of their reduced absence, which means fewer instances of fill-ins by unfamiliar workers and a smaller proportion of the supervisor's time spent fixing absences. However, these are strictly common sense reasons without hard empirical support.

Labor Cost.   The labor cost per hour for job sharing is intended to be equal to that for full-time employment over the long run. Here is XYZ's economic reasoning:

- Fringe-benefit costs for job sharers will be proportionately higher because they are paid the same health and dental insurance benefits as full-timers.

- The chief offset to the higher fringe-benefit cost is expected to be lower overtime costs over a period of years. For example, when 45- or 50-hour workweeks are required, overtime pay is necessary for full-timers. When two people share one job, there will be no such pay premia because job sharers can work more than their usual one-fifth to four-fifths time schedule without individually exceeding 40 hours per week.

- An additional cost offset is the three-way combination of reduced absenteeism, higher productivity, and the saving of fringe-benefit costs for the 5 percent overstaffing that was eliminated.

Participation.   The 60 job sharers, amounting to a bit more than 4 percent of the plant work force, seem to be the maximum number of people who wish to share jobs. Of course, this figure reflects a time in 1980 of deep recession for the company and the local economy because of a depressed construction industry; a few job sharers have returned to full-time work after finding they needed more than half-time earnings. When new hiring commences, following an expected upturn in construction activity and company orders in 1981 and 1982, XYZ expects to permit new employees to be job sharers.

All the job sharers at the company are plant workers except for two occupational-health nurses. Although the company approves of job sharing for plant workers, it believes that job sharing for professionals and managers may be inadvisable, largely because it would increase the difficulty of communicating, a critical function for professionals and one that is not easy even under the best circumstances. Interruptions of continuity might also be a problem if there were job-sharing professionals, according to the company.

The experience of XYZ is that job sharing appeals to a particular kind of person. All 60 of the job sharers are women; and these job sharing positions have always been filled by women. In contrast, only 46 percent of total plant employment is female. There are two specific kinds of women who elect job sharing: young women with young children, and older women with many years of work experience.

Fringe Benefits.   Job sharers get prorated fringe benefits for (1) vacation and holiday; (2) sick leave and other leaves; (3) life insurance—job sharers get $5,000 face amount while full-timers get $10,000 coverage; and (4) retirement, based on annual earnings and funded by profit sharing; all employees who work at least 1000 hours per year are fully vested after three years of calendar time.

Two fringe benefits are paid to job sharers which are extra-cost items for the company. They are unemployment insurance and medical and dental insurance. Unemployment insurance taxes are levied against an $8,000 annual wage base in the state in which XYZ is located. Thus the company pays up to twice as much per labor-hour for these statutory benefits for job sharers (based on a maximum job-sharer's salary of about $15,000). Social Security is not an extra-cost fringe benefit because the two job sharers' combined salaries will always fall below the wage base. Workers' compensation tax is levied against gross payroll dollars in this state and thus is not an extra-cost benefit of job sharing.

The main extra-cost fringe benefit is medical and dental insurance. The company pays the entire premium for these insurances for full-time workers, and similarly offers the same benefits and pays the entire premium for job sharers. The company pays one-half the premium for the elective additional coverage for the worker's family. The company's premium cost for a worker and the worker's family coverage in 1980 was about $750, so that the company's excess cost for two job sharers is also $750 per year.

The additional fringe-benefit cost can be offset by the elimination of overtime pay and overstaffing that was previously needed to cover absences. The dollars and cents of the trade-off between extra fringe-benefit costs versus overtime pay savings due to job sharing is as follows: two job sharers working a combined total of 45 hours per week will save the company five hours overtime pay at time-and-one-half, compared to full-time staffing. At seven dollars per hour (based on an average annual earning rate of job sharers of $14,000 per year), 90 hours of overtime work at straight-time pay of job sharers, or 18 weeks in a year, will make up the extra health-insurance cost.

The reduction of staff by 5 percent made possible because job sharers cover their own absences translates into one and one-half fewer plant workers among the 30 full-time jobs that were converted to job sharing (before job sharing, there would have been 31½ workers for 30 jobs). This amounts to a saving of the company's fringe-benefit contributions for one and one-half workers to medical insurance as well as unemployment compensation and workers' compensation—the benefits that are provided in fixed amounts per worker regardless of time worked.

PROFESSIONALS AND SUPERVISORS AS PART-TIMERS AND JOB SHARERS

by Gretl Meier

Many business people believe that part-time employment is not feasible for high-level employees such as professionals and managers. These jobs all require great skill and long years of training inside as well as outside the company. Managers have to be available all the time and know what is happening in the workplace, it is argued. Continuity is important, and so is a career dedication to the job.

Stereotypes of part-time employment do not fit this mold. But how much of the exclusion of part-timers from high-level jobs is due to ill-conceived stereotypes that are not true in fact? (There are plenty of business people who equate part-time with temporary employment.) To what extent is part-time employment really technologically unsuited to high-level jobs? Is job sharing a good way to use part-time employees in professional and supervisory jobs?

Let us look at a variety of examples of part-time and job-sharing employees in high-level jobs to see just what kind of jobs they are, what kind of organizations they are in, and how these jobs are handled.

Part-Time Professionals

Part-timers, either as single individuals or as job sharers, are now proving to be effective professional and supervisory employees. The most dramatic growth in part-timers employed by the federal government, for example, has been in the higher-grade levels. Some eleven states have initiated programs to create professional-level part-time positions.

In the private sector, numbers are smaller, although a few companies, such as Control Data, employ part-timers at professional levels— accountants, programmers, and personnel administrators. In both the private and public sectors, part-timers are administrators, analysts, planners, social service workers, lawyers, engineers, librarians, teachers, physicians, and other health-care professionals. Some are in positions requiring a great deal of public contact, positions rarely considered suitable for less than full-time coverage. "Now that I've tried it for almost a year," the manager of a part-time supervisor comments, "I have to say it's possible."[3]

One example serves to illustrate several of the necessary conditions for success. Carol Greenwald served on a part-time schedule for several years as vice-president of the Federal Reserve Bank in Boston. She explained:

> In large part, it . . . worked because, while I am the official head of the section, I actually share my supervisory work with the other economist in it. Like team teaching, we have team management, with one member of the team being slightly more equal. I also have bright, well-motivated workers in my section who are happy to take responsibility for their work. I do exactly the same job I used to, but for less pay. I also work harder while at the bank. . . . And of course I take a lot of work home, which I also did when I worked full time.[4]

Working extra, being experienced and organized, having excellent staff back-up, and sharing responsibility, are *some* of the necessary conditions for effective performance by part-time professionals and supervisors.

Based on Massachusetts state agencies' experience, part-time professional work is most easily performed well when (1) work is planned and scheduled in advance, (2) few emergencies arise, (3) work can be carried out independently (even within a team), and (4) work is on-site or in easily accessible geographic areas.[5]

Conversely, this report said that although no single characteristic of a job makes it impossible to do on a part-time basis, a combination of job characteristics taken together can make a job harder to perform on a part-time basis. Examples are frequent tight deadlines, supervisory work which cannot be delegated, coordinating inside and outside the agency, frequent site visits in short time periods, and lack of independence on the job.

The difference between difficult and impossible often lies in the commitment and capabilities of the part-time employees. Part-timers in higher-level positions must be able to (1) set priorities to make the best use of time, (2) consult freely to exchange information, (3) take initiative for information and queries, and (4) act independently to avoid overloading supervisors. They must be well organized and possess good communication skills. In general, they are experienced, often former full-time employees.

For most part-time professionals, extra hours are an expectation just as for full-timers. "My guess is," comments a section chief at the federal Environmental Protection Agency, speaking of the part-time professional she hired, "that she does as much work when she is not here at the office. She leaves on Thursday evening and comes back with a wealth of new ideas on Monday."[6] But part-timers need to set limits. They can be assigned increasingly heavier loads and must learn how to distinguish between the normal periodic crises of administrative work and what may be inappropriate overtime.

Part-Time Supervisors

Part-time supervisors are best used when they supervise other professionals or highly trained staff, whether they are full- or part-timers. In what is called a "consultative" model, supervisors act as advisers rather than as overseers. "I don't plan or schedule their work," explains the part-time manager of a four-person research team which meets weekly to assess tasks. "We agree among ourselves on what to do and how to do it."[7] Part-time supervision is successful when subordinates are able to take responsibility. Both part-time supervisors and workers need to plan carefully to ensure a steady work flow over a long period of time. The organization needs to establish methods of communication between part-timers and other staff, either through meetings, memos, or posted schedules.

Supervision by part-timers is more difficult when work involves frequent crises. Because work usually involves mandated deadlines and is subject to constant emergencies, traditional first-line supervision is obviously far more difficult for part-timers. In these cases, authority must be delegated and the supervisor must be experienced and able to identify the essentials of the job. When first-line supervision also requires coordination within the organization, it can be done on a part-time basis only when work is performed in accessible locations and can be easily divided.

Job Sharing in Managerial Positions

Job sharing may solve and alleviate several of the difficulties apparent in part-time work in higher-level positions. Even more important, job sharing in professional and supervisory positions may often bring a more productive performance than would a single full-time employee.

Job sharing is most effective in higher-level positions which require (1) liaison within and outside of the organization and other agencies, (2) field work in different geographic locations, or (3) time pressure over long or short periods.

Three Mini-Cases.   Among the job-sharing teams who supervise other employees (usually full time) are those who hold positions as office managers at the Stanford University Graduate School of Business, the deputy directors of legislation in the California Department of Employment Development, and the directors of the office of personnel development in a large eastern university. Team salaries range from $23,000 to slightly over $50,000. Two of these teams are responsible for budgets of approximately half a million dollars.

Take a look at these people's responsibilities and working styles to see the conditions that facilitate the successful sharing of these positions.

The office managers are responsible for the maintenance and space utilization of a building which houses 1,000 employees, recruitment of all nonexempt personnel, and supervision of 30 (mostly full-time) secretaries, word processors, and their own office staff. The two women who have been sharing this position for over two years consider themselves interchangeable in dealing with all matters and have no apparent task division. They work consecutive days—one partner for three days, the other for two-and-a-half. They maintain a midweek four-hour overlap and close communication lines with detailed notes. Because of their equipment and building responsibilities and the need to keep in contact with all staff, both spend more time elsewhere in the building than in their office.

The deputy directors for legislation represent the department before the state legislature, present positions on legislation, follow department bills through the process to enactment, and respond to requests for information from legislators and constituents. These two women direct a staff of eight, including four analysts and support staff. They use an alternating two/three-days-per-week schedule and specialize in different task areas. One is more concerned with fiscal matters and the other with unemployment insurance. Each has special responsibilities for each house of the legislature.

The personnel directors are responsible for design, implementation, and evaluation of career and organizational development programs for the university's 8,000 employees, including all levels of managers. They participate in all personnel policymaking bodies at the institution. Their own office consists of seven professionals and three support-staff members. These job sharers work the same hours daily. Their responsibilities have grown from an original 60 percent time to the current 70 percent time each. They consider their skills complementary and work in a totally collaborative manner. Both are out of the office a great deal, at meetings or at off-site training programs. They split many of these responsibilities, feeling that this allows the job function to be in more than one place at a time. They have considerable overlap time which they find important to keep each other informed and to give feedback on work performance. Both are actually involved in all aspects of the job despite splitting many tasks.

Each of these positions is performed especially well because two capable employees share responsibilities. All of these partners are highly qualified and experienced. One of the office managers had been working full time for 18 years in this position, the other for a shorter period in the same organization. The personnel directors, a married couple, both have strong backgrounds in organizational development and had worked together elsewhere for several years. Of the two legislative aides, one had worked earlier with an Assembly caucus and had a strong journalistic background. The other partner had held a post within the department and brought more of a fiscal background.

The "consultative" model is very apparent in these job-sharing positions. Notice that all three positions involve responsibilities conducted outside of the immediate office. The office managers are able to supervise in what they describe as a "hands-*off*" style. They find, as supervisors, little need to directly oversee their 30 staff members, who are located throughout the building. The personnel directors and the legislative aides (all of whom operate in similar physical settings) make a stronger case, describing their style as "involving people in management." The aides operate in as close to an egalitarian model as possible. They hold regular weekly staff meetings with a rotating chairperson at which each staff person sets his or her own weekly priorities. Both sharers do not attend the same sessions, but are in constant communication to learn all the nuances.

These job sharers as supervisors credit high-caliber staff with making this style possible and rewarding. In the legislative aides' office, sharers explain that the lead person below them is a staff manager who is responsible for the day-to-day work flow (a job formerly held by one of the sharers). A mutual sense of trust, they maintain, encourages staff development. Greater initiative and productivity result, one says, when supervisors are able to "look at the product rather than the system."

Consensus between sharers who are supervisors is crucial. All emphasize the need for communication and for the sharing of differences (sometimes by dividing tasks), but also the importance of reaching common positions. To avoid any possibility that the staff will consider them as divided authority, they stress the absolute necessity of adhering to joint decisions. As the vice-president in charge of the directors of personnel explained: "I know what one tells me will represent a common position."[8] One partner points out, "I think it's sort of a myth that if you have two supervisors, people would play them off against each other. . . . If the two supervisors agree anyway, it doesn't make any difference."[9]

Job Sharing in Professional Positions

Job sharing in high-level, nonsupervisory positions also requires experienced and committed employees, management support, and, varying with position requirements, cooperative partner relationships.

Here are three mini-cases of positions which are better suited to two job-sharing employees than to one part-time employee. These cases also demonstrate that some jobs are equally or better suited to two persons sharing a job than to one person working full time.

Internal Consultants.   The organizational development consultant in the City of Palo Alto, California, is responsible for maintaining liaison between the city manager and city department heads. The partner who first shared the position with another consultant of complementary background later helped to hire his replacement. The second pair has since been sharing for over two years. "Such a position," she explained, "would be difficult for one person full time because of the many bases to be covered." Two employees are able to split departments and "work together conceptually" on common issues. Because style and orientation are especially important, job functions are well covered by two employees of complementary backgrounds who frequently overlap to confer.

The fact that the city management is accustomed to job sharing is important. "It's a sort of psychological contract," says one partner of their acceptance by the 14 top executives to whom they report. The sharers' different approaches do not invite invidious comparisons.

Physicians and Social Case Workers.   Job sharing allows improved coverage in other professional positions. It has proved especially advantageous in those which are demanding and stressful, such as health care and social service. In instances where responsibilities are easily divided (such as by case load), job functions are more easily performed by two job sharers. Unlike ordinary part-time employment, and sometimes better than full-time staffing, job sharing allows for extended coverage. Extensive travel, when assignments are based on territory to be covered in a single day, is difficult for part-timers. When job sharers are scheduled in week-on or week-off modes, there is sufficient office time for follow-up work. Emergency coverage is also easier. "We can occasionally cover for each other in crisis situations," says a social worker, "and have come to know each other well enough so that we . . . implement a continuous service to clients even though we are not usually involved with all of them."[10]

Although job sharers (like part-timers) in these and other professional positions are often called upon for extended hours, some find the presence of a partner lessens the sense of pressure and gives "the feeling of having another resource and of wisdom when you feel yourself at your wit's end."[11]

Two physicians who are anesthesiologists in a large city hospital show that job sharing can be used even in typically high-pressure total commitment jobs. "Although individual patient care is not really shared," says one partner, "even when I'm not physically here, I feel that I have someone who is committed to my patients."[12] Their supervisor values their sense of teamwork. There is practically absolute communication between them. "And you can assume that on a given day one knows everything the other one did the previous day or what anybody else did."[13] Most notably, this is not a singular example; a number of shared schedules of internships and residencies are being instituted throughout the United States.

Teachers. Teaching at the elementary-school level has particularly attracted job sharers and school administrators. The earliest employers of job sharers, schools are now faced with fiscal stringency and teacher layoffs, and view job sharing as a way to accommodate staff who wish to reduce assignments *and* save jobs. Job sharing can yield cost savings when teachers at different ends of the salary schedule are paired, and when teachers cover for each other, thus eliminating the cost of substitutes.

These hundreds of positions are now proving especially well suited to job sharing because of qualitative benefits derived from (1) diversified experience levels and the pairing of complementary skills, resulting in versatility and curricular strength; (2) retention of older teachers; and (3) the energy level of teachers who are, as officials point out, "able to spend much more time with the kids" and "go beyond their 50 percent."[14] One administrator points out:

> I think . . . our experience indicates that those who share jobs are able to excite and enthuse each other. Our experience with part-time teaching indicates that there is very little communication . . . even though we do employ (part-timers), the results have not been as satisfactory as when two individuals will actually share the job together.[15]

In teacher job sharing, the same criteria for success hold true: principals supportive of sharing, partners with complementary skills who are compatible and share the same teaching goals, and good communication. Because these conditions have been present in a growing number of cases throughout the United States, sharing in the schools has proved especially successful. Administrators have found it possible to deal equitably with the difficult matters of tenure which are specific to the teaching profession.

College Teachers. Job sharing in college teaching has primarily been by married couples. Although part-time work is possible in many institutions, until recently it has rarely carried the possibility of commensurate salary and benefits or the possibility of a regular, tenured appointment. But these are sometimes associated with job sharing. Organizational conditions which initially appear complicated have been solved in various ways. Institutions have developed different types of contracts: separate, linking, or joint—some temporary, others more regularized. Decisions on voting rights, sabbaticals, and even the sharing of office space have been made to the satisfaction of partners and the organization. Schedules include alternating semesters, joint courses, and divisions in teaching, with collaboration on research. Administrative duties have been performed both separately and jointly by sharing couples.

Equal professional competence and the ability to function as cooperative partners—necessary conditions for all professional-level job sharing—are especially important. The usual skepticism about the value of part-time work is even more strongly articulated in the academic profession than elsewhere. For this reason, too, high-level administrative support is a *sine qua non.* Because tenure is complicated, and because these work settings are also often social settings, successful job sharing cannot be otherwise managed.

One of the longest-term examples is that of the couple who have been sharing an appointment in American history at a California college since 1972. Originally their contracts were linked: in the case of one job sharer leaving, the other had first refusal to take the position on a full-time basis. This arrangement changed over the years, and both have since been granted tenure at different times because of their different qualifications. Both partners have offices, receive travel expenses, take sabbaticals, and vote in faculty meetings.

As for being professionals, one partner says, "When we teach together or have to make decisions together, we treat each other as colleagues. We work our courses, negotiate, compromise, do all the normal kinds of things . . ." The institution is likely to find, as a director of personnel commented regarding three couples sharing three full-time positions, "There is no question we are getting more than a full-time person for each position. And we're getting two sets of talents."[16]

Replicable Conditions

These examples of part-timers and job sharers in professional and/or supervisory positions illustrate the two key special but replicable conditions required for effective job performance:

1. Positive attitudes on the part of managers and the willingness to consider and support qualified, experienced employees, either as

part-timers or as cooperative job sharers, depending on job requirements.

2. Careful planning and consistent follow-through by both part-timers and job sharers to (a) make the best use of work time, (b) ensure communication for daily and long-range performance, and (c) in the case of job sharers, to make best use of complementary skills.

D. Compressed Workweeks in Offices and Factories: Successes and Failures

After a period of early rapid growth from 1970 to 1975, compressed workweeks plateaued in usage until 1979. One of the reasons for the arrested growth during that period appeared to be the fairly demanding sociotechnical conditions for successful use. Compressed workweeks are suited to some work settings but not to others. This is a matter both of the work technology and of the social system in the company. For example, if contact with customers or suppliers is important, a four-day workweek might not succeed while the rest of the world operates on a five-day workweek. If many workers are parents with young children, the long days of compressed workweeks might be quite an inconvenience.

A high rate of failure of compressed workweeks points up the need to carefully assess in advance who can use this new work pattern. In a recent national survey, 28 percent of one-time users of compressed workweeks had abandoned it.[17] Other studies have also reported frequent failures. These failures occurred quite quickly when they happened and were usually caused by trouble with fatigue, coverage, scheduling, productivity, and supervision. They were also caused in some cases by employee discontent.

Now there is renewed interest in compressed workweeks due to their potential role in alleviating energy shortages, congested rush-hour traffic, and air pollution. But which companies are able to convert to this work schedule? Which employees want to make such a change?

In this section some compressed workweek successes and some failures are examined in an effort to find out what attributes of both companies and work schedules make for good rather than bad experiences.

Compressed workweeks include the four-day, ten-hours-per-day schedule as well as three days of twelve hours. We also look at four-and-one-half-day weeks of nine hours for four days, with four hours the fifth day. The newest version of compressed schedules is the 5/4–9 plan: nine hours a day for five days one week and for four days the next week. In all cases, the distinguishing feature of a compressed schedule is that the same number of hours are worked in fewer days. These schedules may or may not also give workers flexibility in their choice of starting and quitting times.

HOW COMPRESSED WORKWEEKS, SHIFT WORK, AND HUMAN-RESOURCE DEVELOPMENT FIT TOGETHER: THE CASE OF THE PHYSIO-CONTROL CORPORATION

The Physio-Control Corporation is an example of a company that has both successful compressed workweeks and attractive shift work. Not just coincidentally, Physio-Control also emphasizes human-resource development and boasts an unusual record on employee education and training. The innovative work schedules are one of the reasons. This is a case study of how innovative work patterns and human-resource development fit together.

Physio-Control, a recently acquired subsidiary of Eli Lilly and Company, is a medium-sized publicly held multinational maker of electronic instrumentation for the medical field. Founded in the 1950s, Physio-Control has a record of rapid growth in sales and profits. The company is located in a new facility in the country near Redmond, Washington, a suburb of Seattle.

The Multitude of Compressed Work Schedules at Physio-Control

There are three different compressed work schedules used at Physio-Control:

- Four days of ten hours a day is used the most, with 566 employees following that schedule, including most production workers.
- Four and one-half days, with nine hours for four days and four hours the fifth day is used by some marketing and accounting employees.
- Three days of twelve hours a day in a Friday–Saturday–Sunday weekend shift applies to 23 manufacturing workers.

In addition to these compressed schedules, there are standard eight-hour days for five days a week followed by 27 people scattered among credit, human resources, and technical services. All the work schedules are fixed hours. Flexitime is not used because the band widths for ten-hour days would be too long, according to the company's human resources director, John W. Price. But there have been requests for flex-itime, and Price acknowledges that it might aid the company's education programs.

Job sharing occurs not as a regular employment option but only as two or three special cases where two diverse skills are needed for one job and where coverage of absences is especially critical. Otherwise, most Physio-Control jobs require a type of experience which in this industry is hard to recruit from the labor market. It must therefore be developed internally, and that is too costly to provide for people who work only half time.

These several varieties of compressed workweeks were started in 1972 when the idea first became popular. Workers asked for these schedules, and the company wanted to be responsive and on the leading edge of new developments.

Why Do Compressed Workweeks Succeed Here?

Because compressed workweeks have not succeeded for a large number of companies that tried them, we need to ask what it is about this company that permitted them to succeed here. This is not a case, after all, of a computer center or a road crew or a police department—some of the types of work units for which compressed workweeks are made to order. What are the sociotechnical conditions at Physio-Control that let compressed workweeks succeed? There are several:

1. There is not one but three compressed work schedules, each tailored to job requirements. There is also a standard five-day schedule. Where coverage is critical, a five-day or four-and-one-half-day schedule is used.
2. The plant operates seven days a week, so interfacing problems are minimal.
3. The work is not physically demanding or mentally tedious, so fatigue is not a problem.
4. The work force is young—the average age of the twelve-hour shift workers is 30 and the average age company-wide is only 32. Typ-

ically, this is the age group that most often prefers compressed workweeks.

5. Although many employees are women (about half), the 4/10 schedule starts very early (6:50 A.M.) so that it also ends only 20 minutes later (5:20 P.M.) than a standard work schedule. (However, there have been requests for an on-site child-care center.)

In brief, the two most common problems with compressed workweeks do not plague Physio-Control: (1) employees do not resist because there is little interference of these schedules with the personal time of the workers, and (2) the work gets done without disruption because the work schedules follow the job requirements and the plant runs every day of the week.

How to Make Shift Work Attractive

Physio-Control has shift work that employees want, and that is a "no-problem" schedule for the company. There are three basic reasons why shift work is running smoothly here when it is such a problem for so many companies elsewhere. First, and most fundamentally, shift work here is nothing at all like conventional shift work in which employees rotate across day, afternoon, and night shifts during both weekdays and weekends. Instead, shift work here is totally three-day weekend work. It is stable; employees can plan their home lives; and they are not physiologically upset.

Second, the weekend schedule that is used (12 hours on Friday, Saturday, and Sunday) gives both the company and the workers an unusual opportunity to do other things that they want to do on Monday through Thursday. In this case, the interests of employees lie principally in higher education.

Third, the jobs are good jobs, perhaps even better on the average than the Monday-through-Thursday workers' jobs. There is very little supervision and a great deal of self-management—as well as an esprit de corps and feeling of teamwork. These attitudes have been fostered by management.

Consider this unusual compressed-schedule weekend work more closely. It was started for the usual reason that shift work is started—to increase production from existing plant and equipment and utilize it more fully. Why wasn't a second shift added during week nights? The main reason was worker preference that translated, in this case, into company gains as well. The weekend or twelve-hour aspect of this work schedule is in no way technologically required. Since the weekend crew is small—only 23 people—it might even have been possible to add that number of workers to the first shift.

The employee appeal of the compressed-weekend shift is demonstrated by (1) negligible turnover compared to a 25 percent turnover rate among weekday workers (those who do leave the weekend shift usually go to the weekday 4/10 schedule but do not leave the company), and (2) a waiting list of people who want the weekend jobs. But why do these workers like the weekend shift when elsewhere one of the reasons why shift work is unpopular is because it means working on weekends? There is a long list, and here are some of the reasons:

- It is altogether *day* work (7:00 A.M. to 7:00 P.M.) even though it is weekend work, and it uses up only three days of the week.
- There is no forced rotation to other work times and days; it is stable.
- The jobs are good jobs: high-skill technicians, final assembly workers, testing and quality-control workers, and preparation for shipping.
- The pay premium is 11 percent—40 hours' pay for 36 hours' work.
- Education can be undertaken in substantial doses from local colleges during the Monday-through-Thursday days off.
- There is minimum supervision (a one-to-fifteen ratio), a team approach to production, job rotation within a day's time, and a resulting entrepreneurial spirit. (All employees at Physio-Control are called "team members" rather than employees.)
- Weekend-shift workers are treated the same in the company as weekday workers.

The company benefits from the weekend shift more than it would from a second shift on weekdays because of the low turnover and high recruiting gains that flow from its attractiveness to employees. The most important advantage to the company, however, is that this work schedule allows the education of employees on a scale that could not otherwise be approached. In a skill-shortage area, this gain is critical. The company also reports higher production rates for weekend workers than for weekday workers.

To gain continuity between the weekend workers and the weekday crew, one supervisor and two lead workers occasionally rotate through both schedules.

Human-Resource Development and Innovative Work Schedules

As a high-skill fast-growth company in an industry that shares these traits, Physio-Control places a premium on human-resource development. That means principally two things: education and training, and performance evaluation with career development. The compressed work schedules facilitate these programs.

The company relies heavily on external providers for technical training for its employees. Correspondingly, the company offers 100 percent tuition reimbursement, paid when the course of study begins (not when it ends). In 1980, there were 158 tuition-aid participants out of 788 total employees—a very high 20 percent. This exceeds national averages of uptake rates by at least five times. Among the weekend shift workers in particular, 85 percent are going to school, mostly to finish four years of college. Indeed, one of the reasons why the weekend work schedule was adopted was to respond to the availability of educational opportunities outside the company and to make it possible for employees to take advantage of tuition aid. The company worked with community colleges to get more electronics education offered, and at the same time it changed the work schedule to permit its employees to take advantage of those offerings.

Although the company has in the past believed, as an article of faith, that tuition-aid expenditures increased employee retention, that proposition will now be rigorously assessed. The company will calculate its return on its tuition-aid investments, signaling a shift in its view to tuition aid as an economic and management program rather than as a fringe benefit or recruiting device.

The educational programs at Physio-Control are complemented by "personal growth" programs. Most employees have group sessions every two months (which is unusually frequent) with trained facilitators. The sessions focus on career development, performance evaluation, and problem solving.

COMPRESSED WORKWEEKS IN A MANUFACTURING PLANT: THE CASE OF THE XYZ COMPANY

Earlier in this chapter, the case of job sharing in a medium-sized manufacturing plant was explained. That company, called XYZ Company, has 1425 production employees out of a total of 1775 employees in a small midwestern town. It is an example of the successful use of a compressed work schedule in quite a different work technology and social system. Much of the factory work is heavy, noisy, and dirty. Much of it consists of machine tending. The industry that uses the company's products—construction—is old and cyclical. This case offers another view of what it takes to get success with compressed workweeks.

The plant normally is a two-shift operation for four and one-half days a week, with a 40-hour workweek for each shift. This is a compressed workweek that was begun in the early 1970s. Here is the shift schedule:

First shift: 6:30 A.M.–4:00 P.M., Monday–Thursday
               6:30 A.M.–10:30 A.M., Friday
Second shift: 4:30 P.M.–2:00 A.M., Monday–Thursday
               12 noon–4:00 P.M., Friday

If overtime work is necessary, the 40-hour workweek is extended to 45 hours for both shifts by having both shifts work the Monday–Thursday schedule also on Friday, and premium wages are paid. If still more overtime is needed, these shifts are repeated on Saturday. A small third shift of 50 people is added only occasionally, in times of extremely high demand, to work in bottleneck areas.

There is no rotation across shifts; the company has little difficulty staffing the second shift, perhaps because there is usually no weekend work. There is no schedule flexibility for workers. No labor union is present in the plant.

Because the failure rate for compressed workweeks has been quite high, it is important to ask why this compressed workweek has succeeded. There appear to be at least four reasons:

1. The workday is nine hours rather than ten, so fatigue is not a problem.
2. The workdays end early—at 4:00 P.M.—because they start early; early starts go along with the rural Protestant work ethic of this community. The early end of the workday means there is not the interference with family life and personal time that compressed workweeks sometimes produce.
3. The plant operates a full five days, so there are no coverage problems for suppliers.
4. All workers in the plant follow the same schedule, so there are no interface problems.

THE 5/4-9 SCHEDULE EXPERIMENT: THE CASE OF THE BOARD OF GOVERNORS OF THE FEDERAL RESERVE SYSTEM

The Board of Governors of the Federal Reserve System changed from fixed working hours to a limited version of flexitime in 1973. When the legal requirement to pay overtime wages after eight hours a day and 40 hours a week was temporarily suspended for federal workers in 1979, the Board of Governors planned an experiment with another new work pattern—the 5/4-9 schedule. This is a version of compressed work-weeks in which employees work five days one week and four days the next, putting in nine hours each day or the usual 80 hours over a biweekly pay period. Every other week, a full weekday is time off.

The Board of Governors employs 1500 people in downtown Washington, D.C. Most of them are white-collar office workers, from clerks to professionals. This case study is about the board's experiment with the 5/4-9 schedule—how a pilot project was designed and implemented, and what the evaluation data show. These data describe the effects of the 5/4-9 version of compressed workweeks when workers also have flexibility in their choice of starting and quitting times rather than rigid hours.

How the Experiment Was Conducted

Before the 5/4-9 experiment began, the board's gliding-hours program permitted employees, with their supervisor's consent, to arrive at work during a flexible band between 8:00 A.M. and 9:30 A.M. The workday then continued for eight and one-half hours and ended as early as 4:30 P.M. or as late at 6:00 P.M. Many employees availed themselves of this program and it operated successfully, especially from the standpoint of employee morale.

When congressional legislation mandated that federal government agencies experiment with alternative work schedules and lifted overtime pay restrictions for this purpose, the board established a task force to study the various components of flexible and compressed workweek schedules. A questionnaire was distributed to all employees in order to gauge the interest of Board of Governors employees in experimenting with alternative work schedules, and a literature review was conducted to determine what effects alternative work schedules might have on productivity, board operations, costs, and benefits and savings to the board.

Since productivity was an important issue, the task force attempted to gather and analyze existing information from previous experiments with alternative work schedules. A consultant assisted the task force in surveying the literature.

The task force was headed by Dr. Neal Hillerman, chief of the Mathematical and Statistical Analysis section of the Data Processing Division. This choice should be well noted. Dr. Hillerman was chosen partly because of his quantitative skills and partly because his Ph.D. would lend credibility to an experiment in an agency populated with well-educated people. A personnel officer was deliberately not chosen, to further communicate that this was a management experiment rather than a personnel innovation.

In January 1980, the board authorized a six-month compressed workweek experiment using the 5/4–9 format to begin in May. Also in January, the board stretched the time ranges for gliding hours to begin the workday one-half hour earlier, at 7:30 rather than 8:00 A.M., and thereby end the workday as early as 4:00 P.M.

The experiment was then announced to all division directors; shortly thereafter the experiment director met individually with all division directors to survey their needs and preferences in planning the necessary steps to implement the experiment. An announcement was made to all employees about the experiment through the board's internal employee newsletter. A consultant again assisted the task force in designing the experiment and its evaluation.

In March, employees who wanted to join the 5/4–9 experiment and whose jobs permitted them to do so volunteered through their supervisors. A representative was appointed from each of the board's eleven divisions to handle coordination. About 250 of the board's 1500 employees (or 17 percent) asked to participate. Participants came from all divisions of the board; no complete work units and no work units whose employees were not able to participate were chosen as experimental units. Participants and nonparticipants were mixed in the same office. In April, an employees' manual was distributed to all participants and supervisors describing the provisions of the 5/4–9 schedule (see appendix, document A-1) and on May 5 the experiment commenced.

The key features of the experiment were:

1. The minimum criteria for success are that "operating efficiency is not reduced and that there are few, if any, abuses."

2. Participation is the employee's voluntary choice, but that choice is contingent on work requirements; supervisors must approve employees' participation, and employees are made responsible for meeting workplace demands. The official business hours of the board remain as they were, 8:45 A.M. to 5:15 P.M.

3. Employees are asked to choose their working hours and days within the flexible time bands and then stick with that choice for quite a long time; there are no debit and credit hours (every workday is nine hours).

4. Overtime is redefined to begin after nine hours (rather than eight) in a day for 5/4-9 participants; overtime must be authorized by supervisors.

5. Evaluation procedures and data to be required from participants are built in and outlined in the manual; they are part of employees' participation.

How the Experiment Was Evaluated

The 5/4-9 Task Force planned a quantitative evaluation of the experiment. The sources of data were questionnaires administered to 5/4-9 workers, supervisors, and nonparticipants, as well as a variety of archival data that were already being collected routinely for other purposes. Questionnaires were administered three times: after four weeks, to assess the impact of the transition and to uncover any problems that needed fixing; at the three-month midpoint of the experiment; and after six months, when the experiment was to be completed.

Results: What Changes Did 5/4-9 Bring About?

The impact of the 5/4-9 schedule on work at the board after three months of operation is described in terms of supervision, resource utilization, energy and transportation usage, and economic results. Here are the main findings:

Supervision:
- Coverage problems increased, but the impact was minor. About 30 percent of the supervisors mentioned coverage problems (for example, getting clerical or professional support), but only 5 percent

thought them serious. Among employees themselves, 10 percent or less had problems getting guidance from supervisors or help from co-workers. However, 28 percent of nonparticipants had these problems after 5/4–9 started.

• Supervisors had less need to adjust schedules to accommodate workers' wishes to do personal business. One out of four supervisors made this response while the rest saw no change.

• Supervisory effort increased, but many supervisors believed it was worth the extra effort. Among the 53 percent of all supervisors who said the 5/4–9 schedule took more effort by them, three out of four said it was worth it. Note here that 76 percent of the supervisors said that their employees performed work tasks that did not require their presence for substantial parts of the day.

• Supervisory skills changed only slightly, but in a positive direction. Improved skills were mentioned by 19 percent and worsened skills by 13 percent of the supervisors.

Human Resource Utilization:

• Quiet-time potential was largely realized. Two-thirds of the supervisors thought there was a benefit from the quiet time before and after core hours, when work requiring concentration could be done.

• Employee decision making and responsibility for their performance increased, according to 27 percent of the supervisors. This result strengthened compared to the four-week transition survey. Employees themselves concurred in this judgment, with one-third giving this answer. Correspondingly, one out of six employees said they had opportunities to learn new tasks because of the 5/4–9 schedule.

• Employees' planning, organizing, and management skills improved. Almost half of them gave this response.

• Communications were somewhat worse. Here there is some disagreement between supervisors and workers, both participants and nonparticipants. The main result is that one-third of the supervisors thought communications within the work unit were worsened. But 80 to 90 percent of the workers saw no change in communications, inside or outside the office (in fact, some saw an improvement, especially in communication across time zones).

• Work-group impact was positive, according to 62 percent of the supervisors.

• Fatigue increased, but only by a small amount. Less than one-fourth of the 5/4–9 workers reported they were somewhat more tired because of the new work schedule.

Economic Results:
• Paid overtime decreased very slightly. Only 4 percent of the supervisors reported this saving, while one percent said overtime pay increased. But 35 percent of the supervisors never have any overtime work.
• The amount of labor input to accomplish the job did not change. Participating employees continued to work the same number of hours with few exceptions.
• Tardiness and absenteeism both went down after the 5/4–9 schedule started. Nineteen percent of both supervisors and participants reported this result for tardiness, while 22 percent of supervisors and 34 percent of participants thought absenteeism went down.
• Neither productivity nor quality of work changed. About 10 percent of the supervisors reported gains and losses, while 80 percent found no change. However, these are opinion reports with no substantiating evidence.

Facility Usage.   Computer usage apparently did not change because of the 5/4–9 schedule. Neither total usage nor peak usage was affected. Cafeteria traffic in the morning for breakfast or coffee did go up. Because the workday could now begin early, some managers feared workers might be inclined to come in early for breakfast at the cafeteria and claim that as work time. Indeed, midweek breakfast counts did go up by 8 percent, compared to 17-week periods before and after the 5/4–9 schedule experiment began. However, limited follow-up counts showed that the midweek increase was for carry-out breakfast, while sitdown breakfast counts remained stable throughout the week. Thus, the level of abuse by 549 participants using working time for breakfast appears to be limited.

Energy and Transportation Usage.   A compressed workweek should reduce energy usage because workers make fewer commuting trips. (If buildings are shut down on the fifth day of the week, that would also reduce energy usage, but this was not the case at the Board of Governors.) However, the energy-saving potential will be more or less realized, depending on (1) how much private-car commuting there is (especially by single occupants) vs. commuting by public transportation, and on (2) how much workers use their cars for personal business or leisure on their extra day off.

The results from the 5/4–9 schedule at the Board of Governors are:

• Commuting time per trip decreased by a small amount, 1.1 minutes per day on the average. Exactly half of the 149 participants who kept commuting time logs for four weeks before and after the 5/4–9 experiment started had reduced commuting time, but 36 percent had an increase. However, the changes were minor, since 79 percent were within five minutes of their former commuting time.

• Commuting modes were unchanged on balance. An unusually high number of board employees (2/3) use car pools or van pools; only 5 percent drive alone. Neither these nor public transportation use was affected by the 5/4–9 schedule. Overall, only 9 percent of the participants changed their commuting mode.

• The number of commuting trips went down, and many trips were easier and quicker. But many employees also used their car for personal business or leisure activities on their extra day off, and some took more long trips because of the three-day weekends.

• Gasoline consumption went down for half the participants, according to self-reports, but only by a small amount for 35 percent of them.

The capability of this compressed workweek schedule to materially affect energy and transportation was limited because (1) flexitime in a limited version was already being used, which meant that some energy and transportation gains would already have been realized, (2) the workday length was nine hours instead of ten, and fixed, thus limiting workers' flexibility and making it possible to avoid only one rush hour, and (3) a large majority of workers were already using car pools.

Leave Usage. Half the 5/4–9 participants reported they consistently benefited from reduced sick leave and annual leave usage after six months of the experiment, and another 35 percent reported occasional benefits.

Morale.   Among participants, 62 percent reported better morale (attitude, cooperation, resourcefulness). Supervisors had similar experiences (58 percent reported better morale of their employees), while nonparticipants were seldom affected one way or the other.

Family Life.   The Board of Governors experiment provides a partial test of the effect of the 5/4–9 schedule on child care and household chores. Only 13 percent (32 employees) had children who required day care before or after school; only 6 percent (just under half this number, or 15 employees) were responsible for arranging this care. Among these parents, about half found no change in day-care efforts. But among the other half, there was an even split—four said day care was harder to arrange, and four thought it was easier. Aside from children, taking care of daily chores at home was made somewhat more difficult for 11 percent of the 5/4–9 participants.

E. Innovative Shift Working

Shift work has been around since the Industrial Revolution, and it has been something of a problem for both workers and companies all that time. Now, as more—not fewer—workers are on shift work, and as their expectations of what they should get out of work and life escalate, shift-work problems are magnified and have to be confronted.

A shift worker is defined in U.S. government statistics as one whose work time falls mainly between 4 P.M. and 7 A.M. About 9.8 million workers, or 16 percent of all full-time nonfarm wage and salary workers, are shift workers by this definition. Some industries and occupations have many more shift workers than others. For example, more than one of three service workers are shift workers and, in some manufacturing industries, the figure is even higher for operatives.[18]

Shift working has grown, along with the overall increase in the labor force in recent years. The big surprise in the trend data is where that growth has come from. Shift working among professional and technical workers was up 17 percent from 1973 to 1978; among managers and administrators, it was up 13 percent; and for clerical workers, the figure was 12 percent. These figures are well above the overall increases in shift working of 8 percent.[19]

The main problem with shift work is that not very many workers like it. They don't like it because of the undesirable work times—nights and weekends—and because of the rotation from one shift schedule to another. Nights and weekends are not good work times for many people because they are off-standard times and out of step with most of the rest of the world. Social relationships are hard to maintain when people work nights and weekends a lot of the time. Rotation from morning to night to afternoon shifts is a problem because it upsets physiological and psychological processes, especially sleeping and eating rhythms. Whether health is actually damaged is not certain, but the social disturbance is beyond doubt.

Companies as well as workers are plagued by the symptoms of shift work: absence and turnover. These problems complicate supervisors' jobs, cause extra overtime pay, and are a drain on training costs. The economic losses from undesirable shift work are surely heavy.

Now that shift work is moving into nontraditional areas, such as white-collar office jobs, there is further cause for solving the economic and social problems of shift work. The nature of technological change in offices, causing heavier capital investments in equipment such as word processors and minicomputers, will compel longer utilization of office equipment each day, and still more shift work.

Solutions to shift-work problems are basically of two types: (1) change the shift-work schedule in any one of a variety of ways, or (2) change the workplace, either its technology or its management. Changing the shift-work schedule means changing the rotation—perhaps from a fast to a slow rotation of as long as six months to a year on one shift to overcome physical adjustment problems. Or it means lengthening the shift and compressing the work time into fewer days—perhaps going from five 8-hour to three 12-hour shifts. This gives less off-standard work time (fewer nights and weekends) and should alleviate the social problems of shift work. Going beyond the shift-work schedule itself, changing the workplace to solve shift-work problems may mean transferring some choice—and responsibility—for work schedules to the workers. It may also mean reducing the hours of work on shifts. And it may mean some redesign of production processes.

These kinds of solutions to shift-work problems are being tried, in this country and in Canada and Europe, and in different kinds of companies. The first to be discussed here is the dramatic case of Shell Can-

ada, Ltd., and then three case studies of British firms, one of which is
also a Shell company.

ATTACKING SHIFT-WORK PROBLEMS WITH COMPRESSED WORKWEEKS AND ORGANIZATIONAL REDESIGN: THE CASE OF SHELL CANADA, LTD.

Problems with shift working have in recent years become more severe
and more often noticed. The problems for workers include physiological
and psychological upsets, and for companies they include high turnover,
absenteeism, and shoddy work. Companies in the petrochemical industry, where shift working is very common, are in the vanguard of innovations to alleviate shift-working problems.

Shell Canada has gone further than most companies. It has attacked
the causes of shift-work problems rather than merely treating the symptoms: in addition to changes in work patterns, it has added a variety of
fundamental organizational redesigns. What Shell Canada has done is
to adopt 12-hour shifts instead of the customary eight-hour shifts,
include a variety of nonshift jobs in the shift workers' schedules, aban-
don job classification and seniority as the basis for pay and promotions
and substitute demonstrated knowledge and skill in several tasks as the
determinant, replace traditional supervision with a participative/facili-
tative self-management system, and include labor-union input in a
cooperative low-strife, problem-solving environment. These sweeping
changes—in effect since 1978—are intended to better meet both the
company's and its workers' needs. The primary focus of this report,
however, is on work schedules.

What kind of work site is this? It is a newly constructed chemical
plant that makes polypropylene and isopropyl alcohol next to a long-
standing refinery at Sarnia, Ontario. The plant is continuous process—
seven days a week and 24 hours a day—and highly capital intensive.
The work schedule that prevailed previously in the refinery next door
was a typical slow-rotation shift schedule with five days on a shift, eight
hours per shift, and a 37⅓ hour workweek. Employment at the plant
consists of chemical-process operators who are shift workers, and day
workers who do maintenance work, warehouse work, and quality control in laboratories. The major union representing both the refinery and
new chemical plant workers is a local of the Energy and Chemical

Workers Union (previously the Oil, Chemical, and Atomic Workers Union).

Why Did Shell Canada Adopt Innovative Shift Working?

The overall goal of Shell Canada for the new chemical plant was to maximize economic and human performance as well as the quality of work life. To do so meant the creation of a learning environment. Management set out to find a new approach to shift work which would be consistent with such an environment.

One of the key reasons that Shell Canada took action to radically reform its use of shift work was shift attrition. Shell Canada shift workers were leaving shift work, bidding into lower-paying day positions, and leaving the company in high and rising numbers. After 15 to 20 years with the company on shift work, many would bid on nonshift day work (which their seniority enabled them to obtain). The company then had to invest in further training for the senior workers in their new jobs and for the new recruits required to replace them, in addition to losing the previous investment. This did not occur because the shift jobs were bad or the pay was low, because neither was the case. They left because of shift working itself.

Of course the time-honored way to induce workers to accept shift work is to offer them pay premia. But at Shell, as is the normal pattern in Canada, these premia were too low—an average of only 4 percent—to prevent attrition. (Shift premia in otherwise similar European situations are often 20 to as high as 35 percent.) But the union's bargaining priority was higher basic wage rates rather than increased shift differentials. Even so, pay was not the real issue for workers. Senior shift workers were commonly taking initial wage cuts of two to three dollars per hour, equivalent to pay losses as high as 25 percent—just to get off shift work.

The economic problems of shift working for the company were worsened by the negative social consequences of shift work for employees. The frequent loss of weekends under the conventional shift-work schedule appeared to be becoming intolerable for an increasing number of employees. (One troubled wife noted that after she turned down three or four invitations to go out on Saturday night because her husband was working on the late shift, the calls stopped coming.) The company felt some responsibility to search for ways to minimize the dislocation its work schedules caused in the private lives of its employees.

The First Step: 12-Hour Shifts and a Compressed Workweek

The Shell refinery at Sarnia converted to 12-hour shifts in 1979. The 12-hour-shift schedule consisted of three days on duty followed by three days off, rotating day (7:00 A.M.–7:00 P.M.) and night (7:00 P.M.–7:00 A.M.) shifts. This shift schedule is now found in most of Shell's Canadian refineries and petrochemical plants. It is becoming the norm in the industry in Canada and, to a lesser extent, in the U.S. Gulf Coast region.

Shell sets out three requirements to be met before conversion from standard eight-hour shifts to the compressed workweek of 12-hour shifts is made. First, the work must not be hot, dirty, noisy, or physically demanding. These conditions guard against fatigue that could be damaging to the safety of the worker and to the productivity of the plant. Second, a two-thirds or three-fourths vote of the workers, depending on the site, is required to begin a 12-hour shift experiment. This vote sometimes fails the first time in Shell's experience and then later succeeds, especially if the work force gets younger on the average over time. Third, there is a one-year experimental or probationary period.

The 12-hour shift schedule is usually favored by Shell workers because (1) they prefer the three-day blocks of time off to the two-day blocks they get under eight-hour shifts, (2) they have proportionately more weekend time off, and (3) they perceive that they have more day work and less afternoon and night work. Under conventional eight-hour rotating-shift schedules there is one-third time day work and two-thirds time off-standard (afternoon or night) work, whereas under 12-hour shift schedules there is day work half the time, if days are defined to be 7:00 A.M. to 7:00 P.M.

While Shell believes that shift attrition may be reduced by the 12-hour shift in a compressed workweek, company management is not altogether happy with this new schedule. Management becomes more difficult. For example, call-ins for emergencies or to fill in for unplanned absences are harder to work out under 12-hour shifts because off-duty workers who might be called tend to go out of town more frequently when they have time off in three-day blocks. Thus a stand-by roster needs to be developed. Another problem is that leave time, such as vacations, needs to be recalculated—on a 12-hour shift of three successive days, a week's vacation is one of these three-day shift sequences rather than a calendar week that might include five days' work in the seven day span. Approval to use 12-hour shifts without payment of overtime must in each case be obtained from the Labor Ministry. While the problem of leave time is a one-time problem that can be solved and then left, the call-in problem is a continuing complication.

Other continuing problems that Shell Canada experienced with the 12-hour shift were that communications were sometimes poor, handovers from one shift to another were rough because of so many days off between working tours, and many shift workers developed principal outside interests, such as farming, which distracted them from their primary job at Shell.

Productivity may also suffer some declines according to subjective speculations of some managers. "If the guy did two tours around the plant checking equipment on his eight-hour shift, I'll bet he still does just two tours on his 12-hour shift." However, there are no hard measures to substantiate these impressions, and the plants with 12-hour shifts appear to function smoothly for the most part.

The Second Generation: Innovative Shift Working in a System of Organizational Redesign

To find a more satisfactory solution to the problems of shift working that faced both the company and its employees meant that the change in the work schedule itself would have to be supplemented by other organizational changes. A system with three major types of changes— in work schedules, in training, and in management style—is now in place in Shell's Sarnia Chemical Plant. Here are the key features:

- The work schedule for shift workers is a combination of 12-hour shifts with nonshift eight-hour days, Monday to Friday, in the laboratory, warehouse, and maintenance shops. This work pattern is intended to reduce the number of off-standard hours worked and to increase job variety, skills, and response capability.
- Job classifications and jurisdictional boundaries between jobs do not exist to the same extent that they do in traditional types of organizations; except for a few craft team members, working exclusively

on days, there are no "jobs" in the sense of a defined activity tied to a certain skill, pay level, or status.

• Shift workers are multiskilled and continually trained.

• The economic reward system is based on what the worker knows—how many skills the worker has acquired, as determined by testing.

• Seniority does not exist for purposes of determining pay or advancement. Seniority continues to be used for protection against layoffs.

• Shift integrity is maintained—the same people work together always, changing shifts together and doing day jobs together. This aids supervision and training and provides for team management.

• Supervision is nontraditional—workers are more self-managing on tasks such as planning, organizing, controlling, and directing. Work teams have a coordinator whose job is employees' team development and coordination, and, in the initial years of organization development, that of team trainer, facilitator, and technical/operational leader for the team.

• The Oil, Chemical, and Atomic Workers Union (now renamed the Energy and Chemical Workers Union) was involved from the beginning and has been a partner in the planning and implementation process. Cooperation has taken place at both the local and the national level.

• The newly-built physical plant is different in layout from the usual chemical plant. It was designed expressly to accommodate the organizational design.

The Shift Schedule.   In order to obtain multiskilled workers and also reduce the adverse effects of shift work, Shell Canada's objective was disarmingly simple and sensible: give Shell workers a variety of skills and reduce the amount of shift working. The strategy was to remove to the extent possible the cause of shift-work problems (that is, shift working itself) rather than merely trying to alleviate its unpleasant aspects. The core of the solution was to rotate shift workers through nonshift work, thus making shift workers only partly shift workers. Of course, this meant that there were fewer exclusively nonshift day jobs and thus diminished possibilities for senior workers to get off shift work altogether. This feature of the Shell Canada plan may limit its attractiveness to other companies.

The staffing requirement in the plant of a full 168 hours per week (24 hours a day, seven days a week), with the preestablished 37⅓ hour workweek requires a minimum of 4½ crews for continuous operation (168 hours per week work requirement divided by 37⅓ hours per week per crew equals 4½ crews). However, Shell Canada uses six crews, or one and one-half extra crews, in order to provide opportunities for each crew of shift workers to do nonshift day work in maintenance, warehouse, and quality-control labs.

The basic outline of the work schedule is as follows: 3D-3O-3N-3O ... (repeat seven times) ... 5DA-2O-5DA-9O.

D   = a 12-hour 7:00 A.M.–7:00 P.M. day shift
N   = a 12-hour 7:00 P.M.–7:00 A.M. night shift
DA = a nonshift eight-hour day assignment, Monday to Friday.
O   = time off

(See figure 2-6 for a sample of the schedule in detail.)

The key facts of this work schedule are that (1) the average workweek is 42 hours, reduced to 37⅓ by two blocks of nine days off during the cycle; (2) the cycle length is 18 weeks; (3) each cycle contains ten full weekends off and four partial weekends off (that is, either a Saturday or a Sunday off); (4) each team (A,B,C,D,E,F) consists of 20 people, and (5) off standard work (the afternoon or night work of conventional shift work) is only 36 percent of total hours worked, and day work is thus 64 percent, where the definition of day work is expanded to include the time between 7:00 A.M. and 7:00 P.M.

Training.   Training as part of employee development is a central and continual activity in Shell Canada's new work patterns. Training is and was required by the complexity of the processes and equipment used in chemical manufacture, quite independent of the work schedule. But now the merging of shift work with day work reinforces the need for training because of the increase in the variety of tasks that workers perform.

While training is complicated because of multiskilling, scheduling is somewhat facilitated by taking advantage of periods of time available during members' "day assignments," when they don't have responsibility for process operations.

	M	T	W	T	F	S	S	M	T	W	T	F	S	S	M	T	W	T	F	S	S	M	T	W	T	F	S	S	M	T	W	T	F	S	S	M	T	W	T	F	S	S
A				N	N	N				D	D	D				N	N	N				DA	DA	DA	DA	DA			DA	DA	DA	DA	DA									
B	D	D	D				N	N	N				D	D	D				N	N	N				D	D	D				N	N	N				D	D	D	DA		
C	N	N	N				D	D	D				N	N	N				D	D	D				N	N	N				D	D	D				N	N	N			
D								DA	DA	DA	DA	DA			DA	DA	DA	DA	DA			N	N	N				D	D	D					N	N	N			D	D	D
E	DA	DA	DA	DA	DA			DA	DA	DA	DA	DA										D	D	D				N	N	N					D	D	D			N	N	N
F				D	D	D				N	N	N				D	D	D	DA										DA	DA	DA	DA	DA			DA	DA	DA	DA	DA		

	3	4	5	6	7	8	9	10	11	12	13	14	15	16	17	18	19	20	21	22	23	24	25	26	27	28	29	30	31	APR. 1	2	3	4	5	6	7	8	9	10	11	12	13
	M	T	W	T	F	S	S	M	T	W	T	F	S	S	M	T	W	T	F	S	S	M	T	W	T	F	S	S	M	T	W	T	F	S	S	M	T	W	T	F	S	S
A	D	D	D				N	N	N				D	D	D				N	N	N				D	D	D				N	N	N				D	D	D	DA		
B								DA	DA	DA	DA	DA			DA	DA	DA	DA	DA			N	N	N				D	D	D					N	N	N			D	D	D
C	DA	DA	DA	DA	DA			DA	DA	DA	DA	DA										D	D	D				N	N	N					D	D	D			N	N	N
D				N	N	N				D	D	D				N	N	N				DA	DA	DA	DA	DA			DA	DA	DA	DA	DA									
E				D	D	D				N	N	N				D	D	D	DA										DA	DA	DA	DA	DA			DA	DA	DA	DA	DA		
F	N	N	N				D	D	D				N	N	N				D	D	D				N	N	N				D	D	D				N	N	N			

	14	15	16	17	18	19	20	21	22	23	24	25	26	27	28	29	30	MAY 1	2	3	4	5	6	7	8	9	10	11	12	13	14	15	16	17	18	19	20	21	22	23	24	25
	M	T	W	T	F	S	S	M	T	W	T	F	S	S	M	T	W	T	F	S	S	M	T	W	T	F	S	S	M	T	W	T	F	S	S	M	T	W	T	F	S	S
A								DA	DA	DA	DA	DA			DA	DA	DA	DA	DA			N	N	N				D	D	D					N	N	N			D	D	D
B				N	N	N				D	D	D				N	N	N				DA	DA	DA	DA	DA			DA	DA	DA	DA	DA									
C				D	D	D				N	N	N				D	D	D	DA										DA	DA	DA	DA	DA			DA	DA	DA	DA	DA		
D	D	D	D				N	N	N				D	D	D				N	N	N				D	D	D				N	N	N				D	D	D	DA		
E	N	N	N				D	D	D				N	N	N				D	D	D				N	N	N				D	D	D				N	N	N			
F	DA	DA	DA	DA	DA			DA	DA	DA	DA	DA										D	D	D				N	N	N					D	D	D			N	N	N

Figure 2-6. Shell Canada team shift schedule for an 18-week cycle at Shell Chemical Plant, Sarnia 1980.

Note: Dates and days of the week are indicated across the top; the six work teams are indicated by the letters A–F along the left side; see the text for the meaning of D, N, and DA.

Source: Shell Canada

While front-end training is more costly, to a large extent it is merely rearranged. Previously shift workers received process operator training over a period of several years. When they acquired enough seniority to get off shifts, they were given craft and technical training for maintenance work. Under the new work pattern, both kinds of training are given at the same time, since both kinds of jobs are done at the same time.

Physical Plant Design.   The introduction of far-reaching work schedule and organizational changes was aided immensely by the construction of a new plant that was designed to accommodate these changes. Here are just three examples: (1) control centers were combined and quality control laboratories were integrated into the production facility rather than physically separated; (2) maintenance shops were reconfigured to provide easier access from production areas; (3) parking lots were rearranged to eliminate status differences; and (4) on-line computer-aided production control was redesigned to provide meaningful feedback to equipment operators.

Flexible Work Schedules.   Because the plant is a continuous-process operation, work stations must be staffed without interruption or overlap. Shift hours, therefore, are fixed rather than individually flexible. However, a system of mutual exchanges is used in which a worker can swap a day or more of his schedule with another worker who is willing and who is otherwise off that day, providing that costs are not increased nor team strength weakened.

The Role of Labor Unions

Once Shell Canada management determined that organization and job-design changes were desirable, the Energy and Chemical Workers Union was asked to participate in planning and implementing change. Despite fundamental alterations in areas traditionally of great union interest—seniority, job classifications, and pay systems—labor–management cooperation was obtained.

Labor–management cooperation in adopting new work patterns in this case was not simply a matter of one local union acting to meet local need without regard to national or international union points of view, as has sometimes been the case in the United States. Because the work-pattern changes were so far-reaching, Shell obtained support from the national union leaders; they would not have been successful with only local support.

Will the New Work Schedules Succeed?

It is still too soon to make a rigorous quantitative evaluation of this innovation, except to note that the multiskilling aspect is valuable. There are problems which require continued management attention. The transition from traditional supervision to self-management is difficult for both management and the work teams, which move at different paces in different ways and with different degrees of success in achieving this transition.

Who Can Use Innovative Shift-Work Schedules and Organizational Redesign?

The immediate question that a business manager would have about one company's new work patterns that incorporate radical changes in ways of doing things is: Can these major changes be adopted in my company? The conditions listed below appear to be necessary for success.

- There must be an uneasiness about shift working before a change is contemplated—workers must be dissatisfied and management must perceive problems in order for far-reaching and fundamental innovations to be successful.
- The shift work must not be physically demanding, dirty, noisy, or hot. If it is, 12-hour shifts will not succeed. Nevertheless, shift workers could still be rotated through nonshift jobs.
- The work technology should be continuous process and heavily capital intensive because these conditions favor multiskilling and training as well as innovations in supervision; the technology should not be an assembly-line technology.
- Training must be highly valued in the company, and provisions must be made to conduct it.
- A new facility and new work force make the innovations easier to introduce. Established workers may object if they are about to be taken off shift work altogether by virtue of seniority, and old plants may not be easily adjusted to accommodate organizational redesign.

• Employees and labor unions need to be participative and cooperative.

• Top managers should endorse the innovations in principle, be willing to risk failure, and let company leaders experiment and fail without reprisal; an underlying question of "Whose head will roll if this thing bombs out?" cannot be tolerated.

Perhaps of most encouragement to potential innovators is this Shell Canada opinion: Even an authoritarian organization can make structural work-pattern changes (such as 12-hour shifts, multiskilling, pay based on knowledge, no seniority, and no job classifications) without having to take the added step of behavioral changes (such as self-management and nontraditional supervision). The structural changes should by themselves solve problems such as high turnover and shift attrition. The behavioral changes should add productivity benefits, but they are not a necessary condition for success.

There is yet another way to look at innovations in the workplace, based on the Shell Canada model. There are three sequential steps that can be taken. First, the organization can change the shift schedule from a standard eight-hour to a 12-hour compressed schedule. That can only be done, as noted previously, if work is not physically demanding, hot, dirty, or noisy—if it is not fatiguing after 12 hours. It also requires flexible labor laws as well as labor union willingness to renegotiate or redefine overtime and vacation rules. If only this step can be taken, with no further innovations, symptoms of shift-work problems are likely to be alleviated.

Second, the organization can add rotation through nonshift work and multiskilling to the initial shift-schedule change. No further conditions for success apply. There must be a good training environment in the company and an adjustable physical plant and work force (especially among senior workers). There must be additional labor-union willingness to experiment. Even if the company stops with this second step, some causes of shift-work problems will be removed and further economic gains achieved.

Third, the organization can add changes in management style and accomplish organizational redesign—such as self-supervision. This last behavioral step is perhaps the hardest to take and may yield large but hard-to-measure results. It is optional. The first two steps do not depend on it; companies need not be deterred from initiating work-schedule changes for fear of taking the last behavioral step.

Finally, it is surely not only refineries and chemical plants that can benefit from dramatic work-schedule and organizational changes. And it is not always necessary that such changes be born out of crisis. Indeed, the Shell Oil Company in the United States also has initiated innovative shift-work patterns at times when management did not have its back to the wall. Shell–U.S. has found that changing management style—the third step—is easier in good times than bad.

The nature of changes in technology suggests that shift working may increase among white-collar workers and in industries where it has previously been rare—for example, in banking and electronics. The conditions for innovative shift working and organizational redesign look quite good in these industries. Transferring experiences from petrochemical plants to these new applications should be high on the business agenda.

BRITISH EXPERIENCES WITH INNOVATIVE SHIFT WORKING: THE CASES OF SHELL CHEMICAL (U.K.), SAVALCO, AND BEECHAM'S PHARMACEUTICALS

by William McEwan Young

Several recent British innovations in shift working are based on the concept of "time flexibility." The principle underlying the concept of time flexibility is a view of an employee's contract of service as an annual time contract rather than a weekly time contract. The application of time flexibility takes many forms, but the concept is constant. It takes the form of a concession by the employer, in return for which the work force undertakes to provide suitable staffing throughout the year, in order to meet the production requirements of the enterprise.

Of course, such a simple statement conceals the complexity of reality. The objectives of the parties in innovations of this type are rarely single objectives. They include reducing overtime without loss of earnings, stemming shift attrition, reducing absenteeism, increasing productivity generally, developing more socially acceptable systems of shift coverage, and other goals.

In all three cases described below, the companies wanted to reduce absenteeism.[20] To do so, management and union people agreed to increase the number of shift workers (deliberate overstaffing) and to reduce the annual hours of work per employee. In return, workers were given responsibility to cover absences, with an incentive system to reduce absences as well. Workers gained some control over their work schedule and the ability to plan their off-work lives.

Annual Time Contracts with Crew Spares at Shell Chemical (U.K.)[21]

At a chemical plant at Carrington, near Manchester, Shell Chemical (U.K.) operates a "Time Flexibility System" with the full agreement and support of the unions involved (Transport and General Workers Union [T&GWU], Association of Scientific, Technical, and Managerial Staffs [ASTMS], and craft unions). The overall objective is to allow the work force to plan its working time and leisure arrangements (within an annual average of 40 hours per week) while cooperating with senior management to provide coverage for any contingency that might arise in the continuous operation of the Carrington Chemical Plant. Here are the outstanding features of the system:

1. The plant is manned with four crews at a level that allows each employee 51 days of leave entitlement per year, made up of 20 vacation days, eight holidays, 13 relief shifts, and ten additional relief shifts. All of these entitlements have to be planned into the shift rotations and taken as time off within a given year.
2. In return for the extra leave entitlements, employees are committed to work 80 "abnormal hours" in a year to cover any contingencies that arise at the plant. They are not paid for the 80 abnormal hours of work. Abnormal hours worked in excess of 80 per year are voluntary and have to be paid for by the company, either in compensatory time off or by payment at overtime rates.
3. Shift employees are organized into work groups, each containing a spare employee(s) to enable the work groups to cover all normal work requirements without recourse to abnormal hours.
4. Work groups are responsible for providing coverage for all *planned* absences from within the group. Coverage arrangements for *unplanned* absences are the joint responsibility of supervisors and the work groups.
5. Work groups (having defined an area where they will work) may choose the shift system (pattern and frequency of rotation) that they wish to follow. There is a defined procedure for changing from one shift system to another. At the moment, no less than seven different shift systems are operating across the plant.

6. Supervisory staff have, in general, the same freedom afforded to the operators. There is nothing to prevent a group of interfacing supervisors operating a different shift system from the operators they supervise. Currently supervisors operate four different shift systems across the plant.

The experience of Shell Chemical (U.K.) shows how an annual time contract can operate in continuous-shift working. The aim throughout has been to provide continuous cover in a situation where, if the work groups cooperate in reducing *unplanned* absences to a minimum, each employee will have more time off. In such a situation overtime working is reduced to a minimum. This was achieved by adding spare workers to the work groups to enable them to cover absences, and by offering a potential extra ten days off if absences were reduced to a minimum (if workers had to cover many absences, they would use up part or all of their extra ten days off). The use of work groups that can set their own shift schedule both fosters a cooperative spirit and increases the ability to reduce absences because individual needs can be taken into account.

Worker Responsibility for Covering Absences at Savalco, Ltd.

Savalco, Ltd. (formerly Philblack, Ltd.), produces carbon black at Avonmouth, Bristol. The plant employs about 120 shift workers in a continuous-process seven-days-a-week operation. In 1972 the company and unions (T&GWU, AUEW, and EPTU) attempted to eliminate overtime by adding a fifth or relief crew. The relief crew was expressly provided to cover holidays and other absences (planned and unplanned). When not required for coverage of vacant places on other crews, the relief crew was obliged to attend one day shift and had to be prepared to carry out such reasonable work as was offered them. Each crew (the original four and the new fifth crew) had a relief week every fifth week of the cycle.

The system worked reasonably well at the outset, but it soon became obvious that the organizational problems of controlling and deploying the crew on relief were enormous. After 18 months the system was radically modified. There have been a number of other changes since then, but the main features of the present scheme have been in operation since the middle of 1974. This system works as follows.

The relief week is now regarded as rostered time off. This means that each crew now works a four-crew system of four weeks, followed by a week off. By manipulating the shift patterns, this relief week off is preceded by two rest days and terminates with one rest day of the regular cycle. In essence, then, each shift worker has ten continuous days off every fifth week, throughout the year.

As a quid pro quo for this concession from the company, the four crews who are currently working at any point in time undertake to provide coverage if any unplanned absences occur. Thus, if crews A, B, and C are working and someone on crew B falls ill, then crews A and C provide coverage for the absence, while they continue to interface. The liability to provide coverage for absences of this sort is 100 hours per year per worker. When an employee has to provide such coverage, all hours worked in excess of the normal eight hours per day are paid in cash at overtime rates.

If any employee exceeds 100 hours of this type, premium pay is received as before (for hours over eight in a day), but straight time is paid for fill-in work that does not exceed eight hours a day (subsequently taken as compensatory time off or paid at straight-time rates at the discretion of the employee).

This system imposes a self-discipline between the interfacing crews, who are confronted with the problem of organizing coverage when any unplanned absences take place. Absenteeism has been reduced dramatically, and the attitudes of the work force are now positive and supportive. An interesting aspect of these rather unique coverage arrangements is the impact they have had on the preferred shift pattern. Whereas under the original (1972) arrangements (coverage provided by the relief shift) a conventional seven-day slow rotation pattern was seen to be adequate, the current (post-1974) arrangements (coverage provided by the working shifts) require a fast rotation continental pattern. In this way no one individual is required to provide an excessive amount of 12-hour coverage in the event of a sustained absence by a colleague on an interfacing shift.

Another point of interest is the role of the personnel officer (an ex-shop-floor worker himself) who plays "honest broker" between line management and operators to ensure that the coverage load is spread equitably over the work force. It is the personnel officer who operates the main control system for the scheme.

The key feature of the Savalco innovation is this trade-off: a fifth crew is added that provides a guaranteed week every fifth week with no call-ins, in return for the elimination of absenteeism as a management concern. Note also that as in the case of Shell Chemical (U.K.), a human-resource management innovation—here in the form of the "honest broker"—accompanies the technical work-schedule change.

Shorter Workweeks in Return for Coverage of Absence at Beecham's Pharmaceuticals

Beecham's has operated a pharmaceutical manufacturing plant in Worthing since 1961, and now employs about 2000 persons. The major product is semisynthetic penicillin. The continuous-production processes involve some 450 process operators, 55 chargehands (or first-line supervisors), 30 supervisors, and 25 maintenance craftsmen.

The plant is highly unionized, and the process operators have a closed shop agreement (T&GWU). There is a comprehensive shop-steward system with communicating representatives on each shift crew. Time off is given for union duties. There are 20 vacation days plus eight holidays. There is a generous sickness and injury scheme, rigorous preemployment medical exams, and a well-equipped medical center manned 24 hours a day. No company transport is provided.

Previously, continuous production was maintained by four crews operating an average 42-hour week plus overtime, following a slow backward rotation (see figure 2-7).

In 1972, management anticipated problems in manning should the workweek be reduced and/or holidays increased. There was also grow-

	Days of the Week						
Crew	M	T	W	Th	F	S	Sun
A	m	m	m	m	m	—	—
B	n	n	n	n	n	n	n
C	—	—	—	a	a	a	a
D	a	a	a	—	—	m	m

m = morning shift, 7 A.M.–3 P.M.
a = afternoon shift, 3 P.M.–11 P.M.
n = night shift, 11 P.M.–7 A.M.

Figure 2-7. Old standard four-crew shift schedule at Beecham's.

Source: William McEwan Young, "Application of Flexible Working Hours to Continuous Shift Production," *Personnel Review*, Summer 1978, pp. 12–19.

ing evidence that operators were reluctant to work the heavy overtime loads associated with the current system and that they considered the sequence of seven work shifts before a rest period was too long. A management working party was set up, and it examined various alternatives, all based on increased staffing. The options were: (1) a five-crew system with relief week, (2) a pool-of-labor system, (3) a lieu-day system (i.e., hours worked beyond those called for by contract can be accumulated up to eight hours and then exchanged for a shift off in lieu of additional pay), and (4) an integrated five-crew system. The working party favored the integrated five-crew plan; but the report submitted to higher management was held in abeyance until the demand for shorter working hours increased. Early in 1973, half a lieu day per shift cycle was granted to reduce the average workweek to 41 hours, but the unions continued pressing for more radical changes. A joint working party was constituted to discuss alternative shift systems.

In arriving at its final recommendations, the working party sought to establish attitudes to shift working at the plant by commissioning surveys from the market research department of the Beecham Group. The results of these extremely detailed attitude surveys were used to devise an acceptable alternative shift system.

The system recommended the originally favored integrated five-crew system, following a sequence of 5m–3r–5n–4r–5a–3r, resulting in a basic 25-day cycle (r = rest days). The repeat period is 25 weeks. The first 25-day sequence of the 25-week cycle is shown in figure 2-8.

Since such a cycle would be equivalent to a workweek of 33.6 hours, the working party proposed that management and unions should negotiate what the new workweek length was to be, what sort of "pay-back" scheme was feasible so that employees could raise their weekly hours from 33.6 hours to a negotiated new workweek length, and how the scheme was to be implemented. The key features agreed to by the unions and management were that (1) contract hours were reduced from 41 hours to 38 hours per week, and (2) the rota hours of 34 (actually 33.6) were increased to 38 by the working of one additional four-hour period (a "covertime") in every "shift week" (that is, a 5-shift block). The rationale for such a pay-back scheme was: Over a period of fifty calendar weeks, each employee works only 42 shift weeks (because the workweek was less than 40 hours while the workday was eight hours, some calendar weeks would have three days off instead of two). Thus, workers would fall 168 hours short of their contractual

Day of the Week

Crew	M	T	W	Th	F	S	Sun	M	T	W	Th	F	S	Sun	M	T	W	Th	F	S	Sun	M	T	W	Th
A	m	m	m	m	m	—	—	—	n	n	n	n	n	—	—	—	—	a	a	a	a	a	—	—	—
B	a	a	—	—	—	m	m	m	m	m	—	—	—	n	n	n	n	n	—	—	—	—	a	a	a
C	—	—	a	a	a	a	a	—	—	—	m	m	m	m	m	—	—	—	n	n	n	n	n	—	—
D	n	n	n	—	—	—	—	a	a	a	a	a	—	—	—	m	m	m	m	m	—	—	—	n	n
E	—	—	—	n	n	n	n	n	—	—	—	—	a	a	a	a	a	—	—	—	m	m	m	m	m

Figure 2-8. New, innovative shift schedule with integrated fifth crew at Beecham's.

Source: William McEwan Young, "Application of Flexible Working Hours to Continuous Shift Production," *Personnel Review*, Summer 1978, pp. 12–19.

obligations. Therefore, employees have to pay back four hours each shift week (four hours for each of 42 shift weeks). But four of these shift weeks are taken as annual holidays, which reduces the shortfall in hours to 152. These are divided into 38 4-hour covertimes; the covertimes are used to fill in vacancies caused by absence due to holidays and sickness.

The first extra four hours worked (in one 12-hour stretch) in a shift week counts as one covertime unless the employee has completed his or her obligation of covertimes. Further 12-hour shifts worked in that shift week may be taken as overtime or counted against the balance of covertime obligation. Covertime credits are given for training, certified sick leave, and other specified absences. Payments (additional to covertime credit) are made for providing cover through quick turnarounds, 12-hour night shifts, and working "into" or "out of" rest periods between shift weeks.

The company has an obligation to offer one covertime per shift week to each employee. This is done through a covertime/overtime rota operated by each crew together with its supervisor and in accordance with detailed procedural rules on acceptance and refusal (devised by the crews themselves) which ensure that an employee has an inalienable right to reject the offer of any *particular* covertime.

In the event that workers have not worked their full 38 covertimes at the end of a 50-week period, they can either give up compensatory time to which they are entitled or carry over a debit balance to the next 50-week period. This happens rarely; if there are extenuating domestic circumstances, the company takes a lenient view on covertime debts. No cash adjustment has ever been necessary.

Because the new integrated fifth-crew shift schedule called for a three-hour reduction in the workweek, annual earnings of shift workers were maintained by (1) increasing basic rates of pay, (2) paying overtime at a higher rate, (3) increasing allowances for night shift and quick turnaround, and (4) initiating a job-evaluation scheme. The outcome was equal annual earnings for the average earner in terms of take-home pay.

Time flexibility schemes are the most interesting shift-work innovations currently taking place in Europe. Their genesis is the movement toward a shorter workweek, which creates conditions for the installation of an additional crew (say, from four crews to five). However, many five-crew installations use work schedules of a conventional type, in which management is seen as retaining responsibility for the deployment and utilization of all five crews.

What distinguishes the time flexibility approach is the involvement of the crews in devising their *own* staffing schedules to meet the operational needs of the enterprise. Such an approach allows the crews to plan on a short- and long-term basis—so that the social needs of their members may be met. The effects on the company appear to be satisfactory: absenteeism and labor turnover are reduced and management is freed from the organizational inconvenience of scheduling for unplanned absences.

The time flexibility concept is capable of adaptation to the needs of discontinuous-shift workers as well as continuous-shift operators and can be used with 3-, 4-, 5-, and 6-crew systems, provided that crewing is such that a pay-back element exists when the annual time contract is calculated. In that sense, the system is also transferable to any industrial culture.

NOTES

1. Based on the author's account, previously published in *Personnel Review* 7 (Summer 1978):12–19. Used with permission.
2. The abbreviation "Fa." is used to indicate a family-owned company or a "firma" that is not a stock corporation.
3. Priscilla H. Claman, *It Works: Part-Time Employment in State Agencies* (Boston: Commonwealth of Massachusetts, Executive Office for Administration and Finance, Division of Personnel Administration, 1980), p. 2.
4. Carol S. Greenwald, "Working Mothers: The Need for More Part-Time Jobs," *New England Economic Review,* September–October 1972, p. 21.
5. See note 3. Jobs studied were classified as field positions, specialists, and research or administrative staff. Professional backgrounds included lawyers, engineers, planners, budget analysts, assistant systems analysts, social service, and welfare.
6. Newsletter of the Association of Part-Time Professionals, Alexandria, Virginia, November 1978.
7. Claman, p. 2.
8. Gretl S. Meier, *Job Sharing* (Kalamazoo, Michigan: Upjohn, 1978), p. 144.
9. Ibid., p. 145.
10. Ibid., p. 75.
11. Ibid., p. 76.
12. Ibid., p. 94.
13. Ibid., p. 96.
14. Gretl S. Meier, et al., *Job Sharing in the Schools* (Palo Alto, California: New Ways to Work, 1976), p. 21.
15. Ibid., p. 2.
16. Karen Winkler, "Two Who Share One Academic Job Say the Pros Outnumber the Cons," *Chronicle of Higher Education,* 3 December 1979, p. 3.

17. Stanley D. Nollen and Virginia H. Martin, *Alternative Work Schedules* (New York: AMA-COM, a division of American Management Associations, 1978), part 3, "Compressed Workweeks."
18. Janice N. Hedges and Edward S. Sekscenski, "Workers on Late Shifts in a Changing Economy," Special Labor Force Report No. 232 (Washington, D.C.: U.S. Department of Labor, Bureau of Labor Statistics, 1979).
19. Ibid.
20. The case studies of Shell Chemical (U.K.), Savalco, and Beecham's Pharmaceuticals by William McEwan Young will form part of a report, *Shiftwork Innovations in the Chemical Industry in the United Kingdom,* to be published by the European Foundation for the Improvement of Living and Working Conditions, Dublin, in 1981. They appear here with permission of the publisher.
21. See also the author's description in "Shift Work and Flexible Schedules: Are They Compatible?" *International Labour Review* 119 (January–February 1980):1–17.

3.

Economic Costs of New Work Schedules

Fringe-Benefit Costs for Part-Time Employment and Job Sharing

The principal economic issue regarding part-time employment and job sharing is their potentially higher labor cost. The reason that part-time employees might be relatively more costly to the company than comparable full-time employees is that some labor costs are fixed per employee. Since part-time employees work fewer hours than full-timers, their per-hour labor cost can be higher. These higher costs are mainly some fringe-benefit costs, although some personnel administration costs may also be higher. If an organization offers the same fringe benefits to part-timers (prorated where possible) as to full-timers, part-timers will cost the organization more per labor-hour worked. If the organization does not offer fringe benefits to part-timers, it denies them equal status and exploits their weakness in the labor market.

Of course, fringe benefits paid on the basis of salary or time worked can be prorated easily and do not pose a cost problem to companies. These include vacations, holidays, sick leave, group life insurance, retirement plans, stock options, and profit sharing. Prorating results in equal fringe-benefit costs per labor-hour for part-time and full-time workers.

Other fringe benefits cannot be so easily handled. Statutory benefits—those required by law—are a case in point. Current contribution formulas for Social Security, unemployment insurance, and workers' compensation have earnings ceilings above which no tax is paid. They are regressive taxes and result in higher fringe-benefit costs per labor-hour to the company for workers whose annual earnings are below the ceiling. Two part-time employees have higher statutory benefit costs than one full-time employee in jobs with annual full-time equivalent earnings above the ceilings.

By far the most troublesome fringe benefit for part-time employment is group health insurance because it is the biggest extra dollar cost for companies, and it is fast getting more expensive. While no law requires companies to provide it, as a matter of fact almost all do—to full-timers. But only half offer it to part-timers. Those companies that do, suffer an extra cost of from roughly $600 to $1200 per year for each part-time employee who gets the benefit on the same terms as full-time employees. The problem with group health insurance is that it cannot be prorated easily for part-timers. The premium is fixed per employee and does not depend on earnings or hours worked.

Some companies pay the full fringe-benefit package, absorb the extra cost, and make it up elsewhere, such as in higher part-time productivity or reduced overtime payments. Some companies that pay the full package would like to get out from under the extra cost burden. Other companies do not pay many or any fringe benefits to part-timers; they save labor costs, but at what price in job performance and employee development? (See table 3-1 for data on how many companies pay fringe benefits to their permanent part-time employees.) Still other companies just avoid the problem by not using part-time employees.

Other solutions to the problem of high part-time fringe benefits are possible. An ambitious and only partly tested plan is cafeteria benefits. More easily, a cost-sharing/waiver scheme might be set up, in which part-timers help pay for the costly benefits or forgo them by choice. A

Table 3-1.   Fringe Benefits Paid to Permanent Part-Time Employees

| | | Offered to Part-Timers | | |
| | | Total | Prorated | Same as Full Time |
Fringe Benefit	Offered to Full-Timers	(percent of all users of part-time employment)		
Vacation	99	80	75	5
Sick Leave	85	55	49	6
Life Insurance	96	51	27	24
Health Insurance	97	52	19	33
Pension	93	59	42	17
Profit Sharing	61	28	20	8

Source: Stanley D. Nollen and Virginia H. Martin, *Alternative Work Schedules, Part 2: Permanent Part-Time Employment* (New York: AMACOM, a division of American Management Associations, 1978).

third possibility is for the company to design a fringe-benefit package for part-timers that meets most of their needs, gives them equal dollar value compared to full-timers, and costs the company no more.

In this section, several company experiences with fringe-benefit costs for part-timers and job sharers are reported. Two of the employers, the County of Santa Clara and the XYZ Company, pay all benefits to job sharers and incur higher costs. Two other employers, the Port of Seattle and the State of Hawaii, have worked out ways to achieve cost parity in their fringe-benefit packages for part-timers and full-timers.

EXTRA FRINGE-BENEFIT COSTS FOR JOB SHARERS: SANTA CLARA COUNTY AND XYZ COMPANY

One of Santa Clara County's innovative work patterns is "split codes," or job-sharing slots negotiated in the collective-bargaining agreement (see pages 134 to 136, for a complete case study of these work patterns in Santa Clara County).

The important reason that the county is pleased to use part-time employees is the recruiting advantage it confers. However, there is one serious problem: part-time employees cost the county more in fringe benefits. While leave time for part-time employees is prorated, full health, dental, and life insurance coverage is provided. Because the benefits are noncontributory, the dollar cost to the county mounts up. For example, the additional cost to the county (the cost in excess of half benefits for half-time work, which would be a cost-parity arrangement) ranged from $346 to $595 per half-time employee per year in 1979 (depending on whether Blue Cross or Kaiser health insurance was selected). Aggregating the 553 half-time employees, this additional cost amounted to $238,333 to $403,231, or about .05 percent of the county's total budget.

Another case of extra fringe-benefit cost is that of a medium-sized midwestern manufacturing company, here called the XYZ Company. The XYZ Company has 60 job sharers who get prorated fringe benefits for (1) vacation and holiday, (2) sick leave and other leaves, (3) life insurance—job sharers get $5,000 face amount, while full-timers get $10,000 coverage, and (4) retirement, based on annual earnings and funded by profit sharing, with all employees fully vested after three calendar years.

Three fringe benefits paid to job sharers are extra-cost items for the company: unemployment insurance, workers' compensation, and medical and dental insurance. Among these, medical and dental insurance is by far the most costly, amounting to an extra $750 in a company-paid premium for each job-sharing worker with a family. The XYZ Company offsets the extra fringe-benefit cost in two ways: (1) overstaffing to cover absences is eliminated because job sharers cover their own absences, and (2) overtime pay is reduced because two job sharers can jointly work 45 or 50 hours a week without either one of them requiring overtime pay under federal law. For a more detailed discussion of fringe benefits and other aspects of job sharing in the XYZ Company, see pages 53 to 58.

COST PARITY IN FRINGE BENEFITS FOR PART-TIME PROFESSIONALS: THE CASE OF THE PORT OF SEATTLE

Part-Time Employment at the Port of Seattle

The Port of Seattle is a quasi-public agency that operates the harbors and airports for the Seattle metropolitan area. Part-time employment began at the Port in 1975 when a management consultant recommended that it be used to better fit the size of the work force to the size of the work load and thus to reduce unit labor cost. Part-time employment was and still is seen as a strictly economic proposition to improve the functioning of the enterprise.

What is the status of part-time employees at the Port? First, they are permanent rather than temporary employees. "Part-time status applies to permanent employees scheduled to work 90 to 130 hours per month (minimum per week: 20.8 hours)."[1] Full-time employees are defined as those who work 30 or more hours per week or 130 or more hours per month. Only the number of hours to be worked distinguishes permanent part-time from full-time employees. Temporary employees are separately defined as people who work full time for less than five months in a year or less than 90 hours per month indefinitely. Temporaries are either full-timers or part-timers.

Second, part-time employees are professionals as well as clerical employees, but there are no part-time managers. Part-time employees may advance within their job classifications as do any other full-time employees. Typical part-time jobs and salaries are listed in table 3-2.

Table 3-2.   Examples of Jobs and Salaries for Permanent
Part-Time Employees at the Port of Seattle

Job	Full-Time Equivalent Annual Salary June 1, 1980
Analyst/Programmer	$27,000
Operations controller, airport	19,000
Data processing operator	14,000
Office assistant	8,000

Source: Port of Seattle Internal Documents

Third, part-timers have flexible work schedules. They set their own
work schedule with their supervisors and may vary it from week to
week. The hours-worked requirement is specified per month, not per
week. Of course, the proper utilization of space and equipment requires
the dovetailing of part-timers' schedules in some cases.

The Port of Seattle is pleased with the part-time employment program. "They are good people," says Rita Fansler Nelson, employee-
benefits administrator of the Port of Seattle. "We get them to work for
us because they are treated right. We think they have better productivity because they are fresher and take fewer breaks. Since they have less
time on the job, they are motivated to get the job done in less time."[2]

Cost Parity in Fringe Benefits

Port management wanted to use part-time employees because of their
claimed productivity advantage; but they wanted to avoid exorbitant
extra fringe-benefit costs. That meant that a fresh look at fringe benefits for part-timers was in order. The Port's objective was to spend proportionately equal amounts of company money on fringe benefits for
both full-time and part-time employees. However, there were some constraints on the Port's ability to make decisions. Some benefits, such as
Social Security, are required by law. Other benefits, such as disability
insurance, have strings attached by the insurer. Still other benefits were
thought by the Port to be more desired by part-timers than other benefits. Considering these variables the Port decided on a package of
fringe benefits that it expected would satisfy part-time employees and
that would result in a proportionately equal fringe-benefit cost to the
company. The benefits included in the package are listed in table 3-3.

Table 3-3. Fringe Benefit Package for Permanent Part-Time Employees at Port of Seattle

Fringe Benefit	Offered to Part-Timers Equal to Full-Timers	Prorated	Not Available to Part-Timers
Social Security		x[a]	
Workers' compensation		x[a]	
Unemployment compensation		x[a]	
Paid leaves			
Sick leave, 12 days per year for full-timers		x	
Civic duty leave, as needed	x		
Bereavement leave, as needed	x		
Military leave, 15 days maximum	x		
Personal appointments, as needed			x
Holidays, 11 days for full-timers		x	
Vacation, 2 to 4 weeks for full-timers, depending on length of service		x	
Medical insurance, employee and family	x		
Dental insurance			x
Life insurance, 2 × salary, $50,000 maximum face amount			x
Long-term disability insurance			x
Retirement[b]		x	
Transportation[c]	x		
Educational assistance	x		

Notes:
[a]Until contribution ceiling is reached, after which part-timers' benefits become more costly to the Port. This usually does not happen with Social Security or workers' compensation.
[b]Vesting after 5 calendar years favors part-timers.
[c]Free parking, 50 percent subsidy of bus fare, or subsidy of van-pool costs.

The Port of Seattle pays the full cost of all fringe benefits (they are noncontributory) except for Social Security (equal contributions from employer and employee as established by law), retirement (the Port pays 7.41 percent of gross earnings and the worker pays 5.51 percent), transportation, and educational assistance.

Offsetting the higher fringe-benefit costs per labor-hour that arise from medical insurance and unemployment compensation, there are four fringe benefits that are not offered to part-time employees. Here they are, with the company's rationale for not paying them to part-timers:

Personal appointment time is not needed by part-timers because they have weekday hours available for these purposes.

Dental insurance, like medical insurance, is more costly per labor-hour for part-timers than for full-timers. In 1975 when permanent part-time employment was started, dental insurance was not expected; now there is a demand for it, however, and a change may need to be made.

Life insurance could be offered just as well as not, and prorated; however, it could add disproportionately to the Port's cost because of the company-imposed ceiling on coverage ($25,000 annual earnings).

Long-term disability is available only to workers who put in 30 or more hours per week, in accordance with an insurers' rule.

How does the Port come out on a fringe-benefit cost comparison for full-time versus part-time employees? The calculations in table 3-4 are based on an actual, and typical, part-time employee:

Table 3-4. Actual Annual Fringe-Benefit Costs for a Part-Time and a Full-Time Employee at the Port of Seattle, 1978

Benefit	Employer Costs		Employee Costs	
	Full-Time	Part-Time	Full-Time	Part-Time
Social Security[a]	$ 965	$ 777	$ 965	$ 777
Workers' compensation[b]	56	39	0	0
Unemployment compensation[c]	234	234	0	0
Sick leave	499	345	0	0
Personal appointment[d]	118	n.a.	0	n.a.
Holidays	811	571	0	0
Vacation[e]	737	519	0	0
Medical insurance	1046	1046	0	0
Dental insurance	316	n.a.	0	n.a.
Life insurance	504	n.a.	0	n.a.
Long-Term disability	178	n.a.	0	n.a.
Retirement	1341	930	1150	797
Transportation[f]	115	115	115	115
TOTAL	$6,920	$4,576	$2,230	$1,689
Percent of Earnings	36.1	34.4	11.5	12.7
Fringe Benefit Cost per Labor-Hour	$ 3.6	$ 3.45		

Notes: Based on a permanent part-time employee in 1977 who worked 26 hours per week and earned $13,287 per year compared to a full-time employee who worked 37½ hours per week and earned $19,164 per year. Assumes no time off for civic duty, bereavement, or military leave, and no educational assistance.
[a]5.85 percent of the first $16,500 of earnings.
[b]Self-insured by the Port of Seattle; charged at three cents per hour for office employees.
[c]Based on 3 percent of the first $7,800 of earnings.
[d]Valued at the hourly pay rate ($9.82 in this case) for 12 hours maximum usage.
[e]Assumes a two-week vacation for full-time employees.
[f]Fifty percent subsidy of van pool monthly pass.
  n.a. = not applicable to part-time employees

Source: Computation by Rita Fansler Nelson, employee benefits administrator, Port of Seattle.

This computation demonstrates that there is cost parity; the fringe-benefit cost to the company for the part-time and the full-time employee doing the same job is very nearly the same percent of each worker's earnings. They are also, of course, the same cost per labor hour worked.

FRINGE-BENEFIT COSTS FOR JOB SHARERS UNDER ALTERNATIVE MODELS: THE CASE OF THE STATE OF HAWAII[3]

As part of a feasibility study for job sharing by public employees in the State of Hawaii, a detailed cost study of fringe benefits was conducted. The dollar costs that would be incurred for two job sharers were compared to those incurred for one full-time employee in the same job. Different jobs with different salaries, different types of job-sharing arrangements, and different family statuses of employees were examined. Existing state statutes and collective-bargaining agreements were followed.

The cost differences between the fringe benefits of job sharing and those of full-time employment are hypothetical in the sense that they are paper calculations rather than archival data from actual experiences, and they allow for no changes in fringe-benefit policy for job sharers. They are predictions of what might happen. Because fringe-benefit rules and policies differ from state to state and company to company, these figures are simply illustrative.

Several fringe benefits were omitted from the Hawaii calculations because their cost to the employer depends on their usage, and that, in turn, depends on events that are hard to predict. These benefits are leaves for education, military service, funerals, and jury duty; they also include workers' compensation and unemployment insurance. Of course, the former category of leaves can be prorated with no additional cost, but the latter two benefits will likely cost more for job sharers (they are levied on a per-capita basis or as a percent of salary up to a low ceiling), unless job sharers have a better accident and unemployment record.

In the fringe-benefit cost calculations shown in table 3-5 the extra cost for two job sharers ranged from 8.8 percent to 16.6 percent, or $445 to $1,549. The cost differences were due mainly to medical insurance for dependent coverage and to the additional cost of Social Security for high-salary workers. Of course, if the job sharing were arranged so that one job sharer worked less than 20 hours per week, or if one job

Table 3-5.   Fringe-Benefit Costs for State of Hawaii Job Sharers and Full-Time Employees, 1977

Fringe Benefit	Employees with No Dependents		Employees with Dependents[a]	
	Full-Timer	Two Job Sharers[b]	Full-Timer	Two Job Sharers[b]
A. Clerk/Stenographer job with $12,960 Annual Full-Time Salary				
Vacation leave[c]	$1,047	$1.196	$1,047	$1,196
Sick leave	1,047	1,196	1,047	1,196
Medical plan	120	240	360	720
Dental plan	—	—	78	156
Life insurance	27	54	27	54
Retirement	2,015	2,015	2,015	2,015
Social Security	758	758	758	758
Total	$5,014	$5,459	$5,332	$6,095
Percent Difference		+8.8%		+14.3%
B. Librarian or Engineer with $24,864 Annual Full-Time Salary				
Vacation leave	$2,008	$2,295	$2,008	$2,295
Sick leave	2,008	2,295	2,008	2,295
Medical plan	120	240	360	720
Dental plan	—	—	—	—
Life insurance	27	54	27	54
Retirement	$3,866	3,866	3,866	3,866
Social Security	965	1,455	965	1,455
Total	$8,995	$10,205	$9,312	$10,861
Percent Difference		+13.4%		+16.6%

Notes: [a] Assuming the employee has a spouse and two minor children.
[b] Each job sharer works 20 hours a week and receives the same salary, equal to half the full-time salary.
[c] Vacation and sick leave are higher-cost benefits for job sharers.

Source: Charles H. Nishimura, Lloyd K. Migita, and Stanley K. Okinaka, *The Feasibility of Job Sharing by Public Employees in Hawaii* (Honolulu: Legislative Reference Bureau, State of Hawaii, July 1977).

sharer with less experience or fewer qualifications were paid a lower salary, then fringe-benefit costs could be reduced.

NOTES

1. "Salary and Benefit Resolution No. 2780," 23 December 1979, Port of Seattle.
2. Personal interview with Rita Fansler Nelson, 24 September 1980.
3. This section is based on material in Charles H. Nishimura, Lloyd K. Migita, and Stanley K. Okinaka, *The Feasibility of Job Sharing by Public Employees in Hawaii* (Honolulu: Legislative Reference Bureau, State of Hawaii, July 1977).

4.

The Role of Labor Unions in Changing Work Schedules

A. Workers' Rights and Responsibilities: Redefining Overtime for Flexible and Compressed Schedules

One of the key issues in the use of new work patterns is the role of labor unions. Both flexible and compressed workweek schedules pose some legitimate problems for unions, but they also hold some promise for them. The key question is: How can labor unions solve the problems of flexible and compressed schedules so that they can realize the potential benefits?

Here are the problems of flexible and compressed schedules from a labor union viewpoint:

1. All compressed workweeks erode the concept of the eight-hour workday. Most collective bargaining agreements call for premium pay after eight hours of work in a day. (In fact, federal labor law requires overtime pay after eight hours for workers on government contracts—the Walsh–Healy and the Contract Work Hours and Safety Standards acts apply here.) But compressed workweeks mean nine, ten, or twelve hours of work a day. Since companies will not want to pay overtime wages for these extra hours of work per day, unions face the prospect of giving up overtime pay after eight hours, or opposing compressed schedules.

2. Flexible schedules that allow credit and debit hours (working more than eight hours one day in return for working fewer hours another day) also run afoul of the long-standing union concept of the eight-hour day. Of course, flexitime with fixed workday lengths of eight hours or less—flexitime or gliding time—do not raise any problems about overtime pay. Labor unions have usually

supported these versions of flexitime. But flexitime that permits variable workday lengths (credit and debit hours) has the greatest potential for quality-of-life gains for workers.

3. Exploitation of workers by management could occur if the eight-hour trigger for overtime pay were taken away. How easy it would be for managers to subtly pressure flexitime workers to stay late some days "voluntarily" in order to meet the company's needs without paying overtime.

4. The long days of compressed workweeks or flexitime with variable day lengths could endanger workers' safety and health, even if the workers choose these long days themselves.

5. Because flexitime is used mainly by white-collar office workers and may not be suitable for many blue-collar production workers, it widens the gap between these two groups of workers. It is inequitable, helping mainly those who are already best off.

Yet there are some gains for both workers and unions in flexible and compressed schedules. By far the most important is the established fact that a large majority of workers like flexitime—it often increases their morale and job satisfaction and makes it easier for them to avoid conflicts between work life and home life. To some extent, these gains are also possible with compressed workweeks. Perhaps union initiatives in obtaining these new work patterns would be a source of new membership and a way of satisfying current members.

There is some noteworthy local union activity in overcoming the problems of flexible and compressed schedules and reaping the benefits. Despite national union opposition, several innovative redefinitions of overtime and methods of protecting workers' rights have been initiated and negotiated by locals. Here are several such cases.

UNION-NEGOTIATED FLEXITIME WITH DEBIT AND CREDIT HOURS: THE CASE OF THE INTERNATIONAL FEDERATION OF PROFESSIONAL AND TECHNICAL ENGINEERS, LOCAL 21

Although national labor union spokesmen have in most cases accepted flexible working hours of limited types, they have usually opposed flexitime that permitted debit and credit hours—working more than eight hours one day in order to work less than eight another day. The two principal reasons are that unions wish to preserve the concept of the eight-hour day, and they fear management exploitation of workers if there are not fixed overtime hours rules to protect them. Local 21 of the International Federation of Professional and Technical Engineers (IFPTE), located in San Francisco, is an exception. Beginning in 1976, Local 21 began negotiating flexitime in labor agreements. As of 1980, there were six contracts with such provisions, some of which included debit and credit hours. Altogether, about 70 percent of the total Local 21 membership of 1500 workers is covered by contracts with explicit flexitime provisions. This number is expected to rise in the future.

The experiences of Local 21 offer a different viewpoint on the issue of preserving the eight-hour day, on the problem of providing protection to workers from exploitation by management when overtime rules are changed, and on the spirit of labor–management relations. We also see in this case some concrete examples of how overtime rules under variable-day flexitime can be changed, and what happens when these departures are made.

Why Does Local 21 Negotiate Flexitime?

Local 21 has six different contracts that include flexitime. Among the employers represented are the City and County of San Francisco, the City of Hayward, and the County of Alameda. These are all public-sector organizations. Local 21's next negotiation will be with a private-sector organization: this negotiation will include flexitime with debit and credit hours. The membership of the 1500-member Local 21 includes engineers, accountants, chemists, rehabilitation counselors, health educators, and inspectors. They are all white-collar employees.

The main reason Local 21 negotiated flexitime, in its business agent's view, is that the workers needed and wanted flexitime, and they asked him for it. "I don't care if this is all I ever get from the union—it is enough that you've gotten flexitime for me," according to one member. Even though some companies have reported productivity gains from flexitime, there was no thought in this case of productivity bargaining. Yet if there should be productivity gains, especially in the public sector in California where revenues are declining, then the objective of flexitime would become one of saving jobs.

The overriding belief in this union is that both workers and managers should reorient their thinking from time to task—that they should look at output rather than clocks.

What about the Eight-Hour Day? What about Exploitation of Labor by Management?

When the labor agreement lets go of the usual definition of overtime as beginning after eight hours in a day, there is a legitimate concern by unions that avenues are opened for management to take advantage of workers. But the union's job is to make life better for workers, and if workers prefer more or less than eight hours some days, they should be able to do it as long as overtime protections are in place to ensure that the choice is the worker's. Of course, workers can keep the eight-hour day under flexitime if it suits them. It is easy to talk about ensuring workers' choices. But how is it done in practice? Here are the two key points according to Local 21:

- The contract must contain explicit language covering the question of workers' protections, including simple grievance procedures.
- Accountability must be designed into the program so that both union and management are in agreement that workers will perform and, hence, that management will be satisfied.

In the case of Local 21, the union (not management) inserted language in the contract that specifies that workers must be on the job when required by their work. If there are any problems of the "you weren't there when you said you would be" type, time accumulators can be installed to account for time worked.

Above and beyond explicit contract provisions, there must also be a departure from adversarial labor–management relations. To make the most flexible work schedule succeed, there must be an attitude of cooperation and good faith.

Work Schedules and Overtime in the County of Alameda

The labor agreement between the County of Alameda and Local 21 of IFPTE that is currently in effect is the second one negotiated to include variable-day flexitime, with redefined overtime (see appendix, document A-2). The key features of this agreement are:

1. Work time is defined in terms of an 80-hour pay period rather than a 40-hour week or an eight-hour day.

2. Employees may put in as many or as few hours as they want in a day provided that:
   - They are present during core time, which covers two fixed periods of two hours each in a day, morning and afternoon.
   - They start no earlier than 7:00 A.M. and quit no later than 6:00 P.M.
   - They are on the job when necessary to get the job done as determined by the agency (these hours may extend beyond core time).
3. The agency cannot otherwise compel workers to follow a work schedule not of their own choosing.

Because working hours of more than eight hours in a day are allowed in this contract, a new definition of overtime was used in the contract (see appendix, document A-3). The usual condition of advance authorization by the supervisor is included. The previous eight-hours-a-day rule was changed to 80 hours in a pay period. To protect employees from subtle pressure by management to alter their work schedules to suit management's needs, there is a further condition: Time worked will only be classified as overtime if "it involves the employee in arriving before or staying after the times at which he would normally start or finish work." So that both workers and supervisor know what "normally" is, the supervisor may ask the workers to submit a tentative schedule of working hours.

Does the flexible overtime definition adequately protect workers? In three years of experience with this contract, there have been two problems. In one work unit, some managers (not union members) did not key out for lunch time (this work unit used time accumulators), although union members were required by the contract to take a half-hour of unpaid lunch time. The union believed this was a bad example, even though it was far from an abuse of workers' time by management. The union asked the managers to key out at lunch just as others did. They did so, and no further grievance was necessary.

In a more serious case, some managers in a work unit asked engineers who were union members to key out after they had worked 40 hours in a week even though they were voluntarily staying for another two hours. While there was no question of abuse of overtime here (since they were voluntarily staying late and overtime was defined to begin after 80 hours in two weeks), these managers were infringing on the engineers' rights under the contract to choose their hours of work. The engineers were losing the debit–credit feature of flexitime. The union asked these managers to eliminate this practice, and they complied voluntarily. There was no need for a formal grievance.

These anecdotes illustrate the importance of informal communications in a spirit of trust and cooperation, even though explicit grievance procedures are present.

HOW A LABOR–MANAGEMENT COMMITTEE STARTED FLEXITIME AND IMPROVED ORGANIZATIONAL EFFECTIVENESS: THE CASE OF GROUP HEALTH COOPERATIVE WITH OFFICE AND PROFESSIONAL EMPLOYEES UNION LOCAL 8

The relationship between labor and management in planning for flexible work hours has often been uneasy and unsatisfying. Unions have worried about the exploitation of workers, and management has worried about the loss of prerogatives. This is a case in which labor and management met these challenges successfully and now have an organization that works better than it did before. This is a case in which the labor union first proposed flexitime with debit and credit hours—the type of flexitime that unions often oppose and that management often thinks impractical. Indeed management did resist, but a joint labor–management committee worked it out.

In this case, the key flexitime question of who is responsible for what was successfully handled. The roles of both workers and managers are simply but effectively spelled out. In this case, we also see how flexitime can stimulate organizational changes for the better. The small amount of cross-training that was required to make flexitime work, the additional formal schooling that some employees undertook on their own off the job, and the new attention given to job responsibilities all have combined to make this a more efficiently operated business.

What the Group Health Cooperative Is and Does

The Group Health Cooperative of Puget Sound is a member-owned health maintenance organization that is both insurer and provider of health-care services. The company owns and operates two hospitals with a total of 470 beds, and it has 11 outpatient centers. With 280,000 members, Group Health Cooperative is one of the two main health-care organizations in the Seattle metropolitan area.

Group Health Cooperative has individual members who each pay $200 for a share of ownership in the cooperative and who get a vote in Group Health's governance, automatic qualification for coverage, and a reduced annual fee for services. There are also people who belong to Group Health because their employers are members. The governance of Group Health is tripartite, consisting of a board of trustees elected by the members, the medical staff, and Group Health management.

The Group Health Cooperative Flexitime Program

Flexitime at Group Health was instituted for all 135 employees of the Health Plan Services Department, which is the accounting and billing unit of the company, in July 1979. Jobs in this unit are clerical and supervisory; the majority of the jobholders are women. Flexitime may be expanded to other work units later on.

Flexitime employees may work between the hours of 6:30 A.M. and 6:00 P.M., observing core hours of 9:30 A.M. to 11:30 A.M. and 2:00 P.M. to 3:30 P.M. Monday through Friday. Business hours requiring coverage remain 8:00 A.M. to 5:00 P.M.

The main feature of flexitime at Group Health is that debit and credit hours are allowed within a week's time; that is, as few as three and one-half or as many as 11 hours may be worked in any one day, as long as the total at the end of the week is 40. Time accumulators are used to record hours worked.

Why Flexitime?

Flexitime is not the first alternative work schedule at Group Health Cooperative. Three years earlier there was a compressed workweek (four days, 40 hours) for some workers, although it was mostly an informal agreement made privately between worker and supervisor as an individual accommodation. And previous union contracts contained language that said "we agree to innovative work schedules" because some 24-hour operations required departures from a standard uniform schedule.

The immediate reasons for the union proposal for flexitime included:

- An increase in the number of workers who were single parents or from dual-career families
- A continuing energy shortage that focused attention on ways to cut gasoline consumption
- Publicity from the Seattle/King County commuter pool on using flexitime to improve rush-hour transportation
- A recent adoption of flexitime by Blue Cross, Group Health's main competitor
- A union business agent whose style it was to introduce at least one innovative idea for each negotiating session

How Flexitime Began at Group Health Cooperative

The Chronology of Events. Local 8 of the Office and Professional Employees Union proposed flexible work hours in October 1978 just before the opening of new contract negotiations. The proposal amounted only to a "capsulized idea," and was one of a very long list of negotiating topics. Group Health management initially opposed the request, believing the proposal was ill-defined, would lead to coverage and control problems unless it was more carefully planned and managed, and would not be suited to very many work units in the company.

The outcome of the negotiations was the formation of a joint labor–management committee in the Health Plan Services Department. This department was thought to be a suitable work unit for flexitime. Meanwhile, the new contract was agreed to without mention of flexitime.

The joint labor–management committee recommended a six-month pilot project, which began in July 1979. There were two criteria that had to be met before permanent adoption of flexitime could take place: (1) there should be an increase in morale, especially in the sense of working together, and (2) no operating problems should arise that could not be satisfactorily overcome. Productivity gains were not an explicit objective largely because there was at that time no performance standard to use for measuring productivity (such standards have just recently been designed). No formal evaluation was planned.

Labor–Management Cooperation. The labor union was the leader and initiator in flexitime. Local 8 wished to represent its members who were perceived to want more flexibility in work hours. In this case there is a history of union activity extending far beyond the usual union role. Labor unions started Group Health Cooperative in the late 1930s, and so they have a sense of ownership. In addition, Group Health is a cooperative, so many employees/union members are literally owners of the company. These factors contribute to a sense of "we are all working for the same goal" and to a spirit of labor–management cooperation rather than opposition.

The joint labor–management committee did two noteworthy things. First, the union contract in force called for overtime pay after eight hours a day; that provision was waived for the flexitime experiment (such a waiver had been used earlier by Local 8 in 1977 when some hospital workers went on a compressed workweek schedule).

Second, responsibilities of employees and supervisors for getting the work done are spelled out, written down, and acknowledged by both parties. Supervisors define job requirements, communicate them to employees, and assure that they are met:

> It is the supervisor's responsibility to plan and schedule requirements for task accomplishment and functional coverage, communicate these requirements to employees, and assure that the requirements are met.[1]

For example, the supervisor sets deadlines for projects, says how many people must be present after core hours, and makes sure that all employees know about all the resources that are available in the office. Workers must manage their time to meet job requirements, assume responsibility for coverage, help solve conflicts between job and personal time requirements, and are held accountable for their time management:

> It is the employees' responsibility to plan and organize their time to meet the job requirements, . . . participate in the solution of conflicts between job and personal requirements for time, and inform the supervisor when coverage requirements are not adequate. . . . employees assume coverage responsibility.[2]

For example, if workers want to change their usual or planned hours of work, leaving a coverage gap, they must arrange substitute coverage, with help from their supervisors.

These responsibility guidelines are very brief and very simple. They are easy to establish. Nevertheless, they deliver two essential messages: first, that *the supervisor's job is planning and communicating;* second, that *the employee takes on new responsibilities and is accountable for them.*

To make sure that all employees understand the terms of the flexitime program, each signs a flexitime agreement (see appendix, document A-4).

Flexitime Experiences: Lessons in Improving Organizational Effectiveness

The effort to define job responsibilities—supervisor versus worker—was required because of flexitime. Going further, job responsibilities among employees themselves—who does what—were also more clearly laid out than before. When not all workers are present all the time, coverage by one for another is necessary, and that means that all employees have to know who can fill in. Quite by accident a preflexitime problem of gaps in customer service and slow interoffice response due to absence was largely solved indirectly by the emphasis on job responsibilities stimulated by flexitime. Now everyone knows who handles the Boeing salaried account and who does cycle billing.

Coverage also meant cross-training. Because of flexitime all employees are now capable of handling one another's jobs (in this office, cross-training was not difficult because the jobs are not very different one from another). Looking back, the boost in cross-training is viewed not as a cost but as a method to improve customer service.

Education off the job has also been stimulated. Some employees have begun for the first time to take college courses either very early, before core hours, or late in the afternoon, after core hours. Their schooling is possible because of flexible hours. This is an investment in human capital that costs the company nothing. Note especially that formal schooling has been undertaken, for the most part, by clerical workers, who earn less and have less previous schooling than the national average.

NEGOTIATING WORK PATTERNS TO FIT WORKERS' NEEDS: THE CASE OF SERVICE EMPLOYEES INTERNATIONAL UNION, LOCAL 6

One of the key issues in the use of new work patterns is the role of labor unions. Compressed workweeks especially pose some threat to union interests. Compressed workweeks, with 10- or 12-hour days, challenge

the hard-fought principle of overtime pay after eight hours. They raise
questions about occupational safety and health. Yet we know that some
workers want compressed work schedules and that these schedules solve
some business production and staffing problems.

In the past, national AFL-CIO union leadership has opposed changes
in overtime pay practices. Nevertheless, local unions have increasingly
undertaken initiatives in this area. Here is a case of one local union that
has done so. The union is Service Employees International Union
(SEIU), Local 6, in Seattle, Washington.

What Has SEIU Local 6 Done?

Several new work patterns are used by Local 6 members, negotiated by
their union. First, 12-hour shift schedules were established for water-
pollution-control plant operators, and the old rules on overtime were
changed. Second, job sharing and permanent part-time employment
were made an option for mental health clinic workers, with equitable
fringe-benefit treatment for them specified in the contract. There are
other versions of compressed workweeks for nonshift workers elsewhere
among Local 6 membership—for example, a four-day workweek with
10-hour days—and here also new overtime rules were negotiated and
written into the labor agreement. Flexitime is also used by some Local
6 members, although it is not yet written into any contracts.

What Local 6 has done, aside from the details of particular new work
schedules, is to respond to a need for change heard from its members.
Workers in different jobs with different employers have different work-
schedule preferences. That is why there are so many varied work schedules among the Local 6 membership—both new work patterns as well
as the standard eight-to-five Monday-through-Friday work schedule. In
every case, the workers themselves initiated the change in work schedules, and their union negotiated the change with a cooperative
management.

New Shift-Work Schedules and Overtime Rules

In both of the Municipality of Metropolitan Seattle's (METRO's)
water-pollution-control plants, about 30 plant operators began a 12-
hour shift work schedule in 1980. Previously, these shift workers fol-

lowed a conventional eight-hour shift schedule, rotating among day, swing, and night shifts. The old shift schedule was changed because the shift workers themselves were unhappy with the rotation and came up with a new plan. There was not a serious shift attrition problem nor was there an acute productivity problem. The initiative came from the workers rather than from management.

The new shift-work schedule that the employees initiated calls for two 12-hour days followed by two 12-hour nights followed by four days off. The shift cycle is eight weeks long; there are four crews. The shift changeover time is fixed at 7:00 A.M. and 7:00 P.M., with a half-hour lunch break and three 15-minute breaks during the shift. During the 12-hour work period, the time actually worked comes to ten and three-quarter hours (however, the half-hour lunch period is an "on call" time [see figures 4-1 and 4-2]).

The new 12-hour shift-work schedule results in an average workweek of 42 hours; half the weeks are 48 hours and half are 36 hours. That means an overtime pay problem was encountered because of the Revised Code of the State of Washington (which requires overtime pay after 40 hours in a week) and because of existing clauses in the labor agreement that called for overtime pay after eight hours in a day.

How did the new 12-hour shift-work schedule come into being? How were the overtime rules changed? First, once the shift workers had come up with a new shift-work schedule that they preferred, they went to their union business agent, who contacted the plant management. The union and management agreed to change the overtime provisions in the contract to make the new shift-work schedule possible, and both parties agreed to a trial period for the new schedule, with the understanding that overtime costs would not increase. After the eight-week trial period was concluded successfully, a memorandum of understanding was appended to the labor agreement which would not expire until more than one year hence (this was done despite a "zipper clause" in the agreement).

The memorandum of agreement redefined daily overtime to begin after twelve hours rather than eight, and it specified that weekly overtime would be taken as compensatory time off at straight-time rates. (Using straight-time rather than time-and-one-half rates is possible for state and local government employees, at the individual employee's option.) To do the latter under the law required that all employees request this provision in lieu of premium pay. METRO made such

Figure 4-1. Twelve-hour shift schedule for METRO (Seattle) water pollution control plant operators, 8-week cycle.

Day	M 1	T 2	W 3	Th 4	F 5	Sa 6	Su 7	M 8	T 9	W 10	Th 11	F 12	Sa 13	Su 14	M 15	T 16	W 17	Th 18	F 19	Sa 20	Su 21
Crew A	*	*	*	*	D	D	N	N	*	*	*	*	D	D	N	N	*	*	*	*	D
B	D	D	N	N	*	*	*	*	D	D	N	N	*	*	*	*	D	D	N	N	*
C	*	*	D	D	N	N	*	*	*	*	D	D	N	N	*	*	*	*	D	D	N
D	N	N	*	*	*	*	D	D	N	N	*	*	*	*	D	D	N	N	*	*	*

Day	M 22	T 23	W 24	Th 25	F 26	Sa 27	Su 28	M 29	T 30	W 31	Th 32	F 33	Sa 34	Su 35	M 36	T 37	W 38	Th 39	F 40	Sa 41	Su 42
Crew A	D	N	N	*	*	*	*	D	D	N	N	*	*	*	*	D	D	N	N	*	*
B	*	*	*	D	D	N	N	*	*	*	*	D	D	N	N	*	*	*	*	D	D
C	N	*	*	*	*	D	D	N	N	*	*	*	*	D	D	N	N	*	*	*	*
D	*	D	D	N	N	*	*	*	*	D	D	N	N	*	*	*	*	D	D	N	N

Day	M 43	T 44	W 45	Th 46	F 47	Sa 48	Su 49	M 50	T 51	W 52	Th 53	F 54	Sa 55	Su 56
Crew A	*	*	D	D	N	N	*	*	*	*	D	D	N	N
B	N	N	*	*	*	*	D	D	N	N	*	*	*	*
C	D	D	N	N	*	*	*	*	D	D	N	N	*	*
D	*	*	*	*	D	D	N	N	*	*	*	*	D	D

D = day shift
N = night shift
* = day off

Source: Service Employees International Union, Local 6

124

Start 7 A.M.	Break 9:30–9:45 A.M.	Lunch 12–12:30 P.M.		Break 2:30–2:45 P.M.	Break 5–5:15 P.M.	Quit 7 P.M.
2½ hours of work	2¼ hours of work	½ hr on call	2 hours of work	2¼ hours of work	1¾ hours of work	

Figure 4-2.   Daily shift schedule for METRO (Seattle) water-pollution plant-control operators

Source: Service Employees International Union, Local 6

requests a condition of its agreement to the new shift-work schedule. Here is the language of the memorandum:

> Employees on rotating shift crews shall work 12 hours per shift . . . compensated at the rate of 12 hours of pay . . .

> Employees on rotating shift crews who are required to work more than 12 hours in any one day shall be paid overtime for such hours at 1½ times the employees' regular hourly shift rate of pay . . . Employees who are required to work more than 40 hours in any one week . . . will be paid overtime for such hours at 1½ times the employee's regular hourly shift rate *except in cases of the employee requesting time off in lieu of overtime pay* (the italics are the author's).[3]

There are other ways to handle the overtime pay problem posed by compressed and flexible work schedules, of course. Shell Canada, we have seen, was able to obtain an exemption from Canadian federal labor law when the company adopted twelve-hour shifts, with some weeks exceeding forty hours (see pages 83 to 93). But that would not be possible in the United States.

Many of the U.S. oil and chemical companies that have also adopted twelve-hour shifts in their continuous-process around-the-clock plants have continued to pay overtime wages for hours beyond eight in a day and forty in a week. But they have reduced the base or straight-time wage rates so that the weekly average earnings come out the same as before. Genuine overtime work ordered by management is then paid at a rate above time and one-half to compensate for the lower base wage rate. These rearrangements have been made with union cooperation (and at nonunion plants). They appear to be within the letter of the law, although some managers are concerned about how they relate to the spirit of the law.[4]

In other cases where compressed schedules call for four ten-hour days, companies have reduced the workweek from forty to, say, thirty-seven and one-half hours (nine and one-half hours instead of ten each day) and paid overtime every day for the one and one-half hours (but not for two hours). These companies have not reduced the basic wage rate, and they do suffer higher wage costs. They depend on productivity gains from the compressed schedule to offset their high wage costs. They also expect that the shortened as well as compressed workweek, with higher wages, will dampen future union demands for higher wages and shorter hours.

B. Negotiated Part-Time Employment

Statements from national labor union officials have often opposed the spread of permanent part-time employment. Companies often see union opposition as a deterrent to using part-time staffing. And, in fact, fewer part-timers are union-represented than full-timers. Here are the main labor-union objections to permanent part-time employment:

1. Expansion of part-time jobs is contrary to the interests of people who need full-time earnings. It will increase job competition and make unemployment worse. Especially in times of high unemployment, converting full-time jobs into part-time jobs merely spreads around the unemployment; it does not create the new employment that we need. If more part-time jobs are available, then probably more people who are not now in the labor force will come in and increase the competition for jobs. Traditionally, part-time employment has been used to overcome labor shortages, while our problem now is labor surpluses.
2. Shorter workweeks or workyears for all people, without loss of pay, is a priority union goal (as permitted by productivity gains), not part-time work for only a few people. A focus on part-time employment may detract from this goal.
3. Exploitation of part-timers is common and easy for companies to do, and thus erodes labor standards. Part-timers are often denied fringe benefits, job security, and promotion opportunities. If part-time staffing were to increase, so would this inequitable treatment.

4. Part-time employment often downgrades occupational status, institutionalizes women in inferior work roles, and helps mainly those who need help the least. Because so much part-time employment consists of low-level jobs staffed by women who do not require full-time earnings, it does not aid the cause of equity in employment.

5. The people who would be part-time employees are likely to be hard to organize and not good union members compared to full-timers, because their main interests are outside the workplace.

There are also advantages of part-time employment that some unions recognize. In some cases, local unions have bargained for part-time staffing and include part-timers among their membership. The union-related gains are potentially these:

1. Because there are many people who want working hours that are less than full time—people now outside the labor force as well as currently fully employed workers—unions can do a service for workers and meet their needs by getting part-time employment as an option for them.

2. Voluntary cutbacks in working time by some full-time workers to what amounts to part-time hours may be an attractive alternative to layoffs in times of economic downturn. More people with less work may be better than fewer people with more work. Both work-sharing and job sharing—special versions of part-time employment—can accomplish this. While their use is intended as a temporary countercyclical policy, some workers may prefer to stay permanently on a part-time schedule, resulting in the creation of new jobs.

3. Some jobs appear to be part time by nature. Workers in these jobs can be organized, adding to union strength, with their work-life conditions improved.

The two case studies that follow describe local union initiatives in negotiating for part-time employment while meeting some of the common labor union objections to this work pattern. They are the cases of Service Employees International Union, Local 6, which has contracts with private-sector mental-health clinics in Seattle, and SEIU Locals 715 and 535, which have contracts with the County of Santa Clara.

NEGOTIATED PERMANENT PART-TIME EMPLOYMENT: THE CASE OF SEIU LOCAL 6 WITH MENTAL HEALTH CLINICS

One of the things that SEIU Local 6 in Seattle, Washington, has done recently is to negotiate job-sharing and permanent part-time employment options for private-sector mental health clinic workers in two separate contracts (see pages 121 to 125 of this chapter for another report on SEIU Local 6 activity in new work schedules). Equitable fringe-benefit treatment for part-timers and job protection for full-timers are built into the contracts.

Part-Time Employment with Fringe Benefits

Both Valley Cities Mental Health Center and Mental Health North, two private-sector health-care facilities, have agreements with SEIU Local 6 that explicitly provide for part-time employment. The Valley Cities agreement states:

Article XVIII — Shared Time

Employees shall be allowed to request part-time employment after the probationary period, provided they work a minimum of eight hours per week and such assignment fulfills the needs of the agency.[5]

This definition of part-time employment has two key features: (1) it ensures that job requirements come first and that part-time scheduling will be used only where it fits with the clinic's business—no wholesale and inappropriate conversion to part-time staffing is possible; and (2) competition for jobs by new labor-force entrants is minimized—only previously full-time employees may cut back to part-time employment. The use of the term "shared time" in this article indicates that many of these part-time jobs will be job sharing.

In Local 6's agreement with Mental Health North, *permanent* part time is defined as one of three employment categories (the others are permanent full-time and temporary employment). Prorated fringe-benefit treatment is required (see figure 4-3).

The fringe benefits to which permanent part-time employees, along with permanent full-time employees, are entitled include vacation, holidays, sick leave, bereavement leave, jury-duty leave, unpaid leaves of absence, group medical and dental insurance (noncontributory), disa-

Article V—Definitions

I. *Permanent Full-time Employee:* an employee who works 37½ hours per week on a regular and continuing basis. Full-time employees are eligible for benefits in accordance with the schedule incorporated in each benefit section.

II. *Permanent Part-time Employee:* an employee who works less than 37½ hours per week. There are two (2) subclassifications of permanent part-time employees:
   A. Those employees who work 20 hours a week or more. These employees are eligible for all benefits on a prorated basis to be scheduled in accordance with the agreed-upon number of hours to be worked between the employer and employee.
   B. Those who work less than 20 hours per week. These employees are ineligible for any benefits.

III. *Temporary Employee:* an employee hired either full- or part-time to fill in for vacation relief or emergency relief. Such an employee is not eligible for benefits.

Figure 4-3.   Definition of part-time employment and fringe benefits at Mental Health North.

SOURCE: Mental Health North, (Seattle, Washington) internal document.

bility insurance (for people who work 30 hours or more per week), and an annuity plan (employee-paid).[6]

Permanent part-time employees are protected from overtime abuse as well as from fringe-benefit exploitation in this agreement. Overtime, which is defined as "any time worked in excess of the number of normal hours of work per week agreed upon by the employer and employee," means that part-timers get overtime for hours short of 40 per week if the employer orders it. "Overtime shall be compensated by equivalent time off . . ."[7] The key point of this contract language is that overtime is defined to be whatever the worker and management choose it to be— overtime is not defined in terms of a set number of hours per day or week. The contract gives both parties flexibility, and yet it protects the employees from subtle pressure by management to work more hours.

LABOR–MANAGEMENT COOPERATION ON INNOVATIVE PART-TIME EMPLOYMENT OPTIONS: THE CASE OF THE COUNTY OF SANTA CLARA AND LOCALS OF THE SERVICE EMPLOYEES INTERNATIONAL UNION

Union leadership in new work patterns for Santa Clara County began many years ago, when job sharing and permanent part-time employment, called "split codes," were started. These special and successful uses of part-time employment have long been part of the collective bargaining agreement. That agreement currently specifies wages, fringe benefits, and conditions under which a job can or cannot be done on a part-time basis. A majority of these part-timers are professional and technical employees.

The unions and county also have an unusual work–leisure trade-off arrangement for workers, called "voluntary reduced work hours," or VRWH. Full-time employees can reduce their work time and earnings without loss of status or benefits, and then resume full-time work and pay six months or a year or more later. This program—also union-initiated—is used to meet employees' needs as well as to solve budget problems for the county.

There is more. Flexible and compressed work schedules are written into some union contracts, but not all. Education and training programs are another fruit of labor–management cooperation—leaves of absence, tuition aid, and on-the-job training are included. Funding levels, types of courses, and participation levels are all written into the labor agreement.

What can be learned from the Santa Clara County experience is (1) how it happens that labor unions here have pushed innovative work patterns that often are opposed by organized labor, (2) what is in it for management—how the employer's interests are served while workers simultaneously get more options, (3) how different work-schedule and education programs fit together to yield results greater than any one could give standing alone, and (4) what the broader effects of these special part-time employment options are on labor markets and on workers' conflicts between work life and home life.

The VRWH — Voluntary Reduced Work Hours

How It Came About.   In the spring of 1976 a substantial county budget deficit was anticipated for the 1976–77 fiscal year to begin October 1, 1976. Work sharing was proposed by the county government—a 75-hour biweekly work period instead of the usual 80 hours. This would have been a mandatory 6.25 percent reduction in work time and pay for all employees.

The major local unions objected, claiming that the county could not unilaterally reduce work hours. The unions instead proposed a voluntary work-sharing plan. The county, in turn, believed that a voluntary plan would not generate sufficient work-hour reductions to provide large enough labor cost savings to close the anticipated budget deficit.

After several conferences between labor and management people, an agreement was made to begin a voluntary work-sharing plan as a starting point in the effort to achieve cost savings. This plan met labor's objective of "free" choice about cutting back work hours and losing pay. It also met labor's wish that fringe-benefit coverages be continued. Because the plan was regarded as a first trial step, management retained the option to take further steps if the voluntary work sharing plan did not succeed. The spirit was one of, "We'll try it and see what happens."

Two features stand out immediately. First, neither the county nor the unions wanted layoffs; the negotiation was about the type of work sharing, not about work sharing versus layoffs. Second, it was clear that the unions' watchword was choice and that management's watchword was experiment.

The voluntary work sharing appeared to run smoothly, although it was never tested under fire. Although the anticipated budget deficit did not materialize, the plan was not scrapped. Later, after employees asked that options to trade work for leisure be permanently available to them, the plan was included in collective bargaining agreements. The county found the plan satisfactory from a cost and service standpoint, and so it became a regular part of employment policy.

A third feature now stands out. A plan that was born in crisis as a temporary arrangement (unnecessarily, as it turned out) matured quickly into a permanent improvement for normal times.

How the VRWH Operates. An employee may request a percentage reduction in work time (and pay) of 2 1/2, 5, 10, or 20 percent for a six-month period. The VRWH schedule may be renewed for the next and succeeding periods. The reduced work time may be taken as fewer hours per day, fewer days per week, or in longer blocks of time away from work.

The department head must approve the employee's request and can say when the time off may be taken. This supervisory decision is officially not grievable; the labor agreement specifies that participation in the VRWH "shall be by mutual agreement between the worker and department/agency head." No supervisory approval is allowed if overtime by other employees would result. Only employees with six months' prior active service may participate; new hires or those returning from leaves of absence are not eligible.

The labor agreement states that reduced output from the county in the form of a lower level of services is expected due to the reduced labor input. There is to be no speedup for other full-time employees nor for the VRWH employees when they are on reduced hours or when they return to full-time work.

The labor cost savings that flowed from the VRWH remained with the department or budget unit according to its VRWH participation, until fiscal year 1980–81, beginning October 1, 1980. The board of supervisors then began to "take" the cost savings to support human-services programs, thus accomplishing a reallocation of funds from some programs to others.

In some cases, temporary employees are hired to take up some of the work load left by the reduction of work time by full-timers. Thus, the budget savings due the county from VRWH are not as large as might first be imagined, nor is the loss of service output as great.

Fringe benefits for VRWH employees are handled as follows:

- Sick leave, vacations, holidays, and seniority (for layoff and pay raise purposes)—benefits that are based on work time—are accrued as if the VRWH worker is a full-time 40-hours-per-week employee. Thus VRWH people get proportionately more fringe benefits and the county pays a higher benefit cost per labor hour.
- Health and life insurance coverage is the same for VRWH as for full-time employees—the county pays the entire premium. Again, VRWH people get proportionately more coverage per hour of work, and the county pays proportionately more.
- Retirement-plan contributions depend on earnings, so this fringe benefit is automatically prorated.

How Well Does VRWH Work?   Looking at the experiences of the 1976–80 period, two main questions are asked: (1) How much participation is there in the VRWH option? and (2) What are the management practices, problems and attitudes?

The number of employees who choose the VRWH option appears to depend on workers' perceived threat of worse to come—mandatory work sharing or layoff from the county—and on the state of the economy more generally (hard times in the job market make people less eager to cut back their work time). The take-up of the VRWH option declined from over 1500 employees in October 1976 (over 15 percent of the total county work force) to less than 450 in October 1979. The average work-time reduction from October 1976 to October 1980 has been about 10 percent per employee.

The original intent of VRWH—to save jobs for employees and to save costs for the county—was fulfilled. These effects continue in the absence of budgetary crisis. The county claims that no new full-time positions have been added because of VRWH. But to some managers and workers, VRWH is similar to a fringe benefit insofar as it is available without regard to the county's budget or employment situation. Most VRWH requests are granted by management—in the range of 90 percent. The county executive has urged managers to approve VRWH requests when possible. Because the reduced work hours taken by full-timers need not be permanent (and because the rate of granting VRWH requests is high), there has been increased hiring of temporaries, thus resulting in more employment opportunities for that category of worker.

Some minor initial implementation problems occurred. Two of them are described here to illustrate the kind of detail that managers have to cope with in new work schedules:

- A question arose whether employees under sponsorship of the Comprehensive Employment and Training Act (CETA) were eligible for VRWH because CETA regulations said, "Part-time jobs shall be allowed only for those individuals who because of age, handicap, or other personal factors are unable to work full time." The county executive decided this language permitted VRWH.
- Some employees became eligible for certain welfare programs (e.g., food stamps) when they reduced their work hours and earnings. The county executive allowed this.

The net cost savings to the county from VRWH have not been determined exactly. Gross savings, which are routinely calculated, were roughly $800,000 in the 1979 fiscal year. The cost savings consist of the gross savings in salaries minus the additional cost of (1) temporary employees; (2) overtime for other full-time or VRWH employees (there should not be any overtime, but there may be some, anyway); (3)

administrative costs of the program (e.g., forms, computer programming, payroll tracking, personal processing); and (4) forgone savings in fringe benefits (due to the proportionately higher fringe benefit cost per labor hour for VRWH employees).

What Is the Future for VRWH? A guess at the long-run outlook for VRWH in Santa Clara County prompts a look at two questions: first, is there a downward trend in employee demand for reduced work time? Second, what is in it for the county?

A quick look at the data on employee participation in VRWH suggests that perhaps it is mainly a crisis management technique rather than a mainstream employment policy. Does the decreased use of the VRWH option now compared to its use at the beginning mean that large numbers of workers want to trade work and earnings for leisure only to stave off more radical mandated cutbacks? Or do the data merely suggest that the work–leisure trade-off is not attractive to many workers when real incomes are declining in the midst of economic hard times? Or perhaps VRWH usage has declined because the less-work/more-leisure option is so attractive that some workers choose to adopt it permanently in the form of half-time job sharing employment (this option has been increasing in the county).

Why does the county continue the VRWH program when there is no immediate fiscal crisis? Of course, it is quite clear that labor unions and workers want the VRWH option. Satisfying these wishes makes for good industrial relations and a smoothly functioning enterprise. And, of course, taking away a popular negotiated program would be extraordinarily difficult. But, in fact, the county does not wish to take VRWH away. Managing it is no problem and, more positively, what VRWH amounts to for the county is a politically easy way to save money and reduce services. It is easier to slightly curtail a large number of services than it is to cut back specific programs with vocal constituencies. Furthermore, the continuing labor costs savings from VRWH permit reallocations of program efforts to be made by management. In a few words, VRWH is a tool that gives management more freedom of action.

Split Codes — Job Sharing and Part-time Employment

For many years the county has had half-time jobs called split codes, which are nominally full-time jobs filled by two job sharers. In practice, many of these jobs are solo permanent part-time positions without partners.

The Labor–Management Agreement.   Split codes are required by union contract. A minimum of 400 half-time jobs are set aside in the agreement (see appendix, document A-5). In practice, there are many more job-sharing and other permanent part-time employees—664 of them in 1979—so that this minimum is far from binding. In addition, the agreement specifies:

- Proportionate salaries are to be paid part-time employees—contract salaries are given in terms of dollars per pay period for full-time service in full-time positions; part-time employees in the same job classification are to be paid at the same rate.
- Workers at half-time or more are to receive all other benefits of the agreement.
- The conditions for management denial of part-time job requests are made explicit.
- Grievance procedures for denial of part-time job requests are spelled out.

The two substantive bases for the county to deny requests for part-time jobs are either that the work is not divisible or that qualified partners, if they are needed, are not available. In addition, management may refuse requests for part-time jobs (but so far has not) if there are already 400 part-timers in the county.

Participation and Costs. The number of part-time and job-sharing employees in the county has been growing steadily over time. The majority of these workers are hospital employees; over 60 percent are professional or technical employees (see table 4-1).

The main reason that Santa Clara County is pleased to use part-time employees is the recruiting advantage it confers. However, there is one serious problem: part-time employees cost the county more in fringe benefits. While leave time for part-time employees is prorated, full health, dental, and life insurance coverage is provided. Because the benefits are noncontributory, the dollar cost to the county mounts up. For example, the additional cost to the county in excess of half benefits for half-time work, which would be a cost-parity arrangement, ranged from $346 to $595 per half-time employee per year in 1979 (depending on

Table 4-1.   Occupations of Split-Code Employees in the
Santa Clara County Government, 1979

Occupation	Number of Part-time Employees
Nurses	198
Case workers	59
Therapists and counselors	50
Technicians	42
Other professionals	17
Clerical	136
Laborers	51
All professional and technical	366
All occupations	553

Source: County of Santa Clara internal documents

whether Blue Cross or Kaiser health insurance was selected). Aggre-
gated among the 553 half-time employees, this additional cost
amounted to $238,333 to $403,231, or about .05 percent of the county's
total budget.

Flexible and Compressed Work Schedules

In some, but not all, union agreements with the county, flexible or compressed work schedules are explicitly permitted in the contract. In other
agreements the contract language specifies that negotiations on alternative work schedules should take place: "The county agrees to meet
and confer on alternate work hours commencing April 15, 1980."[8]

The alternative work schedules that exist currently include 10- and
12-hour shifts in addition to the regular eight-hour shifts, and flexible
hours, with debit and credit option. These schedules have been developed on a work-unit-by-work-unit basis, depending on their suitability
and employees' needs. For example, both a unit of probation officers
and a unit of social workers, represented by two different SEIU locals,
have flexible schedules, whereas no building-trades union employees
have either an alternative work schedule or voluntary reduced work
hours.

Because both the 10- and 12-hour shifts, as well as the debit–credit
hours version of flexitime, may involve more than eight hours of work
per day, the labor agreement specifies that overtime shall commence for

these employees after ten hours in the workday rather than after eight hours. Thus the union has made an accommodation in the usual rules governing overtime pay in order to permit flexible and compressed schedules to be used. Of course, county employees who are working directly on federal government contracts are still required to be paid overtime rates after eight hours a day because of the Walsh–Healy or the Contract Work Hours and Safety Standards acts.

Education and Training Programs

Labor–management cooperation in Santa Clara County extends to a wide range of negotiated training opportunities for workers. Employees can undertake education off the job via unpaid leave, paid leave, or tuition-aid arrangements; they can also undertake on-the-job county-provided training.

Educational Leave of Absence.   Leave without pay up to one year, with an extension up to another year, can be undertaken when the education "will benefit the county." If a course of study is available only during working hours, then half of the time away from work is forgiven and the other half must be made up by the employee or deducted from vacation leave. Some categories of workers, such as nurses, get 40 hours per year of fully paid educational leave in order to maintain their licenses. The State of California has a continuing education requirement for relicensing. All of these educational leave provisions are written into several different union contracts.

Tuition Aid.   Tuition aid is available to workers if the training "is related to the worker's occupational area or has demonstrated value to the county." A typical negotiated tuition-aid agreement includes a specified pool of reimbursement funds to be set aside by the county. During 1979, total county spending out of such funds exceeded $300,000. There is a maximum reimbursement of $300 per worker in a year. The aid is distributed on a first-come-first-served basis; the reimbursement is made when the tuition payment is made by the worker, at the beginning, not the end, of the course. If the employee who received tuition aid leaves county employment within one year after course completion, the worker is required to repay to the county half of the aid.

The recent history of tuition aid in Santa Clara County indicates two unusual features. First, all the tuition-aid funds are always exhausted. Second, the take-up rate of tuition-aid resources is disproportionately high among clerical and blue-collar workers—precisely those workers who ordinarily have the least education and the poorest jobs. Thus, it would appear that the county's tuition-aid plan serves the cause of equity.

On-the-Job Training.   County-provided on-the-job training is similarly required in some union agreements. For example, in the case of SEIU Local 715, a joint labor–management committee is directed to agree on a list of in-house training courses for particular classifications of workers. A fund is set aside in the union contract to provide these courses (above and beyond the tuition-aid fund).

There are two notable features of the on-the-job training programs. First, the purpose of these programs is promotion to higher skills and better-paying jobs. The training is provided for entry-level unskilled employees, who then have a chance to advance. Second, the salaries of the trainees are slightly reduced during the period of training. Thus the trainees are sharing in the cost of the training by accepting less pay and thus reducing the county's payroll outlay (see appendix, document A-6).

Lessons Learned: Can Other Employers and Unions Follow the Santa Clara–Local 715 Examples?

What succeeds for Santa Clara County and Local 715 may or may not succeed for other employers and unions. How transferable are these results? Here we focus on three issues: (1) How do we explain the labor union role? (2) What are the broader labor-market effects of these new work patterns? and (3) Are there favorable effects on home and family life flowing from this case?

The Labor Union Role.   Local 715 favors several work patterns (and has acted to implement them) that are opposed by national AFL-CIO officials. Why has this happened? Why has Local 715 initiated (not merely gone along with) part-time employment both in the form of reduced work hours and job sharing? Why does Local 715 also favor flexitime, with debit- and credit-hours options? There appear to be two answers. First, the union believes strongly in giving maximum choice to workers—the more options the better. (Of course, voluntary reduced work hours [VRWH] started as a response to a crisis, as the lesser of two evils. But it continues when there is no crisis because workers want it.) These local workers' interests are represented by their union.

Second, the dangers that the new work patterns could pose to the union's interests are avoided by contract guarantees. For example, part-time employees at Santa Clara County are not second-class citizens and are not exploited precisely because they are union members and get good fringe benefits and the right to return to full-time work if and when they want to. Cooperation between labor and management to achieve mutual interests is the underlying climate that makes it possible.

Labor-Market Effects.   The Santa Clara County–Local 715 experience shows that changes in the linear life plan are viable. There are other ways to organize the education–work–leisure lockstep. Alternating time between full-time and part-time employment is practical for some people. There are some people who will, in fact, choose to work less and earn less if they have a decent option to do so. And that means that the VRWH form of part-time employment is an employment-creating work pattern. Although Santa Clara County does not use it this way, quite clearly the work time vacated by full-time employees is available for new labor-force entrants if there is work to be done. Work sharing is not only a temporary alternative to layoffs; it is also a permanent way to redistribute work to the workers who want and need it.

If the work is not available, there is another redistributive labor-market effect. Because the reduced work hours taken by full-timers were not permanent at Santa Clara County (and because the rate of granting VRWH requests was high), there was increased hiring of temporaries, thus resulting in more employment opportunities for that category of worker.

Finally, this case shows graphically that part-timers can be career employees and professionals. Part-time is not synonomous with temporary and low-level jobs.

Why is it that one employer has so many different innovative work patterns and training opportunities? What are the relationships among these various programs? In one sense voluntary reduced work hours, split codes, flexitime, compressed workweeks, educational leave, and tuition aid are all independent, one from the other. Any one of these programs could operate successfully without any of the others. There is no system to which they all must belong, but there is a relationship among some of them.

The presence of one new work pattern affects the other. For example, the possibility of reducing working time without loss of status via job sharing (split codes) apparently diminishes the popularity of VRWH during normal times. Thus, in this case the increased use of one work pattern decreases the use of another. This means also that the success and continued availability of VRWH should not be evaluated in isolation from other programs.

In another vein, voluntary reduced work hours, split codes, and flexitime all support the successful operation of the education and training programs. Although the evidence is only anecdotal, it appears that some workers who reduce their work time via VRWH or split codes use the time so gained to undertake education and training activities. The fact that both work-schedule options and training funds are available makes it possible for some employees to participate in training opportunities whereas, in the absence of either, they might not be able to do so.

C. Using Job Sharing and Work Sharing to Improve Employment Outcomes

The customary way for companies to cope with cyclical downturns in their business is to lay off temporarily the employees who are not needed and then rehire them when economic fortunes improve. This strategy has the obvious advantage of quickly saving large sums of money for the company. It also has the longer-term disadvantage of losing some human-resource investments if and when some recalled workers do not return.

There are other problems with layoffs. If they are based on seniority, there may be a disproportionate loss of blacks and women, and that just makes achieving equal-employment-opportunity goals that much harder. Despite generous unemployment compensation benefits, being idle against one's will is surely socially maladaptive.

The search for alternatives to layoffs is intensifying. One not-so-new idea is work sharing: a group of workers choose to reduce their hours of work and accept less pay. The choice is terribly constrained, of course, if the alternative is layoffs. The trade-off is between less work and pay for more people versus more work and pay for fewer people. (Opponents of work sharing would call this sharing the unemployment, and insist on macroeconomic policies to create jobs rather than spreading too few jobs around more thinly.)

The main problems with work sharing as an alternative to layoffs are: (1) laws governing the payment of unemployment compensation make it impossible for work sharers, who are partially unemployed, to get partial unemployment compensation, while fully unemployed workers can get government assistance; (2) carrying work sharers on the payroll means the company continues to pay fringe benefits, whereas laid-off workers get no such benefits, thus making work sharing potentially more expensive for the company; and (3) work sharing will usually mean that senior people give up work and pay, just as junior people do; senior employees may resent the loss of their ordinarily more favored position.

The State of California is experimenting with a change in legislation that will permit partial unemployment compensation to be paid, and thus overcome a major problem of work sharing.[9] The U.S. Congress has similar new legislation under consideration, and the AFL-CIO has endorsed the concept behind these experiments.

Meanwhile, another idea to cope with cyclical downturns is being tried: job sharing instead of layoffs. This idea is very similar to work sharing, but it differs in that (1) the decision to reduce working hours and pay is an individual employee decision, and (2) seen from the company's standpoint, full-time jobs remain, even though there are fewer jobs and some employees work part time. Job sharing as an alternative to layoffs may not accomplish the same scale of employment reduction as work sharing because job sharing is individually voluntary, and thus some layoffs may still be necessary. But the feature of choice will stave off equity problems.

In this section, a case study of job sharing instead of layoffs is presented. It is a case of labor union leadership and labor–management cooperation. Next, a case study of California state government efforts to foster work sharing and other forms of part-time employment is presented. These efforts, aimed at improving employment outcomes, have obtained labor union support.

JOB SHARING INSTEAD OF LAYOFFS: THE CASE OF UNITED AIRLINES

A job-sharing program was necessary because United Airlines was losing business and losing money.[10] It was possible because of a brand-new climate of labor–management relations. It worked because both the company and its employees were better off with it than without it. What it did was let some flight attendants choose to share their jobs with other flight attendants and cut back their hours of work so that not as many people would be laid off. This is the case of United Airlines and its union-negotiated job-sharing program for flight attendants.

United Airlines has 8,600 flight attendants who are represented by the Association of Flight Attendants (AFA), an international union. The year 1980 was one of financial adversity for the company. Higher jet-fuel costs led to higher ticket prices, and that in combination with the business recession meant fewer passengers than in 1979. This was all apparent early in 1980, and so the company projected a reduced schedule of flights and a reduced number of flight attendants, as well as pilots and ground personnel.

How Job Sharing Got Started

Faced with an imminent surplus of flight attendants, why did not United simply furlough as many junior flight attendants as necessary? (Furlough is the airline-industry term for layoff.) Other airlines had already done so. United had customarily furloughed people in the past in similar circumstances, and the policy was already spelled out in the labor contract. What motivated the change?

A New Climate of Labor–Management Cooperation.   According to Norman Reeder, director of personnel for the Employee Services Division at corporate headquarters in Chicago, job sharing started as an alternative to layoffs because of a new approach the company was taking to working with labor unions. Using help from the Quality of Work Life Center in the Institute of Industrial Relations at the University of California at Los Angeles, the company approach was simply one of talking about problems with the union before taking action. The company did not expect to issue edicts, nor did it intend to give away management prerogatives. The basic truth the company accepted was that a union problem would eventually become a company problem. A cooperative posture rather than an adversarial posture was adopted. In this case, the new approach meant acting as a partner with the flight attendants and giving them a chance to have their say.

Not all companies and not all unions will be ready to fundamentally alter their industrial relations climate in this way. Exchanging the adversary relationship for a cooperative one is not an easy step, although it is surely recommended by many U.S. experts and followed extensively in Europe. Of course, United Airlines had suffered a damaging strike in 1979 which served as an immediate stimulus to improve labor–management relations.

Negotiating a New Solution.   In the end, the job-sharing program was the union's idea. Here is how it happened. The company presented the hard, cold facts of its financial hard times to the union leadership in a meeting asked for by the company in early February 1980. The data showed that the company needed to cut 200 flight attendants by April and save $275,000 because of a reduced flying schedule. The company asked the union, "Do you have any ideas about how we can save this money other than by furloughs?" Of course, company management had already looked for such ways, but had come up blank and thus did not expect anything from the union.

The union people responded positively, agreed to look at the problem, and thanked the company for telling them about it ahead of time. In a few days, the union came back with three ideas, two of which had been considered by the company already and rejected. The third idea was the job-sharing idea, called "partnership time off."

"We were pleasantly surprised," said Norman Reeder, "in that the job-sharing proposal they offered was innovative and, with refinement, workable." So management and union people met for several days and worked out an agreement. In just two weeks time, from first meeting to final agreement, partnership time off became a reality. The program was to commence April 1, 1980, and end August 1, 1980.

How Partnership Time Off Operates

Here is how the union describes the job-sharing program it negotiated: "Partnership time off is another way of providing time off from the workplace while at the same time providing partial pay and continued benefits (insurance, passes, etc.)."[11]

The key features of partnership time off are these:

1. Only senior flight attendants with seven years of experience are eligible to job share. Later on, the eligibility requirement was cut

to four years. United wanted this provision because more money would be saved for each job sharer if senior flight attendants joined the program. The salary scale is fixed by union contract over a 14-year tenure span, with salary dependent on length of service.

2. The two partners work out their own schedule. The company sets no restrictions, and does not get involved in scheduling the flight attendants anymore than it would normally. United Air Lines describes the program as follows: "Under the program two flight attendants bid together and are responsible for one line of flying. So long as one of the partners covers the flying assignment, there are no constraints on how they divide their time. . . . partners will function as one flight attendant, they will bid for and receive a single line of flying. . . . they will be responsible for determining which trips each will fly."[12]

3. Job sharers' responsibilities are to (1) find their own partner, (2) stick with that partner for the four-month duration of the program, (3) submit a pay allocation for each month so that the company knows how to distribute salary and benefits between the two partners, (4) alternate work, that is, not work at the same time as one's partner, (5) be accountable as a partnership for missed trips or absences until they inform the company which partner is responsible, (6) resolve their own disputes, and (7) sign an agreement that states their rights and responsibilities (see appendix, document A-7). "If one of the partners is sick, the other partner can choose to fly the trip, or the partnership can go on sick leave."[13]

4. The junior partner of the two is paid at the senior partner's salary rate, and the senior partner's bidding rights are used to determine which line of flying the partnership gets. This financial and schedule incentive to junior partners (who still have at least seven, or, later on, four, years of service) was intended to stimulate participation by flight attendants at lower salary levels, who might otherwise not want to trade any earnings for time.

5. Vacation and sick-leave benefits are accrued at a half-time rate for all job sharers, but health and life insurance and pension benefits continue to be paid by the company as before. This arrangement was adopted for reasons of administrative convenience.

The Experiences: Mostly Good, Some Bad

For the partnership time off program that ran from April 1, 1980, to August 1, 1980, 270 flight attendants volunteered. That saved 125 jobs, and so 75 people still had to be furloughed. But that number was less than the 200 furloughs originally planned (125 rather than 135 jobs were saved by the partnerships because of the higher salary and fringe-benefit costs of job sharing required by the program's design).

A great variety of partnership schedules were chosen. In some cases, partners would alternate months—one month on, one month off. In other cases, partners would decide who would fly on a trip-by-trip basis. At one extreme, one team had the senior partner do no flying, while the junior partner flew the entire schedule. As several partners pointed out, "You have to make sure you team up with someone you can trust."

What did United Airlines gain and lose from partnership time off? Compared to the alternative of layoffs, the company lost nothing. (As noted above, the way in which salaries and fringe benefits were paid raised the company's payroll cost per-labor-hour worked, but this only meant job sharing did not prevent as many layoffs as it might have. If the program were to be permanent, this would be quite a different matter.)

But what did the company gain for its trouble?

- *More even distribution of cutbacks.* The United flight attendant work force tends to have junior people clustered in Chicago, New York, and Cleveland, with senior people located more frequently in the western part of the country. Furloughs would have hit the western locations hard, but because all attendants participated in partnership time off, the cutbacks were geographically quite even.
- *Retention of trained flight attendants.* Had all the furloughs taken place, the laid-off flight attendants would, in most cases, have had only six months of actual flying time. The company's training investment would have been made with almost no recovery of that investment. These very junior people are also the ones least likely to come back after a layoff (they cannot afford to wait it out); as it turned out, the recession in air travel was so long that the company could not have rehired them.
- *Some reduction in absenteeism.* Although the scale of partnership

time off was not big enough to make much difference and the absenteeism reduction not that large, the program began to get at a very big problem. In air travel, if a flight attendant misses just one flight because of illness, he or she may actually miss three days of flying because the downtime segments of the schedule also have to be filled by reserves. Thus, absence due to sickness or any other reason causes administrative problems. Flight attendants have an unusually high incidence of sick-leave usage because of their irregular schedules, varying climates, and continual exposure to so many different people.

• *A demonstration to employees that the company cares about its people.*

Advantages of partnership time off for the flight attendants are clearcut. For very junior employees, the advantage was a reduced probability of being furloughed. For quite senior people, the advantage was the option to work less if they chose. These comments of flight attendants appeared in a newspaper article describing partnership time off programs.

It's given me a lot more time to be home and to travel—that's a hobby of my husband's and mine.

Reaction has been extremely positive. Some of my friends gave me a bridal shower a week ago and all but one of them—six or seven—were on special leave. They were furthering their education, traveling, exploring things they'd always wanted to but never had time for. With a flying schedule it's not easy to do long-term things, like take a regular class schedule or even develop a personal relationship.[14]

For people of intermediate seniority who were eligible for the program, the gain, in addition to choosing time off if they wanted to, was the option to earn at a higher rate and get more desirable flying schedules.

Did anything go wrong? Was there any trouble? Yes, some backlash from flight attendants was noticed. Some of the senior nonparticipating people found themselves suddenly at both a psychic and relative monetary disadvantage. Because the junior partner got the senior partner's pay and bidding rights, some nonparticipants saw flight attendants who were less senior than they were getting more desirable flights and higher pay. Of course, this was only temporary, and only relative—no senior nonparticipant lost bidding rights or pay.

Next Steps

The original partnership time off program was extended through December 1980 and expanded in the face of even more labor cutbacks than were anticipated. For all of 1980, 1,175 flight attendants would have been furloughed, but because of partnership time off the number was reduced to 810 furloughs. Altogether, 365 jobs were saved at one time or another during the year. At the end of 1980, 508 flight attendants were job sharing. Of course, 810 furloughs is still a large number and United wishes it could be less, but partnership time off is an individually voluntary program.

The success witnessed by partnership time off for flight attendants prompted the spread of the job-sharing concept to other units of the company—for example, to ground personnel, such as ticket agents. Aside from the flight attendants' success story, this spread was possible partly because United Airlines has long had permanent part-time ground employees, in a variety of jobs, who have always gotten full fringe benefits. The transition to job sharing was not that radical—only the partnership aspect was different.

Could job sharing as a temporary alternative to layoffs become a permanent and regular employment option? Recognizing this as a matter for negotiation with labor unions, management is willing to consider it favorably. Job sharing could be another way to help cope with seasonality in labor demand. Right now, United uses leaves of absences and without-pay status (a very short maximum of 30 days informal leave of absence) as tools to adjust the number of flight attendants on duty. Job sharing could complement these efforts.

PUBLIC POLICY INITIATIVES IN NEW WORK PATTERNS: THE CALIFORNIA STATE GOVERNMENT

Since the mid-1970s, the California state government has encouraged the use of various forms of part-time employment, most notably job sharing and work sharing. The purpose of inquiring about the State of California's experience is to assess the role that public policy can (or needs to) play in expanding work-schedule options. Three questions about this case need to be answered: (1) what happened, (2) why did it happen, and (3) what lessons can be learned?

What happened in the California state government was a series of actions in both the legislative and executive branches, beginning in 1975. New events are continuing to take place—we are glimpsing an "experiment" that perhaps has only started. But there has been no grand design and no single program. As in most public-policy initiatives, there are multiple reasons why changes are taking place.

A chronology of events follows.

1. The California State Personnel Board initiated a job-sharing experiment, running from 1975–1977. The purpose of this experiment was to evaluate job sharing as an aid to women reentering the labor force.

2. Senate Bill 570 mandated a permanent part-time employment demonstration project in the Department of Motor Vehicles (DMV) in 1976 and funded an evaluation of it. DMV was chosen because it was a statewide employer, had many women employees, and agreed to cooperate. The purpose of the project was to determine the feasibility of a statewide policy encouraging the expansion of part-time employment opportunities. The following potential advantages were to be tested: increased employment opportunities for certain categories of persons; decreased unemployment; furtherance of affirmative action; and increased job satisfaction, quality of life, and productivity.

3. The DMV demonstration project took place in 1977 and 1978. The evaluation was completed in January 1979. The findings were that all of the potential advantages of part-time employment were realized but that the employer's fringe-benefit and administrative costs increased.

4. "Leisure-sharing" hearings were held in the California Senate in November of 1977. These were informational hearings and not related to particular pieces of legislation or administrative regulations.

5. Proposition 13 was passed by the California electorate in June of 1978. This event is important in the chronology of the California state government policy process because the property-tax reduction figures of Proposition 13 were widely expected to cause an economic downturn and rising unemployment.

6. Senate Bill 1471 was passed in July 1978. This bill, prepared in advance of Proposition 13 and passed only a month afterwards, permitted company-wide temporary shared work unemployment compensation as an alternative to layoffs. The bill permitted employees to be paid

partial unemployment compensation, up to 20 weeks, if their employer faced a 10 percent or greater reduction in hours of work and voluntarily joined the program. The compensation was to be equal to the same fraction of full benefits as work hours were reduced. The State Employment Development Department was to approve employers' plans; employees had to be available for full-time work to qualify. This was an emergency statute due to expire at the end of 1979.

7. Senate Concurrent Resolution 94 was passed in August of 1978. This resolution merely urged local public agencies to consider temporary reduced-work-time alternatives to massive layoffs because of cutbacks due to Proposition 13. It further urged the State Employment Development Department to provide technical assistance in consultation with local agencies, using existing departmental and legislative resources. There was no additional funding and no mandate.

8. Senate Bill 210 was enacted, extending SB 1471 to December 31, 1981.

9. Senate Bill 370 was passed in September 1979. It permitted a reduction in work hours for individual state employees as an alternative to layoff. This bill permits individual employees in state agencies, as opposed to groups of employees, to reduce their work time voluntarily if the state agency faces a reduction of as little as one percent of work time, as long as the individual reduction is administratively feasible and contributes to the preservation of jobs. These employees have first priority to return to full-time work when it is available. (The law is effective as an emergency statute only to June 30, 1982.) This legislation was needed for state agencies because state law otherwise required 40-hour weeks; private employers, on the other hand, could choose their own length of workweek. The work-sharing route was offered because, otherwise, employees would have to go to part-time status to reduce their work hours and save jobs, thereby losing seniority rights.

10. Senate Bill 371 was also passed in September of 1979 as a means of encouraging private industry to employ more workers. This legislation mandates a demonstration project on job creation via voluntary work-time reduction in the private sector. It establishes a three-year experiment in which employees of private-sector companies can voluntarily reduce their work time, even if not under the pressure of layoff. They may do so by working shorter days, weeks, or years; taking sabbatical leaves; or sharing jobs. The legislation asks the Employment Development Department to obtain federal and other grants to award

to participating employers to induce their cooperation with the experiment and to offset their potentially higher labor costs attributable to the experiment (for example, nonprorated fringe benefits, recruiting, training, and evaluation costs). The Employment Development Department is mandated to evaluate the experiment.

11. Senate Bill 1859 was passed in 1980. It established full-rights, voluntary, permanent part-time employment for state workers. It makes reduced work time a usual option for state employees, not contingent on layoff threats; it gives equal rights during layoff to part-timers and prorated fringe benefits, except for pension and health insurance. However, unionized part-timers in state government already have full health insurance and prorated pension coverage if they are employees working half time or more. Thus, this legislation would extend these fringe benefits to unorganized workers and part-timers working less than half time.

Why It Happened — the Forces at Work

There are several explanations as to why this unusual succession of legislative initiatives should be taking place in California. One of them is the original concern in the state about employment reentry for women. This concern in the state legislature is what occasioned the first part-time employment experiment. Perhaps the role of women in California may have a higher profile than in other states.

Second, there were from the beginning activist groups and a few key people in the legislature, in the administrative branch of state government, and also among the activist groups, who have been consistent long-term supporters. The policy process has been a sustained effort, building on small successes, with indigenous leadership.

Third, labor unions have not been opposed to these changes in work patterns. In fact, some locals have favored these changes and, when asked, have helped in the passage of legislation and in the experiments.

Fourth, most of the state-government experiments in new work schedules have originated in the legislature rather than in the executive branch. This approach is favorable to new policy because (1) it spreads the risk of change, with a larger number of people and organizations necessarily involved; (2) it is a grass-roots effort, with citizens (via hearings) all the way up to the governor involved, broadening the base of support; and (3) the bills reported out of the legislature have compelled evaluations and reports. Useful data have been collected for further policy initiatives, and the evaluations have necessarily involved the executive branch as well as the legislative, resulting in a high profile for the various programs.

Fifth, the passage of Proposition 13—an exogenous occurrence that could not be planned or anticipated in the beginning—made unemployment an immediate and dramatic problem for which a solution (of almost any kind) was needed. Proposition 13 hastened the policy process and created an environment conducive to change.

NOTES

1. Group Health Cooperative internal documents.
2. Ibid.
3. "Memorandum of Understanding between the Municipality of Metropolitan Seattle and the Service Employees International Union, Local 6," 18 June 1980.
4. Herbert R. Northrup, James T. Wilson, and Karen M. Rose, "The Twelve-Hour Shift in the Petroleum and Chemical Industries," *Industrial and Labor Relations Review*, 32 (April 1979).
5. Agreement between Valley Cities Mental Health Center and SEIU Local 6, 4/11/79–2/28/81. The probationary period is defined as 90 days for clerical staff and 180 days for clinical staff.
6. Collective Bargaining Agreement between Service Employees International Union Local 6 and Mental Health North, 1980–81.
7. Ibid.
8. Agreement between the County of Santa Clara and Local 535, affiliated with Service Employees International Union, AFL-CIO, July 1979–October 1982, page 26.
9. See the forthcoming evaluation and report by Fred Best for the California Employment Development Department, Sacramento, California.
10. The author is indebted to Nan McGuire and New Ways to Work, San Francisco, California, for their assistance in presenting this case study.
11. From a memo by Susan Rohde, chairperson, Master Executive Council, Association of Flight Attendants, February 21, 1980.
12. "Partnership Time Off Program," United Airlines internal document, 1980.
13. Ibid.
14. Reported in the *Los Angeles Times*, 30 November 1980. The second quote refers to Pan American program similar to the United Airlines program.

5.

The Effects of New Work Schedules on Family Life and on Men and Women as Individuals

A. Family and Life-Cycle Changes Due to Job Sharing
by Gretl S. Meier

Because job-sharing workers have more time away from work than full-timers, they have a better chance to solve the conflict between work life and home life than full-timers. Yet they can have a serious labor-force attachment and earn some income. Of course, many people cannot afford to do with anything less than full-time earnings. But the increase in dual-earner families makes job-sharing possible for some.

Based on the experience of job sharers themselves, it appears there are three main ways in which job sharing aids family life and personal time needs. First, job sharing allows a better balance between work and family responsibilities. Second, job sharing permits men and women to change stereotyped sex roles if they wish. Third, job sharing helps accommodate work-life changes over the life cycle—it helps the transition from primary parenthood to careers, and from full-time work to retirement. And it permits workers to more easily pursue education on their own or with company support.

Family and Work: A Better Balance

Job sharing is likely to enhance the well-being of the family as a whole because it enables mothers who wish to work outside the home to better balance work and family responsibilities. "It gives me the best of both worlds," these sharers frequently explain. Women who are mothers— the great majority of job sharers—feel better able to be responsible and committed both as employees and as parents.

A social worker, for example, mother of an 18-month-old child and pregnant with her second, found that she could not "hack a 40-hour week and be a decent mother, wife, or worker."[1]

At work, sharers find satisfaction from higher energy, partner support, and a feeling of control over tasks and time. But beyond this, these women value the sense of a worthwhile and "regular" job. They are more likely to find work for which they have been trained, at jobs with higher salaries—and carrying fringe benefits—than would be true of other part-time work.

Sharers attribute balancing at home to the daily flexibility of job sharing, even more effective than that of the more usual part-time arrangements. The ability to trade time with a partner often means being able to cope better with families, whether children are toddlers or teen-agers. Partners need not stretch lunch hours, negotiate special time off, nor necessarily be tightly restricted to a fixed time schedule. "There's no way I could manage our family life," says a secretary with four children, "if I couldn't sometimes ask my partner to cover."[2]

Sharers can also manage child care better by using nonwork time as needed for illness and emergencies, medical appointments, and maintaining contact with children's schools—the last item a growing concern among educators when both parents work full time.

In a larger sense, the ability to balance affords a better perspective on both work and family responsibilities. Many women would echo the comments, "I'm better at work, better at home; I can look forward to both." "I'm a better parent when I can come home refreshed and know that I've been doing a worthwhile job."[3]

Changing Sex Roles

The number of men who are job sharing is still quite small. Those who are working full time and wish to change to part-time work or job sharing encounter great difficulties, given the still prevailing attitudes about less than full-time work. Men who are job sharing tend to be younger (in their thirties) or older (over 50) compared with women. Those who are married are more likely to share household and parenting tasks when both they and their wives are working part time or job sharing.

A few resemble the city planner who restructured his full-time job (a two-year process) in order to have more family time after the birth of his first child. As another (a young probation worker) reported, the experience helped his relationship with his wife. Not only was he less exhausted when he came home, but, he added, there seemed to be some "carryover" in rearranging household tasks.

The most significant change in traditional roles is illustrated by married couples who share the same job. Although a small proportion of all sharers, they represent the modern version of family work sharing and the deliberate attempt to reestablish the earlier close connections between the two worlds. Most of these couples are employed in college and university teaching and administration. They have chosen to share in order to combine professional and family responsibilities. Others have rejected commuting marriages and turned to sharing in order to find jobs in the same community. Whatever the reason for the initial decision, most couples find, as one commented, "It's essential that the stuff at home is also shared."[4]

Many of these men find that rearranging domestic responsibilities so that each parent shares cooking, cleaning, and child care benefits all the family. One reports:

> The clearest advantage of our arrangement has been to our family life. We both have more free time on weekends and more energy at the end of the day. When our daughters come home from school, one of us—and not always the same one—is there.

She adds:

> After ten years of relatively polarized roles, we are returning to the shared housekeeping of our early married life. We choose tasks by preference and divide up the ones neither of us likes.

> We realize now how good an arrangement like our present one would have been for all of us when our children were babies and preschoolers.[5]

Two special concerns may face such couples. The first is the problem of restricting the job so that it does not become the center of family life. This goes beyond the issue of fitting work into allotted hours, which affects job sharers in other professions. It is a matter of achieving the delicate balance of enjoying the benefits of work–family unity and yet of still having "time to play."

Secondly, job-sharing couples may also find stress, even more than other job sharers, as a result of the ways they are perceived by others. Some feel greater need to be treated as separate entities. Others, particularly in administrative roles, need to be viewed as a team. This dilemma is complicated, of course, because as academics, couples' work settings are usually also social settings.

Most job-sharing couples find that the advantages outweigh the disadvantages compared with the stress when both are working full time. Not only is there "more time for parenting, more research and study time, and more leisure" but the feeling of "unified lives" in which children know both parents and each parent is aware of the other's problems and tensions as they alternate work and child care.[6]

Life-Cycle Changes

Stages of Motherhood and Careers.   Women who are mothers best illustrate the flexibility over the span of working years which job sharing often affords. Together with other work options, sharing may help alleviate the choice of "children or career" facing an increasing number of young women entering the labor force each year, including those who are well educated and highly trained.

Until recently, many job sharers were "reentry" women—those who had completed years of motherhood on a full-time basis. Few had opportunities of less than full-time paid work. These were women like the job-sharing clerical worker who, after 33 years as a housewife, felt "closed-in" but feared a full-time job.[7] Many have used job sharing as a way to return to the labor force. Some have teamed with partners of similar work backgrounds. Others have arranged to share with partners possessing more current skills—women who were working full time and wished to reduce working hours.

Women are now waiting fewer years after childbearing to return to work. A teacher whose daughter entered kindergarten last fall explained, "She's my only child, the only one I plan to have. I'd hate to miss that just for my career. But I can't consider not working with today's economy."[8]

Still others are even less willing to forgo careers because of any time interruption. They begin to consider job sharing when working full time. "I didn't want a three-to-five-year interruption in my career," said a young woman job-sharing personnel representative at an electronics firm, "just when I was finally doing what I wanted. I didn't see giving up everything I'd worked for because I'd be away from Jonathan just four out of twenty-four hours each day."[9]

Older Workers.   A few older workers use job sharing to return to the labor force after long periods of absence. "As an older woman returning to the job market," a secretary comments, "in an area that was not my original career, I feel that I received much good on-the-job training and current experience."[10]

Some others are beginning to use job sharing to phase toward retirement. "I find job sharing an unexpected, unforeseen boon in my later working years," reports a participant in a special project for older workers. "While many jobholders eagerly accept full retirement, it had loomed up before me as a 'sign-off' from life that I could not cope with."[11]

Poor health and family responsibilities are the reasons generally given by older workers when they reduce their hours through job sharing (or other part-time arrangements). An older woman began sharing after her physician advised her to stop working full time or be forced to quit. "I'd have preferred giving up my right arm," she responded, "to giving up teaching altogether after 19 years."[12] Although her health improved markedly, she had no desire to return to a full-time assignment. Others who reduce their hours resemble another woman who had been working full time for 18 years and wanted more time to spend at home with her elderly husband. She found that job sharing in the last few years before her retirement made this possible.

These cases do show that job sharing in the later years can bring easy transition to retirement for those who wish to continue work but slow down gradually. In general, however, older workers have yet to make use of job sharing in large numbers. Many are not able to make difficult choices which affect income for the rest of their lives. For the potential of job sharing's flexibility to be realized, and thus influence more extensive changes in the life cycle of older workers, certain organizational and legal changes will be required.

For workers under age 62 (the age at which a person can first collect Social Security benefits), the problem is especially acute. The size of most annuity benefits is based not only on the length of service, but also on the highest annual pay received for three consecutive years. In some instances (e.g., in the federal government), an employee who chooses to work part time before retirement is given full credit toward the annuity. This preretirement work can serve to raise the amount of the pension. However, promotions or pay raises which occur once the employee becomes a part-time employee cannot be used to increase the amount of the pension.

A few organizations have amended the system of calculating retirement benefits. When the City of San Francisco faced teacher layoffs in early 1980, it sought to attract more older full-time teachers to job sharing. New interest was aroused in 1974 state legislation which permits teachers to work half time in their last five years of service. In such cases, a job-sharing teacher receives full benefits because both employer and employee continue paying into the retirement fund at the full rate.

The Social Security System also penalizes those who wish to continue working into their late sixties. Even a half-time salary above the earning limit of $5,500 reduces benefits. Under this level, of course, workers over 62 can collect Social Security, and a half-time salary may mean higher income than would retirement. Wisconsin's Pre-Retirement Work Options Program has calculated the sums for several salary levels and points out that, in addition, such workers will still increase retirement benefits and may be taxed at a lower rate.[13] But because this depends on each individual's circumstance, considerable individual counseling is required so that older workers are able to make knowledgeable decisions.

Some kind of transition to the Swedish model of partial retirement, however, would encourage the use of job sharing and other part-time arrangements. Swedish workers are using sharing in part because workers are allowed to reduce their hours and a partial pension makes up some of the lost wages.

Changes in Education and Training Time. Traditional work schedules leave little time for those employees who wish to continue their education or training. Job sharing allows nonwork hours to be used for study—either for career advancement or career change. It also means that others, like the mother of five teenagers, a medical clerk who had never been to college, may have a "late beginning."

Two men in their thirties, one a probation officer, the other working as a tax auditor in state government, best illustrate job sharers who return for advanced degrees while working. The first had found it impossible to study and to carry on with his demanding caseload, even though he could not afford to quit his job. The other, who already had an M.A., also needed further training to advance beyond his current job. He was able, after several years of negotiating, to share his job and make time for clinical and class study time.

Beyond the time freed for study, job sharing itself may be used as a training period. In some cases, sharers have been able to use their shared jobs to renew skills, and they have then moved to full-time work. Elsewhere, in one type of work–study program, the Continental Bank in Chicago arranged for 500 teenagers to work half time. This program proved so successful that management suggested that a second shift of students might be added to share full-time jobs.

For the most part, apprenticeship arrangements have been on an individual basis. In these cases one partner, usually receiving a proportionately lower salary, is paired with a more senior partner. A chemist at a food-processing plant wanted to return to school and arranged to share with an assembly-line worker, whom she trained as her technician. A young teacher who became pregnant and wanted to reduce her teaching load, which had become more burdensome because of disciplinary problems, was paired with an older man in his late fifties who had returned to teaching after several years as a principal. The result was not only a better combination for students and two employees whose personal needs were met, but a sense of mutual learning for both partners. The younger teacher commented: "We've really had to get together to make sure that our methods are consistent. He's really well organized and he's able to perceive a problem before it actually happens."[14]

These examples illustrate that job sharing has made it possible for a growing number of individuals to make adjustments in the ways they organize their lives over the span of working years. Better balance at various stages has been possible, encouraging these workers to continue education, continue working rather than retiring, and more evenly maintain family responsibilities. Because it has afforded flexibility, job sharing has enabled them to enrich their lives as individual social and economic beings.

B. Flexitime and the Work-Life/Home-Life Conflict

The fact that there is a conflict between work life and home life for many workers has recently been established empirically. The theoretical arguments are also quite clear by now. In brief, the most compelling pieces of evidence about the work-life/home-life conflict are these two:

1. Over one-third of all workers in the nationwide 1977 Quality of Employment Survey who had a spouse and/or children said that their job and their family life interfered with each other "somewhat" or "a lot." The biggest reason for the interference was excessive or inconvenient hours of work.[15]
2. The strongest policy recommendation adopted by the 1980 White House Conference on Families was that employers should adopt work schedules that enable employees to accommodate workplace demands to family-life demands.[16]

These should not be surprises. The dual-earner family is not as unusual, as it used to be; it is becoming the norm. Single-parent families are also on the rise. The husband–breadwinner, wife–homemaker family with two lovely children is already a small statistical minority. There are more people working outside the home than ever before, and they have less discretionary time than ever before.

Flexible work hours, in principle, ought to help. The main thing flexitime can do is let workers juggle their work schedule so they can match personal needs with workplace needs. Since most institutions, such as schools and public transportation, run on fixed and uniform schedules, a switch from fixed to flexible schedules in the workplace could help workers make accommodations.

Of course, flexitime cannot lengthen the day beyond 24 hours, and it does not shorten the workweek of 40 hours. Flexitime cannot create time for workers to meet family needs. But flexitime can let workers organize their days more efficiently and come up with more time for themselves, even though they work no less time. Saving commuting time is one example. This, however, is all theorizing.

What happens in practice? We know only a little. It is a rare company indeed that feels any pressure from its employees about conflicts between work life and home life. The topic is out-of-bounds. It is not discussed at work. Women suffer the conflict more than men (society thrusts the dual roles on them); no career-oriented woman employee dares to reveal any family problems or let any work–family conflict intrude on work. Male managers, not feeling the conflict themselves, do not take action. As one CEO remarked cynically, "Most CEOs don't care about their own families, so why should they care about problems their employees have with their families?" And so actual company experiences dealing with work-life/home-life conflicts are very hard to find. Many companies have adopted flexitime, but almost none of them have looked at what flexitime does to the conflict between work and family.

While evidence is scarce, some does exist. A handful of case studies is in hand, collected and analyzed in the first place by people outside companies but with company cooperation. That evidence is presented here.

MORE AND BETTER FAMILY AND PERSONAL TIME: THE CASE OF TWO GOVERNMENT AGENCIES

When two federal government agencies in Washington, D.C., decided in 1978 to change from fixed to flexible work schedules, a team of outside researchers was permitted to keep track of how the agencies' employees changed their use of time. By taking a variety of before-flexitime and after-flexitime measures and also by looking at a comparison group that did not use flexitime, some actual experience with how flexitime affects family and personal time was obtained. This section reports the results of the twin case studies.[17]

The Workers and the Work Schedule

The employees whose family and personal time was studied met two conditions: (1) they had at least one child age 12 or under, and (2) they changed their work schedule when flexitime was implemented by at least 30 to 45 minutes. As it turned out (not by experimental design), nearly three-quarters of these workers also were either members of dual-earner families (in which both parents were full-time employees) or single parents. On the average, there were 1.6 children per family; the average age of the children was 5.2 years (see table 5-1).

These workers clearly were candidates for conflict between work life and home life. If flexitime could do something to ease the conflict—in the face of other institutional and social constraints—this surely was the place for it.

The flexitime program that was adopted, however, did not give much latitude for change. It was the conservative flexitour version of flexitime, in which eight hours are required every day (no debit or credit

Table 5-1.   Demographic Characteristics of Flexitime
Employees

Characteristic	Result
Sex: percent who were women	53
Age: average age, in years	32
Children: number of children, average per family	1.6
age, average per child	5.2
Length of service: average years on this job	4.8
Family structure: percent from dual (full-time) earner or single-parent families	71

Note: The sample size was 34 employees in two agencies.

Source: Richard A. Winett and Michael S. Neale, "Results of Experimental Study on Flexitime and Family Life," *Monthly Labor Review,* November 1980, pp. 29–32.

hours) and in which the worker must pick a work schedule and stick with it for a time (in this case for a biweekly pay period). Core hours started at 9:30 A.M. and ended at 4:00 P.M., with a lunch break. The arrival-time and departure-time "windows" were only two hours long. And of course there was no assurance that the spouse of the agency's flexitime employee would also have flexible hours. So this is a case of workers who clearly needed help with work-life/home-life conflict and who were offered a fairly modest tool to alleviate it.

Change In Family Time

Compared to standard fixed work hours and compared to other employees in the same agencies who did not change their work schedule, this is what happened to the flexitime workers' use of time:

• They spent nearly an hour a day more (55 minutes) with their families; that amounted to a 25 percent gain in family time. Most of that increase was time spent with spouse and children together (there may actually have been a slight loss of time spent with spouse alone).
• They started work 51 minutes earlier in the day, at 7:42 A.M. instead of 8:33 A.M., and got up in the morning 19 minutes earlier to make that possible.

The preferences these workers had that flexitime let them act on were to start the day earlier, reduce family time in the morning, and get more nonwork time in the afternoon and evening. Morning time was judged less pleasant than evening time, and so these workers managed to increase the quality of their family and personal time by trading in morning time for evening time.

Where did the extra 55 minutes of family time come from? It came from less time at home in the morning, less time commuting (both ways), and nearly a half hour less sleep (see table 5-2). In one agency, flexitime workers also reported working a few minutes less each day. Perhaps the transfer from sleep time to family time would not be sustained forever (although the postflexitime logs covered 14 weeks in one agency and 28 weeks in the other agency), or perhaps the easing of several household and child-care chores made less sleep possible.

The two agencies from which these averaged results come differed somewhat on the magnitude of the changes, but the substantive conclusions were the same. The comparison groups of workers in the same agencies who stayed on standard fixed-work schedules did not show these changes. Of course, other workers in different work settings might behave differently.

Table 5-2.   Changes in Family Time for Flexitime Workers

	Before	After	Change
Time spent with:			
children alone	1 hr. 11 min.	1 hr. 27 min.	16 min.
spouse alone	1 hr. 0 min.	56 min.	−4 min.
both spouse and children	1 hr. 31 min.	2 hr. 13 min.	42 min.
family, total	3 hr. 41 min.	4 hr. 36 min.	55 min.
Work-start time	8:33 A.M.	7:42 A.M.	51 min. earlier
Waking-up time	6:05 A.M.	5:46 A.M.	19 min. earlier
Going-to-sleep time	10:56 P.M.	10:43 P.M.	13 min. earlier

Notes: All times are daily averages of 34 employees in two government agencies.

"Before" data obtained from time logs kept by employees for five weeks in one agency and seven weeks in the other agency. "After" data spanned 14 weeks in one agency and 28 weeks in the other agency.

Flexitime workers are those who changed their work schedule by at least 45 minutes in one agency and 30 minutes in the other agency.

All changes are statistically significant compared to a group of similar employees in the same agency who did not change their work schedule, except for time spent with spouse and going-to-sleep time.

Sources: Richard A. Winett and Michael S. Neale, "Results of Experimental Study on Flexitime and Family Life," *Monthly Labor Review,* November 1980, pp. 29–32.

Richard A. Winett, Michael S. Neale, and Kenneth R. Williams, "The Effects of Flexible Work Schedule on Urban Family with Young Children: Quasi-Experimental, Ecological Studies," unpublished paper (Blacksburg, Va.: Virginia Polytechnic Institute and State University, 1979).

Changes In Family Life and Personal Activity

It is difficult for a worker to find enough time to spend with children and spouse—and the family is not all that interests working parents. What about the difficulty of taking educational courses, engaging in recreation, seeing friends, or shopping? Here also the government agency workers who switched to flexitime reported several changes for the better (see table 5-3). These are the highlights:

- The most difficult thing to do (in a list of 15 activities) under fixed work hours was to spend afternoon time with children; flexitime's major effect was to make that easier.
- Pursuing educational opportunities (formal or informal) was one of the most difficult things for these working parents to do when their work hours were fixed; flexitime made that substantially easier.
- Shopping and household chores were other activities that were similarly made easier to do with flexitime.
- Spending time with spouse or partner and having relaxed evenings during the workweek were rated somewhat difficult to do before flexitime but easier to do afterwards.
- Time for recreation and seeing friends during the workweek was easier to find when work schedules were flexible.
- Having breakfast time with children was the second most difficult thing to do under fixed work hours. Flexitime may have made it even a little more difficult (recall that these working parents chose to squeeze morning time in return for more evening time).
- Picking up children from school or providing child care in the afternoon was another moderately difficult activity; flexitime did not help (core hours at work extended to 4:00 P.M., too late for school pickups). Getting children to school in the morning was easier and not at all affected by flexitime.
- Commuting with a fixed work schedule was "somewhat difficult"; flexitime brought about a modest swing to "somewhat easy." There was no reduction in use of car pools.

What these working parents' self-reported experiences with flexitime amount to is this: Faced with conflicts between work life and family life and personal time, a limited version of flexitime lets workers make adjustments to get more time for their own needs. It can also make it easier for them to engage in several child-care, spouse-relating, and per-

Table 5-3. Effects of Flexitime on Family Life and Personal Activity

	Score[a]
With standard fixed hours, the most difficult things to do are:	
Spend afternoon time with my child	5.9
Have breakfast time with my child	5.3
Pursue educational opportunities (formal and informal)	5.2
Shopping and household chores	5.1
Engaging in recreational pursuits and hobbies	4.9
Spend time with my spouse or partner during the week	4.9
Pick up my child after school or from child care	4.7
Have relaxed evenings during the week	4.7
See friends during the week	4.5
Commute to and from work	4.5
With standard fixed hours, the least difficult things to do are:	
Share lunchtime or coffeebreak with friends at work	3.4
Have dinner with my spouse or partner and child during the week	3.7

	Change in Score
The biggest positive effects of flexitime are that it is easier to:[b]	
Spend afternoon time with my child	2.3
Spend time in the evening with my child	1.8
See friends during the workweek	1.7
Engage in recreational pursuits and hobbies	1.7
Pursue educational opportunities (formal and informal)	1.6
Do shopping and household chores	1.6
Spend time with my spouse or partner during the week	1.5
Have relaxed evenings during the workweek	1.3
Have dinner with my spouse or partner and child during the week	1.0
Commute to and from work	.9
The negative effects of flexitime are that it is harder to:[c]	
Have breakfast time with my child	− .3
Share lunchtime or coffeebreak with friends at work	− .2

Notes:

[a]Average of 34 employees in two agencies on a scale where 7 was "very difficult" and 1 was "very easy"; midpoint = 4. Both pre- and post-flexitime surveys were taken during the school year.

[b]These changes are statistically significant compared to fixed work hours and a comparison group.

[c]Not statistically significant.

Source: Richard A. Winett, Michael S. Neale, and Kenneth R. Williams, "The Effects of Flexible Work Schedule on Urban Family with Young Children: Quasi-Experimental, Ecological Studies," unpublished paper (Blacksburg, Va.: Virginia Polytechnic Institute and State University, 1979).

sonal activities, such as education. Some other of these activities are not
touched by flexitime.

Based on this case study, the conclusion can be drawn that flexitime
is an easy and inexpensive way for companies to let workers help themselves out of their own work-life/home-life conflicts. Perhaps a more
flexible flexitime would do even better. But as long as institutions and
social roles remain fixed, even if work schedules are flexible, we should
not expect too much. Flexitime is just one small step.

WORK–FAMILY STRESS, FAMILY TIME, AND SEX ROLES: THE CASE OF THE MARITIME ADMINISTRATION

The Maritime Administration in the U.S. Department of Commerce in
Washington, D.C., uses a flexitour version of flexitime: employees
choose starting and quitting times but are expected to stick with those
times except for infrequent changes. Eight hours must be worked every
day, and no debit or credit hours are allowed.

When this flexitime program was over a year old, the Family Impact
Seminar (an organization devoted to the study of family problems) took
some measurements of three personal effects that flexitime might have.
These effects were (1) the degree of stress felt by employees in managing their family life and personal time and in resolving conflicts
between job and family roles, (2) the amount of time employees spent
in "family work," and (3) the sharing of family responsibilities between
women and men.[18]

Employees, both men and women, who answered questions about
these aspects of their lives covered all job levels and marital and family
status. Fifty-seven percent of these employees actually changed their
work schedules when they got flexitime; the rest continued to follow
their old work schedules even though the agency permitted them to
change (often employees did not "use" flexitime because car pools or
the schedules of other family members stood in the way). Responses
from both changers and nonchangers are included in this study because
the researchers believed that the availability of a flexitime option might
alter people's perception of work–family stress, even though the option
could not be taken. (This approach is in direct contrast to the Winett
and Neale study reported on above, in which only those employees who
actually changed their work schedule were included in the flexitime
results; the others were treated as a comparison group although they

were in the same agency.) Questionnaire responses were obtained only after flexitime had been operating for some time, so there are no before-and-after comparisons. However, workers on standard fixed hours in another government agency were asked the same questions and served as a comparison group.

Family-Management Stress and Job-Family Role Strain

The conclusions that come out of this case study are based on the self-reports of Maritime Administration employees compared to similar employees on standard fixed work hours. While no cause-effect relationships can be proved, the simple differences between flexitime and fixed-hours employees stood up to further analysis, using other variables (family-life-cycle stage, total hours worked, occupational level) that might also have affected family life and personal time. Here are the key results:

1. Overall stress was lower for people on flexitime than for those with fixed schedules. Among flexitime employees there was substantial stress reduction for some but not for others. Flexitime helped some employees—but not most of them—to manage family stress by a modest amount.

There are some very good reasons that in this case flexitime had minimal results—and accomplished the least that could be expected from its use. First, flexitime in this agency was not very flexible. Employees still had to work eight hours every day, and they were not supposed to change their work schedule from day to day.

Second, these employees may not have had a high degree of family-management stress in the first place. The problem was not that great (by their own self-report), and so a solution could not be that striking. The midpoint of the five-point question scale was 3.0. Among standard fixed-hours employees, the average response was between 3.1 and 3.2, only slightly on the difficult as compared to the easy side of handling family tasks. (Of course, the flexitime employees may have experienced more stress initially.)

Third, only a few more than half of the employees in the flexitime agency actually followed a work schedule different from their previous fixed schedule. Many of those who did not change to flexitime when offered the option could not do so because (1) supervisors constrained them, (2) the spouse's schedule was a problem, or (3) other institutional rigidities discouraged them. Therefore, the effects of flexitime are diluted by the mixture of nonchangers and changers.

2. Flexitime appeared to help reduce family-management stress among workers who did not have primary child-care responsibilities: single men and women without children, married women without children, and married men who had children and whose wives did not work outside the home.

3. The workers whose family-management stress was not reduced despite flexitime were those who would seem to need help the most: married women workers who had children and whose husbands also worked. These women had the highest stress scores of all employees in the flexitime agency. Single mothers were too few in number to yield a reliable result (see table 5-4).

Flexitime, limited as it was, did not leave workers with objectively the most serious family-management problems any better off than their fixed-hour counterparts in this study. Limited flexitime is, perhaps, not

Table 5-4. Family-Management Stress and Job–Family Role Strain for Flexitime and Standard-Fixed-Hour Workers (Mean Scale Scores)

	Family-Management Stress		Job-Family Role Strain	
	Flexitime	Fixed Hours	Flexitime	Fixed Hours
Employees with children	3.0	3.2	2.5	2.6
Women with employed husbands	3.2	3.1	2.8	2.8
Men with employed wives	2.9	3.2	2.4	2.6
Men with nonemployed wives	3.0*	3.5	2.4	2.5
Single mothers	2.8	3.1	2.7	2.8
Employees with no children	2.6*	3.1	2.5	2.6
Women with employed husbands	2.6*	3.5	2.5*	2.9
Men with employed wives	2.8	2.9	2.5	2.4
Men with nonemployed wives	3.0	2.7	2.5	2.4
Single women	2.5*	3.2	2.6	2.6
Single men	2.4*	3.3	2.4*	2.8

Notes: Scale scores are means for all employees in each category across several questions; scale scores ranged from 1 to 5, where 5 was most stress, and 3 = midpoint. Sample sizes for the respondent categories range from 11 to 50.

Scales for employees wih children whose results are reported here included questions about children, while scales for employees without children did not.

* = statistical significance for the difference between means of flexitime vs. fixed hours groups.

Source: Halcyone H. Bohen and Anamaria Viveros-Long, *Balancing Jobs and Family Life: Do Flexible Work Schedules Help?* (Philadelphia: Temple University Press, 1981).

potent enough to make a dent in these problems in the face of other strong institutional rigidities. But other workers, with objectively smaller family-management tasks (no children, for instance) but, subjectively, not much if any less stress, apparently found flexitime sufficient to make a difference. These people surely had fewer external obstacles to low stress, and so even a small innovation like flexible work schedules can help.

4. Strain generated by conflicts between job roles and family roles did not seem to be serious on the average for these workers. There were few differences between flexitime employees and employees with fixed hours.

Results such as these will, of course, cast doubt on the use of flexitime to relieve workers of the stress generated by work–family conflicts (when they do occur). But these case studies make it very hard to show the effects of flexitime even if they do occur. For example, among the Maritime Administration employees, those who chose to "use" flexitime by changing their work schedules were more likely than nonchangers to have regular demands on their time outside of work and family demands (second jobs, volunteer activities, and educational activities led the list for these workers). These people were also more likely to live with another person(s) than to live alone, and so their family or personal-time demands were probably greater. And while the flexitime users did not have more children than nonusers, they did have younger children. Perhaps the results of this case study would have been quite different (more like the Winett and Neale study) if only those workers who actually changed their work hours were studied, both before and after the change.

Time Spent in Family Work and the Sharing of Family Responsibilities

Family work in this study was taken to mean home chores and child care. Sharing of this work was a matter of its division between spouses. The chief results from employee surveys were these:

• Both men and women in the flexitime agency reported spending more time in home chores than employees in the fixed-hours agency—about 2.3 compared to 2.0 hours a day for men, and 3.7 compared to 3.3 hours a day for women. But almost all of the additional time was spent by men who did not have children and by single mothers.

• Married men in the flexitime agency did not spend more time on home chores than men with fixed work hours, nor did married women spend less time. Married women employees who had children spent almost twice as much time on home chores as did married men with children.

• Employees in the flexitime agency apparently did not spend more time in child care than employees in the fixed-work-hours agency. Here also, mothers spent 50 to 100 percent more time in child care than fathers, even though both parents worked full time (see table 5-5).

• Married-women employees claimed that they were responsible for about two-thirds of the home chores and child care whether they were

Table 5-5.   Time Spent on Home Chores and Child Care

	Flexitime	Fixed Hours
Average hours per day spent on home chores		
Married women employees		
with children	3.9	3.8
without children	2.9	2.7
Single mothers	4.2	3.1
Married men employees		
with children, wife employed	2.4	2.5
with children, wife not employed	2.2	2.0
without children, wife employed	2.2	1.6
without children, wife not employed	2.2	1.7
Average hours per day spent on child care		
Married women	3.8	4.0
Single mothers	4.3	4.1
Married men		
wife employed	2.2	2.3
wife not employed	2.5	2.1

Notes: Average hours include weekend days; workday averages alone are much less.

Sample sizes range from 14 to 51 in each category; differences between flexitime and standard-hours groups are not statistically significant.

Source: Halcyone H. Bohen and Anamaria Viveros-Long, *Balancing Jobs and Family Life: Do Flexible Work Schedules Help?* (Philadelphia: Temple University Press, 1981).

Table 5-6.   Division of Family Work between Spouses

	Flexitime	Fixed Hours
Percent of total time spent on home chores		
Married women employees		
with children	71	64
without children	63	66
Married men		
wife employed (with children or not)	42	42
wife not employed (with children or not)	27	23
Percent of total time spent on child care		
Married women employees	64	63
Married men		
wife employed	40	45
wife not employed	33	39

Note: Sample sizes ranged from 15 to 50 for each category; no differences between flexitime and fixed-hours groups were statistically significant.

Source: Halcyone H. Bohen and Anamaria Viveros-Long, *Balancing Jobs and Family Life: Do Flexible Work Schedules Help?* (Philadelphia: Temple University Press, 1981).

in the flexitime agency or had fixed work hours. Men with the flexitime option did not do proportionately more, whether or not they had children. What altered the men's share of home chores and child care was whether their wives were employed, and not whether they had flexitime (see table 5-6).

These results taken together do not speak well of flexitime as a social innovation intended to reform and improve family life and men's and women's roles. Surely flexitime did not damage. Workers liked it, and a third of them said they used flexitime to spend more time with their families. Yet, when measured objectively, flexitime had little effect on employees' home lives. Flexitime, after all, slightly alters the facts of work life and home life (although it has other advantages). Limited flexitime can have only limited effects.

NOTES

1. Interview, data bank for national survey, 1978.
2. Ibid.
3. Ibid.
4. Gretl S. Meier, *Job Sharing* (Kalamazoo, Mich.: The W. E. Upjohn Insitute, 1979), p. 146.

5. Catherine Christie Nicholl, "Will the Real Professor Please Stand Up?" in *Careers and Couples: An Academic Question,* edited by Leonore Hoffmann and Gloria DeSole (New York: Modern Language Association of America, 1976), p. 36.
6. Barbara Riegelhaupt, "Half a Job for Two is Better Than One," *Valley News,* 25 June 1980, section 3, p. 1.
7. See notes 1–3.
8. "Job Sharing," *Good Housekeeping,* June 1979, p. 66.
9. Meier, *Job Sharing,* p. 59.
10. "Pre-Retirement Work Options, Quarterly Progress Report, March 1, 1980–May 31, 1980," State of Wisconsin, State Division of Human Resource Services, p. 1.
11. Ibid.
12. Meier et al., *Job Sharing in the Schools* (Palo Alto, Calif.: New Ways to Work, 1976).
13. Ibid., appendix II.
14. Meier, *Job Sharing,* p. 103.
15. Robert P. Quinn and Graham L. Staines, *The 1977 Quality of Employment Survey* (Ann Arbor, Mich.: The University of Michigan, Survey Research Center, Institute for Social Research, 1979).
16. White House Conference on Families, *Listening to America's Families: Action for the 80's* (Washington, D.C.: The White House Conference on Families, 1980), pp. 24–25.
17. This section of chapter 5 is based on Richard A. Winett and Michael S. Neale, "Results of Experimental Study on Flexitime and Family Life," *Monthly Labor Review,* November 1980, pp. 29–32, and on unpublished material from this study obtained from the authors.
18. This section of chapter 5 is based on a study in Halcyone H. Bohen and Anamaria Viveros-Long, *Balancing Jobs and Family Life: Do Flexible Work Schedules Help?* (Philadelphia: Temple University Press, 1981).

6.
Managing New Work Schedules

A. Strategic Management and New Work Schedules

Before management can begin to implement a new work schedule such as flexitime or compressed workweeks, some questions must be answered—questions that concern long-term planning and strategy rather than short-term day-to-day administration of new work schedules. How will these schedules fit into the company's overall management structure and processes? What kind of management philosophy and organizational climate is needed? How will new work schedules relate to human-resource development?

We know that the use of new work patterns is not rigidly and technologically determined. It is true that some work operations are not well suited and others are naturals—but companies themselves report that how the work schedule is managed is very important.

Our objective in this section is to observe what the managements of model flexitime and compressed workweek companies are like. Of course, this does not mean that all companies have to be like the models described here in order to get good results with new work patterns. The cases are selected precisely because they are innovative and perhaps a bit different from most managements.

The case of Control Data Corporation is presented in this section, followed by a summary of the management features of the Hewlett-Packard and Corning Glass Works flexitime programs.

HOW NEW WORK PATTERNS FIT INTO HUMAN RESOURCE
DEVELOPMENT: THE CASE OF CONTROL DATA CORPORATION

Control Data Corporation is one of the first flexitime users in the United States, beginning in 1972 and extending now to most employees in the company nationwide, including manufacturing workers. In addition to flexitime, the company's work force consists of about 10 percent permanent part-time employees—an unusually high figure. One Control Data plant, located in the St. Paul inner city, manufactures computer manuals and has been completely staffed for several years by permanent part-time workers, including supervisors. Flexiplace, in which employees work at home—in this case communicating via computer terminals—got started in 1980.

Going well beyond innovative work patterns, Control Data also operates programs to assist workers in their personal lives—from on-site child care at some locations to the Employee Advisory Resource (EAR). This is an employee counseling and referral service with a 24-hour telephone call-in service as well as an in-house staff. Any problems of a personal nature, work-related or not, are handled, ranging from personal conflicts between a worker and the worker's boss to marital conflicts between a worker and the worker's spouse, and from alcoholism to suicide.

The obvious question is, why does one company have these employee-centered programs? What accounts for this collection of new work patterns and employee-assistance programs? Are there linkages between them? What kind of human-resource management system does this company have?

Look first at some easy answers that may explain the company's unusual interest in its employees. Control Data is a profitable and growing company in a growing high-technology industry. Money and growth make innovation easier. The company is quite young and does not carry the baggage of either old factories or old ideas. In addition, the headquarters are in Minneapolis, thought to be a city with an unusually homogeneous population and quite free of urban strife. No doubt these factors make a difference by facilitating change, if not by directly causing it. They are favorable background factors. But they are surely not enough to make the company take the positive and concrete steps that it has taken over the last decade.

Nor is any one business operating problem the immediate reason for Control Data's human-resource programs, as is so often the case. Flexitime does not happen in this company because of high absenteeism or low productivity or low morale. Permanent part-time employment does not happen only because of labor shortages or unusual business hours. Economic rationale is clearly in evidence for all these programs, but not as a narrowly focused solution to a single operating problem that is pinching the company.

The underlying reasons for Control Data's interest in human-resource programs are threefold: (1) the values of top management, led by the founder and chief executive officer, Mr. William Norris; (2) a management philosophy that pervades the entire company; and (3) a long-range planning process that encourages the inception of human-resource programs. Here is a closer look.

Management Philosophy

Several aspects of Control Data's management philosophy stand out:

- The short run is sacrificed for the long run. It is desirable but not necessary that this quarter's earnings exceed last quarter's. This long-run orientation is especially noteworthy in view of recent criticism of American management's preoccupation with immediate results.
- Social problems are seen as potential business opportunities, in which Control Data technology and capabilities can be utilized. Social problems are not seen as a thorn in the side of the company or as a drag on the company's freedom of movement. For example, "Homework," the company's flexiplace program, saves energy and aids the handicapped, but it also sells computer terminals.
- Behavioral approaches take high priority. Even in a technically oriented company, and even among engineers and scientists, human needs and social science are genuinely important. This starts with the values of the top two or three executives. They simply believe that human-resource programs are the right thing to have.
- The corporation is made to fit employees rather than employees adapting to fit the corporation. This is accomplished through planning and human-resource programs. There is an underlying respect for individual differences.
- Human-resource programs, such as flexitime and EAR, are regarded as management tools to improve the business, not as social welfare programs. They are more nearly privileges extended to employees rather than rights or entitlements; yet they are not used as a weapon by management. They are just part of the business.

The Employee Advisory Resource (EAR) illustrates this last point. Even though EAR is a radical departure in company attention to workers' personal lives, it can also be regarded as a sound economic invest-ment. In its first five years of operation (1974–79) it has saved a doc-umented $6 million and an estimated (undocumented) additional $4 million. For example, if EAR prevents even one employee's suicide, it saves the company $100,000. Of course, that is not why EAR exists, but the company is aware of such economic implications. Less dramat-ically, supervisors and line managers often do not know how to handle employees' personal problems manifested on the job, and so an in-house counseling and referral service has a role to play. In addition, EAR is a barometer of stress and picks up employee problems to feed back to management. About 40 percent of the presenting problems are work related (even if stemming from the employee's personal life), and so can be partly alleviated by company-sponsored human-resource programs.

Human-Resource Planning

But how is management philosophy translated into human-resource programs? And how does one program relate to another? The answer is in the planning process. The linkage among various human-resource programs (alternative work schedules, counseling, training, and health) is that they are all solutions to related macro problems. They all have a social issue (which is ultimately a business problem) as their common origin. They are linked by the planning process, during which issues affecting the company are identified and programs to address these issues are proposed.

These human-resource programs reinforce one another insofar as they contribute to the organizational climate. They are systematic, but they are not a system of programs; they are a system of beliefs. They are not dependent on one another in a sequential way (Program A does not necessarily precede Program B) or in an enabling way (Program A does not necessarily make Program B easier or more effective) (see fig-ure 6-1).

The human-resource planning process itself is marked by several key features:

- It is institutionalized—i.e., it is a regular formal process governed by well-understood procedures and responsibilities, not by personali-ties. It is a rule of law, not of men.
- It has a long-run five-year strategic plan and a short-run one-year

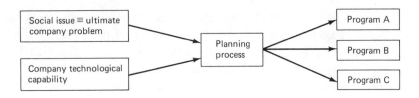

Figure 6-1.   Schematic view of human-resource program generation.

Note: ≡ means *is identical to.*

operating plan; the latter depends on the former and comprises the actual programs.

● Evaluation, including quantitative measurements where possible, is built into the plan rather than added on later.

● Employee-attitude surveys are taken annually so that needs and problems can be anticipated (for example, when employee dissatisfaction with performance appraisals was detected in 1975, a new system was designed and implemented before a crisis arose).

● Communication occurs both across functions (operating line managers meet in planning sessions with human-resources staff) and up the management hierarchy (giving feedback) as well as down.

● The planning function is a coordinating function rather than a decision-making function; its task is to integrate the needs of various divisions of the company to harmonize their priorities, and to relate people needs to the goals of the business plans. Human-resource managers do not make the plans (operating managers do), but they make sure the plans are made and made well.

The chronological sequence of tasks and the people who are involved in the year-long and continuous human-resource planning process are sketched below and in figure 6-2 (see page 182).

1. Macro issues that affect the company are identified by a small number (six to ten) of the operating and personnel executives in October.
2. Company goals and strategic objectives are proposed by a larger group (15) of personnel managers in February to deal with the issues.

3. Operating objectives, specific goals, and programs are designed by the 12-member corporate personnel policy committee in March and sent to the planning function in the divisions of the company.
4. The business plans, incorporating personnel programs, are constructed in the divisions and reviewed by top corporate executives in June.
5. Budgets and operating plans are adopted in September.

For examples of macro issues, company goals, strategic objectives, and human-resource programs from the actual 1980 Control Data plan, see the appendix, document A-8.

Linkages between New Work Schedules and Training

The relationship between new work schedules and other human-resource programs, such as training, in the planning process is one of problem solution. A needs-identification approach is used. First, determine training needs on the dual basis of (1) career orientation of employees, and (2) labor-market conditions. Then see how new work patterns might support this training. For example, the growing tendency of employees toward career switching—major shifts in jobs in roughly five-year cycles—calls for periodic major inputs of formal classroom education as well as on-the-job learning. These training needs can be accommodated by offering permanent career part-time employment opportunities for career switchers to use while they are undertaking new training. Training and work-schedule needs that are identified from career orientations of employees will have to be modified according to labor-market conditions. For example, skill shortages mean more training sponsored by the company, and more alternative work schedules.

Another training need that the company has identified is that of combating skill obsolescence. In a high-technology environment with rapid changes in knowledge, this is a problem that is best solved by managing people to prevent it from occurring. This means using small doses of training continually—mostly in-house but formal, up to two weeks per year. Employees can also be encouraged to take continuing education courses on their own time. They will be more likely to do so when they have flexible working hours, in large measure because they can mesh work and training schedules better.

MANAGEMENT STRUCTURE AND STYLE: THE CASE OF HEWLETT-PACKARD

Another company noteworthy for certain elements of its management structure and style is Hewlett-Packard, an electronics firm whose flexitime program is described more fully in pages 24 to 28. Hewlett-Packard, a long-time flexitime user, established its program in the United States in 1972. Currently every H-P employee, worldwide, has some degree of work-schedule flexibility.

Here is a review of the management features of Hewlett-Packard that relate to its successful use of flexitime.

- Management is decentralized; because authority is widely dispersed, employees are more likely to accept responsibility.
- Human-resource management is integrated with operating business management; line and staff divisions are blurred. Every manager and supervisor is a human-resource manager. One of the chief duties of every supervisor—and one on which he or she is evaluated—is employee development.
- Jobs—even production jobs—are designed to give workers maximum responsibility. Workers rotate jobs regularly; cross-training is continual.
- Rules are scarce; policies are treated as guidelines. Individual responsibility and judgment are substituted for rules.
- Employee performance appraisal depends mainly on output (not time input), on interpersonal qualities such as teamwork, and (for supervisors) on innovation as well as planning, organizing, and controlling. The organizational climate is one of informality, trust, and equity. The company believes that "men and women want to do a good job . . . and that if they are provided the proper environment, they will do so." The system "places great responsibility on the individual concerned. . . . the dignity and worth of the individual is a very important part of the H-P way."

B. Implementation and Supervision for Flexitime

Among all the new work patterns, flexitime is the one for which implementation and supervision are the most critical. The odds of success with flexitime are high, but management is important. Flexitime usually is adopted as a "program"—as a formal written policy for many or all workers (unlike part-time employment, which often is an ad hoc feature for a few people). Flexitime is applicable in a wide range of work technologies (unlike compressed workweeks, which are technologically determined to a great extent). Flexitime is a change in spirit and style as well as substance for many workers and supervisors—behaviors have to change. These features mean that flexitime has to be managed.

In this section, we first look at a case study of how a recommendation to adopt flexitime in the first place was arrived at, focusing on the internal company study and deliberation. Then we look at an actual flexitime experiment at Corning Glass Works—how the flexitime idea was presented to managers and workers, how the experiment was conducted (including the implementation guidelines), and what the main results were for supervision and productivity.

Several actual company implementation "manuals" appear, in whole or in part, in the appendix of this book in connection with other case studies (e.g., Physio-Control Corporation, Board of Governors of the Federal Reserve System, Group Health Cooperative of Puget Sound, as well as the Corning Glass Works). To these have been added the "flexitime administrative guidelines" of the General Motors Corporation, one of the largest and most successful users of flexitime (see appendix, documents A-9, A-10, and A-11).

ARRIVING AT A FLEXITIME PROPOSAL: THE CASE OF ABC CORPORATION

How does the idea of adopting flexible work hours get started in a company? How is a recommendation to use flexitime made? What is the decision-making process? This is a case study of the early stages of flexitime implementation—of the internal company study of flexitime as an alternative work schedule rather than of the administration of flexitime once a decision to use it has been made. The ABC Corporation is a multi-billion-dollar multinational corporation.

Where the Flexitime Idea Came From

The flexitime idea came from a personnel official who was knowledgeable about flexitime because of his participation in a local industrial relations society. The immediate reasons for suggesting flexitime were the operating problems the company was expected to suffer when it moved its offices. A commuting problem was foreseen because the new office had only limited access points, and no public transportation service. A shortage of labor was foreseen because the company expected to lose 60 percent of its nonexempt work force when it moved, and the new labor market might not be able to supply that many replacements.

These are unique motives for suggesting flexitime. Perhaps no other company is in this situation, nor was the ABC Corporation until the office relocation came along. General concepts of raising productivity or boosting morale did not figure in the flexitime idea. And this is often the case. Particular operating problems for which flexitime might be a solution are often the reasons for getting flexitime started. (Of course, there are notable exceptions: Corning Glass Works started flexitime in its research and development division because of a general mission to improve productivity, and both Hewlett-Packard and Control Data adopted flexitime because of a top-management belief that it was the right thing to do for employees.)

Should Flexitime Be Adopted?

Given the flexitime idea and the anticipated operating problems, the question was: Should we adopt flexitime? The study that went into this question consisted of a needs assessment and a feasibility analysis. The method was to form a task force with an outside consultant as a resource person.

The Task Force.   The mission of the ten-member task force was to (1) gather information about the company's anticipated problems and about flexitime, (2) determine if flexitime should be recommended, and (3) if so, sketch the key design features of the recommended flexitime program. The task-force membership was intentionally diverse. It included employee-relations managers, a building manager, support-services managers, product managers, a financial officer, and a research-and-development manager.

An outside consultant was brought in at an early stage to assist in identifying the questions that would need answers, to help plan the feasibility study itself, to report on the experiences other companies were known to have, and to generally serve as a resource person. The special features of the relationships between the company and the consultant were that (1) the company integrated the consultant into the task force (i.e., he participated in all its deliberations), and (2) the company used the consultant as a resource person (i.e., he did not deliver a particular product such as a written report).

Questions and Answers.   This is a summary of what the task force asked and what they found out.

1. Access to the office by commuter traffic would be a problem. Based on a simulation study, ABC Corporation work schedules would have to be coordinated with other local employers in order to avoid rush-hour congestion and also air pollution. Van pools could be required in the future with a usage rate of 10 to 20 percent of all employees needed at this site. Flexitime and van pools with standard hours were regarded as alternatives. Flexitime would cause some problems for van pools, but they could be worked out by employees themselves. Staggered hours were universally opposed.

2. The labor market into which the company was going to move was actually a net exporter of labor, principally in high-level jobs. There were shortages in other jobs. In the future, employment opportunities in this labor market were expected to grow much faster than population (constrained by housing supply), and the market would become a net importer of labor. The company could expect to tap high-level people who were currently living in the area but working out of it, but entry into the labor force would have to be stimulated for many other jobs. Other nearby employers were offering flexitime, so the ABC Corporation might need to do likewise. Job sharing and part-time employment were seen as the best solutions to the labor-shortage problem, but fringe benefits would be a problem.

3. Utilities and security would not be affected by flexitime. Building open hours would be 7:00 A.M. to 6:00 P.M. in any case, which would accommodate a flexitime band width. Security would be around-the-clock and could accommodate early arrivers or late stayers.

4. Support services such as audiovisual, library, mailroom, travel service, and cafeteria should be available during normal 8:00 A.M. to

Service	Can Flextime Apply?		
	YES	NO	
Employee Store	X		Store would only be open during core hours.
Newspaper and notions counter		X	
Food services (contracted labor)		X	
Corporate library		X	Unless additional person hired ($13,000).
Duplicating		X	Unless personnel are staggered to cover flexible hours.
Central mail		X	Unless employees are staggered to handle workload.
Administrative support centers (copiers, coffee, teletype)		X	Could add $121,000 for part-time help during flexible hours.
Stationery stockroom	X		If client service during core hours only is acceptable
Corporate information center	X		Assumes answering of outside calls during official building hours is acceptable.
Video/Audiovisual communications		X	$25,000 for personnel needed to service equipment during flexible hours.
Purchasing	X		If client service during core hours only is acceptable.
Art and design	X		If client service during core hours only is acceptable.
Photography	X		If client service during core hours only is acceptable.
Slides and charts	X		If client service during core hours only is acceptable.
Meetings and travel (contracted labor)	X		If client service during core hours only is acceptable.
Printing and literature distribution		X	
Exhibit design and construction		X	
Mailing lists		X	

Figure 6-2.   Suitability of flexitime to marketing and support services.
Note: Services not operating on flexible time will have a morale problem affecting turnover, undesirability of these jobs, and so on.

Source: Internal company document, ABC Corporation.

5:00 P.M. business hours, and could be stretched to cover an entire 7:00 A.M. to 6:00 P.M. band width, either by voluntary coverage agreements among employees or by job sharing, converting a full-time 8:00 A.M. to 5:00 P.M. librarian into two half-time job sharers, one working 7:00 A.M. to 12 noon and the other working 12 noon to 6:00 P.M. (see figure 6-2).

5. Company policy required overtime pay for all nonexempt workers after eight hours a day, even though there is no labor-union representation at the office and neither the Walsh-Healy Act nor the Contact Work Hours and Safety Standards Act apply. Overtime pay at the office amounted to a sizeable $350,000 to $500,000 in the most recent year. The options were to change the company overtime policy or limit flexible hours to a maximum of eight hours per day. Since the workday was to be eight hours after the move, this would mean no debit or credit hours.

6. Management prerogatives vs. employee rights or privileges was a major issue. It was raised by the coverage problem. "Does flexitime mean a $100,000 executive can't tell his secretary that she has to be in at 8:00 A.M. to take dictation?" "My secretary has five other men on her telephone and she's got to be there to pick it up, otherwise the secretary across the way has to get it." (Perhaps this is not only a management question, but also a male vs. female role question.) The resolution was that flexitime must be controlled, beginning with only limited flexibility.

7. Productivity outcomes were questioned. On the one hand, different jobs have different work-schedule requirements, and some workers won't be able to have flexibility. That might cause a morale problem because of the inequity, and that might ruin productivity. In addition, some workers might loaf when their supervisor isn't around, and flexitime could make this worse. You must mentally watch the nonexempt. On the other hand, new office technology, such as word processing, will require longer hours of operation, and flexitime and job sharing might make that easier. Computer terminal usage might be evened out also. All this debate led to further calls for controlled and limited flexitime. It also emphasized the role that organizational climate and managerial style has to play.

8. Some key experiences that other companies reported in interviews with the task force were:

- When AT&T moved an office across town in Washington, D.C., flexitime helped the company retain good employees.
- Fewer jobs needed continuous coverage over the whole band width than expected at AT&T.
- Advance approval from supervisors of employees' work schedule plans was important at General Motors headquarters; people soon settled into a pattern.
- Traffic problems were relieved at American Can Company when its 2200 headquarters office employees in Greenwich, Connecticut, went on flexitime.

9. A survey of 22 managers in one division showed that flexitime was the first choice of 10 managers, while 8 preferred staggered hours, and 4 wanted to keep standard hours. The chief doubts about flexitime concerned the possible incompatibility of managers' and workers' schedules, lack of managerial control, and communications problems. Four out of six divisions favored flexitime, while two saw it only as a last resort.

The Flexitime Proposal

The outcome of the task force's work was a one-page proposal to adopt flexitime, including these key features: (1) flexitime would apply to all employees in all divisions of the headquarters office except for those in some units of building services, (2) workdays would be fixed at eight hours, with two-hour "windows" at each end and six hours of core time, (3) individual work units could set up their own work schedules within these guidelines to meet their own business needs, (4) employees should give one-week advance notice of their planned work schedule, subject to supervisory approval, and (5) timekeeping would remain unchanged, with time cards for nonexempts and honor system for exempts (see appendix, document A-12).

The proposal was conservative and designed to assuage the doubts of skeptics. It was also quite general, leaving details and interpretations to be filled in later.

Although the plan received preliminary endorsement by employee relations people, senior management of the corporation vetoed it and it was never put into effect. The reasons for the plan's demise—and some lessons to be drawn from it—are discussed in some detail on pages 209 to 211.

ADOPTING FLEXITIME: MANAGEMENT, PRODUCTIVITY, AND EMPLOYEES' PERSONAL NEEDS AT CORNING GLASS WORKS

by Stanley Nollen, Andres Steinmetz, and Gary Wydman[1]

Many companies use flexible working hours because their employees want it and because they believe that morale and job satisfaction will improve. The top managers of these companies typically have a value stance that says flexitime is good because it gives employees more choice and more control. Because these companies believe that flexitime will do little or no damage to business operations (and may even help), they adopt flexitime as an article of faith.

Some companies use flexible working hours because they have a particular operating problem, such as high absenteeism or turnover. These companies see flexitime mainly as a way to solve a business problem. Because workers usually like flexitime anyway, they go ahead and adopt it. Notions of productivity improvement due to flexitime in these cases are quite vague, or cast in terms of narrow variables, such as saving $200,000 a year from reduced absenteeism.

The case of Corning Glass Works is quite different. The unit of the company that experimented with flexitime did not have any particularly pressing business problem that required immediate solution. There was no single or narrowly focused reason to try flexitime. Instead, there was a combination of (1) a continuing sense of a mission to improve productivity, broadly conceived, and (2) an understanding that the personal needs of employees were important to the business success of the company and that the company would be better off both ethically and economically if it assisted employees to meet their personal needs. Flexitime at Corning Glass Works is thus a planned experiment, designed by management to be one component of a grander human-resource development program.

Corning Glass Works is a large company, with about 30,000 employees (some of whom are outside the United States) located in the small city of Corning in upstate New York. The company has long been a major producer of glass and ceramic products, both for consumer and industrial use. Recently, however, the company has diversified somewhat into several technically related fields. There is a precedent for innovation in human-resource management in the company. A well-known organizational development effort took place in recent years, one of the lasting results of which is an advanced performance-appraisal system.

Why Flexitime?

The research and development unit of Corning Glass Works, called Sullivan Park and located in a separate facility in the hills outside Corning, New York, had been looking into the advantages and disadvantages of flexitime for several years. In 1980, the personnel department at Sullivan Park decided to try flexitime. The overriding reason was productivity. There was no manifest R&D productivity problem. In fact, by a variety of quantitative measures, R&D productivity was showing steady gains and good payoffs in the last decade. But there was a company-wide general productivity improvement program, and the R&D laboratory perceived itself as a leader in the company in both productivity and innovation.

The second reason to try flexitime was to improve the use of time as a resource available to management. Time management was reckoned to be one of the key ways that productivity could be improved. In turn, improving the use of time meant (1) improving supervision, and (2) making it easier for workers to meet their personal-time and family-life needs. For example, there ought to be less time taken from work for personal needs and less supervisory ambivalence about granting personal time if flexitime is used.

Third, Corning Glass had some desire to do what it could to make it easier for employees to resolve conflicts between work-life demands and home-life demands. This consideration would not in itself have caused the flexitime experiment to be initiated, but it was an acknowledged background consideration.

A closer look shows how some managers at the R&D facility view productivity improvement and the relationship of flexitime to such improvement.

Productivity improvement is a long-term proposition, and it depends on many factors. To believe that one can tinker with a single variable, such as work schedules, and solve all workplace problems, or that one can increase productivity simply by putting people on a different work schedule, is naive. But looking at the possibilities for productivity improvement through human resources, the first truth is that work is an individual matter first, even before it is a cooperative matter. There are productivity factors that workers can control directly, such as gaining more technical knowledge or improving interpersonal relationships. And work schedules have something to do with these concepts.

The company can take simple and concrete steps to respond to this very micro concept of productivity. Start with the premise that management's responsibility is to define work objectives and organize resources to get the work done. Two resources are people and time; organizing those resources means setting work schedules. Organizing people and time is bound to be easier and more efficient if managers have some leeway beyond a fixed 8:00 A.M. to 5:00 P.M. Monday–Friday work schedule. From the company's standpoint, there is no single best way to organize. There are innumerable different situations that require unique attention. From the workers' standpoint, everyone's effectiveness is different at different times. So management's task of getting the right person on the right job at the right time with the right support is bound to be helped by work-schedule flexibility.

Immediately, an experimental problem is confronted. Even if flexitime has a strong positive effect on productivity, by whatever mechanism, that effect probably cannot be measured by any quantitative indices over the short duration of a flexitime experiment.

But, optimistically, we can be alert to how productivity might be influenced day to day by events that happen in the workplace or at home. We do have experience and observations and judgments. We can look at mediating variables, and at the productivity process. Nothing is gained by failing to try an experiment even though you know before you start that you cannot quantitatively prove a cause–effect relationship. Nothing is gained by giving allegiance to habit.

A summary of how Gary Wydman and Andres Steinmetz of the personnel department at Sullivan Park presented flexitime to R&D top management is shown in the appendix, document A-10.

How the Flexitime Experiment Was Performed

The first step in planning a flexitime pilot project was to get both an endorsement of the concept of flexibility in work schedules and the go-ahead to do some experimenting from the senior vice-president for research and development as well as from the corporation's vice-president for personnel. This support was obtained, consistent with what Gary Wydman knew was a top management value placed on openness and employee responsibility. Three different departments, with a total of 70 employees, were selected for the flexitime experiment. The departments were chosen to maximize diversity in work technology as well as in management style. For example, internal communications were critical for some departments, while contact with clients was more important for others.

Once the managers of the three departments (biochemical research, technical services, and consumer products development) agreed to participate, meetings were held with the manager and supervisors in each department to work out the operating details of the flexitime schedule, anticipate issues and problems in advance, and build in some evaluation. Here are the key flexitime design variables that were worked out:

- Core hours were set at 10:00 A.M. to 12 noon, and 1:00 P.M. to 3:00 P.M., Monday through Friday in two of the departments, while the third department established only a 10:00 A.M. to 12 noon core period Monday through Thursday.
- All the departments permitted debit and credit hours within the workweek. At most, one department permitted an eight-hour-plus-or-minus balance as long as 40 hours were worked when the week was over. This scheme permitted a four day workweek, and thus amounted to a maxiflex schedule.
- All departments required a minimum lunch period of 30 minutes.
- Timekeeping was left unchanged; employees recorded their working hours on a time card, using the honor system.
- Two of the departments asked employees to post their planned work schedule for the week ahead so that everyone could see when each worker would be on the job. This was intended to improve planning and guard against communications breakdowns, but was in no sense an ironclad commitment to which the worker was required to adhere. (That would have destroyed the very flexibility that was desired.)
- The company's policy to pay overtime wages to all nonexempt workers, whether or not they were union members, working on government contracts, was waived for the experiment by the corporate personnel vice-president. This change was required to permit debit and credit hours.

• The hours of business in the three departments remained 8:00 A.M. to 5:00 P.M. as before; all of the department's usual activities were expected to remain operational during those hours.

• Excused paid absences for personal business during the workday, which some supervisors were in the habit of granting, was not explicitly forbidden under flexitime, although clearly the company expected employees to make accommodations.

The key feature of these flexitime ground rules is that they were different for every experimenting work unit. This is because they were worked out cooperatively between the personnel department and the department manager, and thus were tailored to the differences in work technology and labor-force characteristics of each department.

Before the flexitime experiment began in July 1980, a meeting was held for all the employees in each of the three departments separately during which a brief flexitime "manual" was given to each employee (see appendix, document A-14), and a general meeting was held with all Sullivan Park employees, including those who were not participating in the experiment, so that everyone would understand the strange things that some of their colleagues were about to do.

How Workers Responded: Job Satisfaction, Personal Well-Being, and Training

Employee response to the flexitime experiment was measured by both a pre- and post-experiment survey and by questioning of supervisors during and after the experiment.

Subjectively, there was no doubt that many—even most—employees liked flexible working hours. But some supervisors objected, saying it required them to do more work than they had before. Here are some quotes from workers who liked flexitime.

This is the best thing the company has done in the seven years I've been here. It shows they care about us.

I've been here one year, and I'd be gone by now if it weren't for flexitime. I'm really involved in community activities, which is important to me in a small town like this. If it weren't for flexitime, I couldn't do these things very easily.

I like it and hope we can continue it. It makes me feel like I have some control over my own destiny for once.

The good response from workers occurred despite the fact that very few of them made big changes in their work schedule. Most often, the change was only to take just 30 minutes for lunch (instead of the previously required one hour); some workers came in a bit earlier—half an hour or so. The fact that flexitime did not cause big changes in work schedules is probably due to the fact that (1) some of these workers already had de facto flexitime—59 percent of them carried the job title of scientist, and half of these had Ph.D. degrees and used considerable work-schedule latitude; (2) the work force is unusually old—the average age of the people in the flexitime experiment was 44 years; and (3) the work force was overwhelmingly male (79 percent).

Nevertheless, there were a few changes in people's attitudes about their work. Comparing pre-flexitime with post-flexitime answers to the same questions, about one out of ten workers thought they had:

- Greater opportunity to use my knowledge and skills at work
- A larger number of different kinds of tasks I do that enlarge and enrich my job
- Increased degree to which employees are treated fairly
- Stronger social relations at work
- Decreased stress felt about my job

However, there were dissenters on both the social relations and the stress questions. (None of these conclusions are statistically grounded despite the before and after surveys because there were no comparison groups and no statistical inference tests applied; the small number of participants and the infrequency of change would have made the latter useless.)

Family Life and Personal Time.   The preflexitime fixed-hour schedule did not interfere too much in the family life or personal time of these workers. This is surely because of the mostly male and mostly older workers in this experiment, few of whom had young children at home. But 19 percent of all the survey respondents said the amount of personal time they spent with friends, family members, or with themselves increased after flexitime. This moved the average scale score on this question in a favorable direction (see figure 6-3).

My present nonflexitime work schedule interferes with my family life or personal time

a great deal	3.71	a negligible amount

The amount of quality personal time I now spend with myself, friends, or family members is

too little	2.49 before flexitime	2.75 after flexitime	sufficient

My work schedule makes education off-the-job

inconvenient to take	2.33 before flexitime	2.57 after flexitime	easy to take

My nonflexitime work schedule makes training at the workplace

inconvenient to take	2.65	easy to take

Figure 6-3.   Family life, personal time, and education effects of flexitime.

Note: Scores are averages of 70 employees on flexitime.

Source: Corning Glass Works internal survey.

Education and Training.   Education off the job was judged quite incon-venient to take because of fixed work hours, although training at the workplace was easier to mesh with fixed hours. Some employees (11 percent) reported that education off the job was easier to take after flexitime. These results are surely minimum estimates of the training effects of flexitime that other companies might expect because of the age and terminal degrees that many of these employees had, as well as their already not-so-fixed work schedules prior to flexitime (see figure 6-3).

In the January–October 1980 period 29 percent of all employees in the experiment reported taking organized educational courses. This is quite a high number; tuition reimbursement is available.

Productivity and Supervision

What was measured? Employees were asked about their work output in the survey, and several "hard" measures of physical output were pro-posed: turn-around time for laboratory tests, number of experiments run per day, number of technical reports written, changes in furnace utilization—but a three-month-long experiment is much too short to have any effect on research productivity. And flexitime was only one of a multitude of productivity determinants, the rest of which were not measured. Perhaps the best insights came from interviews with supervisors in which changes in how work was done were elicited.

From the before-and-after survey of employees, 11 percent reported that the quantity of work they did increased. This number is small compared to the experiences of other companies, but then there were limitations on these effects being manifested (see above).

If some factors are examined that might affect productivity (in the absence of measuring it directly), work-time input quickly comes to mind. Although the work-output–time-input relationship is surely not that strong, the company was especially interested in finding out if flexitime would cut down on the hours of paid absences for personal business that many supervisors granted their employees. (While these leaves were intended to be made up, often they were not.) The survey showed that 78 percent of all employees took time off from work for personal business before flexitime, averaging 2.2 hours a month for all employees. After flexitime, 68 percent of all employees were continuing to take personal time, and the average for all employees dropped to 1.7 hours a month. That amounts to a 23-percent gain to the company in recovered paid absence, or about 35 hours per month for the three departments.

However, equal numbers of employees were in the habit before flexitime of working more than their required 40 hours. The average figure was 3.5 hours a week or about 15 hours per month. Since much of this was unpaid "overtime" by exempt professional employees, it was a gain to the company that far offset the loss from personal time. After flexitime, the "free" hours worked dropped slightly to 3.2 hours a week for all employees, or just under 14 hours a month per employee, and the number of employees working extra hours came down to 70 percent. Some of these changes, however, may have no connection to the flexible work schedules. If they do, the loss of unpaid "overtime" was twice as great as the gain from fewer paid absences. Of course, the unanswered question that remains is whether these time gains and losses have anything to do with productivity.

What did supervisors say about how people's work behavior might have changed? Most supervisors thought that people did make changes in how they spent their workday. Sometimes long experiments could be done more efficiently because technicians could vary the length of their workday. Sometimes the set-up time for experiments was reduced because early arrivers could do that without interruption. But in other cases the pace of work was driven by equipment that was not flexible. There was one case of a marginal long-employed technician whose whole workplace demeanor and performance was turned around after flexitime was started.

Communications seemed not to suffer. Taking and delivering messages had to be handled on a makeshift basis, but apparently it worked. There was one important exception. If the departmental secretary chose an early schedule, such as 7:00 A.M. to 3:00 P.M., someone else had to cover the telephones until 5:00 P.M. In one department, scientists and supervisors found themselves doing that. It worked for the three-month experiment, but it clearly could not continue if flexitime were permanent. (Another department installed a telephone-answering machine to take messages.) There was a trade-off. The secretary did a better and faster job of typing reports in the early hours of the day when there were no interruptions, but the telephones were not well handled in the late hours of the day.

Insight into the linkage between flexitime and productivity comes from open-ended responses made by supervisors to a variety of productivity questions. Here are the key results (see figure 6-4).

● What productivity means to supervisors in research and development is usually not how much work is done, but rather how efficient the work unit is and how good the work is.
● Supervisors' own productivity depends most frequently on the people they work with (especially how good they are) and on the supervisors' own time (both how much and how good that time is). The quality of time here refers mainly to quiet time and uninterrupted time. Physical resources rank near the bottom of the list. This is probably due to the fact that the company has amply supplied these resources.
● Nearly two-thirds of the supervisors believe that flexitime does not affect their own productivity, but those who do believe so say that the effect results from their better use of time.

The story these few results tell is simply that for many people flexitime won't make any difference to productivity. Yet what productivity

Question	Percent
What productivity means to supervisors (n = 28):	
Efficiency, meeting deadlines or objectives, completing tasks	39
Quality of work, effectiveness	25
Creativity, ideas	21
Quantity of work, amount of output	14
Supervisor's own productivity determinants (n = 41):	
People I work with	32
how good they are	17
how much teamwork we have	10
how many there are	5
Time I have	27
quantity of time	15
quality of time (interruptions, quiet time, etc.)	12
Organizational commitment and clear signals, and management effectiveness	20
Money, equipment, accessible resources	12
Freedom I have	10
How flexitime affects supervisor's productivity (n = 22):	
No effect	64
Affects my use of time—how I deploy resources, schedule work, use personal time	23
Other (affects trust, morale, colleague interactions)	14

Figure 6-4.   Productivity and supervision.

Source: Supervisors at Corning Glass Works research and development facility; "n" refers to number of responses to open-ended questions; some supervisors gave multiple responses.

amounts to is mainly people and time and quality and efficiency—and that is what flexitime can improve.

What happened to the supervision function itself? The way employees saw it, there were a few changes for the better.

- It increased the leadership I get from my supervisor, according to 10 percent of the workers.
- It increased the support I get from my supervisor, said 10 percent of the workers.
- It increased the degree to which I supervise myself, said 16 percent of the workers.

But two effects were split. Some workers said flexitime increased the extent to which they talked to their supervisor, and some said it increased the extent to which they talked to their colleagues. But there were nearly equal numbers of dissenters who reported the opposite effect.

Here is how some supervisors saw the change to flexible hours:

It means more planning for me to organize my work schedule for my people, but that's okay.

It takes a lot more effort from me to get the same work done. Because my technicians come in early, I have to also; I don't like it.

The people who worked different hours some days turned into clock watchers; they didn't have to do that before flexitime.

One conclusion that several supervisors agreed on was that there may well be some jobs that don't lend themselves very well to flexible scheduling. Some technicians and some secretaries are genuinely needed at times that may not be of their own choosing. They may have to be on the job from eight o'clock in the morning until five o'clock in the afternoon. While it would be a simple solution to make such hours part of the job's requirements, supervisors were sensitive to the equity question. That solution contradicted their belief that if some workers are permitted to vary their work schedules, then all workers should be permitted to do so, especially when the jobholders whose jobs would be so restricted—secretaries, more often than not—would be low-paid and women. This is the classic efficiency–equity conflict. It will take skillful management to innovate a suitable compromise.

C. SOLVING MANAGEMENT PROBLEMS OF JOB SHARING

by Gretl Meier

One of the attractions of job sharing as a new work pattern is that it overcomes some of the management problems of ordinary part-time employment. With job sharing, the job is full time while the jobholders are part time. From the company's standpoint, that means no problems with coverage because a job sharer is always there. And the potential recruiting and productivity advantages of part-time employment are retained. Job sharers themselves can more easily do managerial work than part-timers (see pp. 61 to 64).

But nothing is free; job sharing introduces some management problems while it solves others. Here are the difficult aspects of job sharing:

1. Brokering—getting the right match between the workers and the job and between the workers as partners. Of course, the worker–job match also has to be made with full-time as well as ordinary part-time employment. But with job sharing it is harder because there are two workers involved.
2. Complementarity—ensuring that workers perform cooperatively. The payoff from achieving complementarity is the synergy of "two heads are better than one." The problem areas are getting each job sharer to accept responsibility rather than to pass it off, and to see his or her role in the context of the larger job.
3. Scheduling—deciding who will work when.
4. Communication—making sure that one job sharer knows what the other is doing, and that both job sharers give clear messages to co-workers and managers.

In this section, the experiences of many companies with job sharing are distilled into several guidelines that can be used to solve the management problems of job sharing.

BROKERING, COMPLEMENTARITY, SCHEDULING, AND COMMUNICATION: LESSONS FROM SEVERAL EMPLOYERS

Brokering

Job-sharing experiences are growing in number throughout the United States in diverse occupations. Their success has been based, in large part, on the effective management of one of the more difficult aspects of this work option—ensuring the right match between workers and the job and between workers as partners. The key elements here are (1) task analysis of the job, (2) assessment of skills required, and (3) careful recruitment and interviewing procedures. Each calls for both employee and employer responsibility.

Task Analysis. In the past, most shared jobs have been initiated by workers—either by current full-time employees, singly or in pairs, or by two outside applicants who have teamed themselves in search of a particular position. This pattern is now shifting as more organizations look for ways to realize the potential advantages of job sharing. Whether sharing is organization- or worker-initiated, a fundamental first step is a careful task analysis of the position or positions being considered. Task analysis for job sharers means outlining the job objectives and activities.

Public-sector employers, the organizations which employ the largest number of sharers, have found that this analysis serves to (1) define duties, (2) clarify job descriptions, and (3) form the basis for judging the accountability of both individuals and teams.

A useful format has been developed by the State of Wisconsin's Project in Job Options and Innovations (JOIN), which restructured full-time positions for 115 job sharers. In it, major goals are listed and tasks elaborated under each goal.[2]

Skills Assessment.   After doing task analysis, the organization (together with job-sharing applicants) is then able to clarify the skills needed from workers and to assess the ways in which two applicants may best fill these needs. In some jobs, employers have hired two workers who have similar, if not identical, skills. Computer programmers, clerks, social workers, and bank tellers are among those who divide jobs by identical tasks or case loads (that is, they have split assignments and standard time arrangements). Jobs which are monotonous, repetitive, emotionally stressful, or those which require extended daily coverage are often better performed by two sharers rather than one full-time employee. In these jobs, the two employees need have little contact with each other.

In other jobs, however, employers have wanted two employees with a greater variety of complementary skills in order to have a broader range of expertise to fill job requirements. For example, the director of operations of a university medical school needed a project coordinator to oversee immediate renovation of a research laboratory. He hired a man trained as a mechanical engineer and a young woman with a Ph.D. in anatomy, explaining: "Their backgrounds complemented each other perfectly."[3] Generally, one partner dealt with choosing and installing equipment and the other planned the use of the equipment after its installation. Similarly, a publisher who hired a former schoolteacher and a former librarian to share an assistant editorship found that they had a " . . . common ground of experience, but they (had) different skills . . . which means they bring an aggregate of maybe ten years or more of experience."[4]

The ability to analyze combined skills for total job requirements enables employers to make most effective use of the advantages which two job sharers can bring.

Prospective job sharers themselves, seeking positions that did not exist, have shown the way. Often aided by local employment resource agencies (now developing into a national job-sharing network), prospective applicants (1) analyzed jobs which were advertised as full time and then listed functions and methods of dividing responsibilities according to their individual strengths; (2) prepared joint resumes describing each individual's skills; and (3) interviewed both singly and jointly as a team.

Recruitment: Interviewing and Matching.   Many ways of finding a partner for a job sharer have proved effective. In the majority of cases, the recruitment of partners has been assumed by current employees (or by applicant teams) who wish to reduce hours. In cases where the organization has assumed responsibility, some have accepted applications only from teams whereas others use the usual part-time recruitment methods, such as advertisements, bulletin boards, and so on. A few organizations advertise jobs as open to two part-timers or one full-time applicant, allowing themselves the option of filling the position in either way. (Such a technique also helps to determine whether or not applicants genuinely wish part-time work.)

When the City of Palo Alto, California, wanted to fill the position of organizational-development consultant (with responsibility for maintaining liaison between the city manager and city department heads), the administration wanted to combine the expertise of two individuals who would bring a greater variety of skills than might one full-time person. Its interview process was thorough. Applicants appeared singly and with each other, in turns, alternating the pair arrangements.

Elsewhere, too, employers have themselves paired the two partners. In Project JOIN, because State Civil Service regulations precluded applications from two individuals for the shared job, each sharer was recruited singly. This type of selection reportedly proved successful in matching cooperative and compatible partners.

Whether sharers pair themselves or are matched by the organization, the interview process presupposes that the organization and prospective

sharers—individually and as a team—have considered and will discuss
these issues:

1. Suitable schedules, including the question of coverage in case of
   illness and emergency, and the question of meeting company or
   personal needs for extra time.
2. The division of task responsibility—to what degree it is circum-
   scribed by the organization and to what degree partners may be
   flexible.
3. Partners' experience in working together and anticipated means
   to ensure consistency and to manage shared pressure.
4. Ways to ensure adequate communication with supervisors and co-
   workers.
5. Accountability for raises, promotions, and firing.

(All of these assume, of course, that the equitable division of salary and
prorating of fringe benefits have been agreed upon.)

No definitive conclusions can be drawn as to whether the organization or the sharer is best responsible for the matching of partners. Much
depends on the level and nature of the job involved, especially on the
degree of closeness required. Certainly there are outstanding examples
of success when sharers have arranged their own partnerships. This is
particularly true in higher level positions and in jobs requiring close collaboration. But there is also some evidence to the contrary. Two workers
matched carefully by a supervisor may often develop an effective pattern as they work together, although they may require a slightly longer
adjustment time.

In either case, a period of adjustment may be necessary, again
depending on the nature of the position. Some sharers have used the
period immediately prior to working officially together to discuss routines and tasks and to become better aware of each other's work styles.
Many later recognize that their partnerships are dynamic relationships.
"We keep learning how to relate and be consistent," comments a sharer
in a high-level administrative post.[5]

The Several Criteria for Successful Brokering. What matters is not so
much who does the matching but how the matching is accomplished. In
addition to matching both partners' skills to job requirements, crucial
elements are:

- Clear agreement between employer and workers on total job requirements.
- Clear understanding between employer and workers as well as between partners on the ways in which these responsibilities are to be divided—the degree of latitude open to sharers and the degree to which division is determined by the organization.

Beyond this, to ensure that the initial brokering is maintained and developed for effective job performance, the key factors are complementarity, communication, and scheduling.

Complementarity

Ensuring that workers perform cooperatively depends on a mix of both organizational factors and the personal relationships between job sharers. Because organizational support is of equal importance for the successful management of job sharing (and often of greater importance because it can create the climate for personal relationships), it demands more attention than has been generally recognized.

Supervisory Support.   Immediate supervisory support is particularly crucial. This is likely to occur when supervisors:

- Are informed about job sharing—are shown examples of different positions and types of job sharing, and the variety of schedules and communication systems that can be used.
- Are involved in the job division and description and in the selection of sharers. Because supervisors need to work cooperatively with sharers, such knowledge and participation in planning are likely to help avoid potential problem areas and find solutions should problems occur.

Certain conditions will facilitate positive attitudes. When a supervisor knows one or both employees who will share a position to be converted to job sharing, or when the organization is accustomed to sharing, supervisors and co-workers alike will tend to react positively.

Will there be an extra supervisory work load with job sharing? If there is, or if supervisors perceive that there will be, how does one handle the situation? Consider these two cases:

- More than 75 percent of the supervisors of 256 part-timers and job sharers in an experiment at the California Department of Motor Vehicles felt that two part-time workers did not require much more supervision than one full-time person. They found advantages in improved morale, scheduling flexibility, and equal or higher productivity, and they valued the ability to keep trained personnel who might otherwise have left.[6]
- Project JOIN concluded that although slightly more time was involved in training job sharers, this was an initial cost only. The fact that in the end both employees have more training than one would receive may well have accounted for job sharers' higher productivity.[7] Moreover, when one sharer is trained by the other, training time by supervisors may be lessened. As a supervisor elsewhere commented, "They motivate each other. I don't have to spend my supervisory time worrying about that."[8]

A supportive supervisor (together with conscientious efforts by job sharers) will influence the attitudes of other co-workers. Potential resentment by full-time co-workers can be mitigated when these employees are informed of the specifics of job sharing, including the salary and benefits rights as well as the schedules of job sharers.

Partner Relationships.   Employers considering job sharing will also want to look at how the partners need to relate to each other on the job. Although some teams will need to be highly collaborative and some not at all, most will lie between these extremes. Many partners need to cooperate in coordinating daily details or in planning and problem solving, especially to eliminate inconsistencies in dealing with others within and outside the organization.

Compatibility, flexibility, and, above all, trust, have proved essential to good working relationships. Employers should seek those who value cooperation rather than competition. "You need mutual respect," says a typical job sharer, "and you must not try to outdo each other."[9] Successful sharers are characteristically those who do not need to "own" their own work, who are often able to forgo much of the ego connection with their jobs. Personal recognition is still important to many partners, however. A well-planned division of tasks will ensure that some work is performed individually.

A sense of accountability is as important to job-sharing employees as to the organization. This is especially true because partners often sense that they are perceived by others as unusual or outside the norm. Once accountability procedures are established, job sharers are more likely to feel that their responsibilities and commitment are recognized to the same degree as those of full-time employees.

Scheduling

Scheduling of job sharers' time is best managed when (1) work time follows job requirements, and (2) supervisors and co-workers are informed of each partner's time at work.

A variety of schedules can be used. Split weeks are most common— two-and-one-half days each week for each person or alternating two- and three-day weeks for each person. Other sharers work half days, while others work a week on and a week off. Teams of civil engineers, probation workers, and others have worked six months on and six months off.

Partners in "seasonal" positions—for example, two state legislative assistants in Wisconsin—have both worked full time during busy times and "banked" hours for nonwork time during quieter intervals. In other cases, when special projects required extra work, sharers have worked full time. As one explained, "There is someone to do the extra work who does not need to be trained," or "There is the availability at all times of at least one member of our office."[10]

In jobs which require a great deal of public contact or continuity in response to consumers, some organizations have found that four five- hour days, and five four-hour days, or even the six month pattern pro- vided a better routine than alternating two- and three-day weeks. When scheduling is complicated by extensive travel requirements, sharers need to arrange their time to allow full days (rather than half days) for follow-up time in the office.

Many schedules allow for overlap time so that sharers may confer either on a daily or weekly basis. Some use regular or occasional lunch hours. Others allot one day when both are "on" (and then both may have another day free of work), and a few sharers overlap regularly for shorter times or at special periods. This is an especially valuable use of sharers' time because it allows both to keep current and to check on individual and total job assignments.

Scheduling arrangements need to be made clear during the initial period of sharing, when responsibilities of the team are agreed on. To avoid ambiguity, supervisors and sharers must agree on such questions as (1) the degree of flexibility for the organization and employee; (2) whether sharers are able to trade time off freely as long as job responsibilities are fulfilled; and (3) whether partners are expected to work full time on occasion. When full-timers are accorded overtime, the question of overtime pay for hours worked beyond regular schedules must be decided as well as the means to record compensatory time.

Communication

As the number of shared jobs increases and patterns become more regularized, job sharers need to pay more attention to formal communication systems as well as to overlap time, rather than relying on time taken outside of scheduled hours. "People who share a job," comments a supervisor, "have to work out a lot of things between them. They must have excellent communication skills."[11]

Methods include: log books, notes, staff meetings, and regular telephone calls. A team may typically keep several folders—one for appointments on hand by dates, another for pending matters, and a third for current data and procedures needed to perform duties. The team may also use a system whereby both check all information before filing and both check memos before they are sent out.

Sharers acknowledge that it takes valuable time to communicate with each other and to relay, in writing, information to other staff members. But except for those whose jobs are essentially separate, both they and their supervisors cite the absolute necessity of consistent communication. This not only prevents potential problems but serves as double coverage.

A further benefit may also occur when the process of communication and recording of information by sharers, together with the need for efficient use of time, encourages the entire office unit to reassess general procedures and thereby increase efficiency. "Our office has been forced to reexamine and streamline certain processes," comments a supervisor of a shared job. "Apparently one gets a much better view of what constitutes wasted effort from a four-hour-day perspective."[12]

Good communication, appropriate scheduling, cooperative partners aided by evenhanded supervisory support—all these reinforce the initial brokering between employee skills and employers' job requirements. These conditions are consistent with good management practice for all jobs. They are even more important when two workers share. The "difficult" aspects, properly planned and executed, can be turned to the advantage of both employee and employer.

APPLYING THE MANAGEMENT GUIDELINES: THE CASE OF XYZ COMPANY

Earlier we looked at a large-scale use of job sharing by a medium-sized midwestern manufacturing company, which we called XYZ Company (see pp. 53–58). Several of the management guidelines discussed above were successfully followed by the company in its job-sharing program. They are described below.

1. *Task analysis* was simple for these machine-operator factory jobs. Output is visible and measurable. Goals and activities are self-evident.
2. *Skill assessment* was only minimally necessary because job sharing is restricted to low-skill jobs. These jobs are split jobs where each job sharer does the same set of repetitive tasks. Complementary skills are not required.
3. *Recruiting*—including finding a partner—is entirely left to employees. The first job sharer is usually a former full-timer who wants to cut back work hours (no recruiting needed there), and the partner must be found by the first job sharer. The company serves as an information clearing house.
4. *Supervisory support* is gained because job sharing is a plantwide program, endorsed by top management, and because the supervisors already know some of the job sharers beforehand. Salary and benefit rights are well known.
5. *Supervisory work load* due to job sharing is actually reduced because job sharers (rather than supervisors) are responsible for covering absences.
6. *Partner relationships*—the job sharers work independently of each other, except for arranging their own coverage of absences. They are explicitly accountable for this aspect of job sharing.
7. *Scheduling* is up to the job sharers themselves. Any combination is satisfactory to the company as long as job sharers work at least one day per week and an entire shift. These conditions are laid down to meet job requirements.

8. *Communication needs* are minimal because the jobs are quite separate; however, the fact that the plant is in a small town in which most workers know one another makes communication easy.

D. Problems and Failures of New Work Schedules

All of the company case studies in this book have been successful uses of new work schedules. Of course, not all the company experiences have been uniformly happy ones, but whenever there were problems, they were successfully solved. However, not every company that tries to use new work schedules has successful outcomes. What about failures of new work schedules? There are some, and we can learn from them.

How frequent are failures of new work patterns? Using the narrow definition of failure as "tried but dropped," the failure rate for flexitime is very low—8 percent in the most recent national survey, and even lower, 3 percent in another survey.[13] The failure rate for compressed workweeks is quite a different story. It is high—28 percent in the largest and most recent survey, 23 percent in two other earlier and smaller surveys, with other estimates ranging as low as 8 percent to as high as 44 percent.[14] Failure rates for permanent part-time employment or job sharing are unknown because so few of these work patterns are conceived as formal programs and so many part-timers and job sharers are scattered around companies in ones and twos. It is quite impossible to come up with a single meaningful failure-rate figure.

Several vignettes of failure in one of the major new work schedules, flexitime, are presented here. For each vignette, two questions are asked: (1) what went wrong? and (2) why did the failure occur? In particular, we want to find out if the problems can be traced to the work technology—was the work schedule badly suited to the kind of work that had to be done? Or, looking back, could managers have done something differently to make the work schedule succeed?

FLEXITIME PROGRAMS THAT DID NOT WORK

First, consider three organizations in which flexible work schedules were unsuccessful. All three of these companies dropped flexitime after problems appeared. However, one company retained flexitime for some work units while it dropped it for others, and another company subsequently restarted flexitime successfully. Second, we look at a company that proposed flexitime but was unable to get it implemented.

Delaware Valley Regional Planning Commission

The Delaware Valley Regional Planning Commission is a multijurisdiction public agency for the Philadelphia metropolitan area that deals with public concerns, such as transportation and air quality. The agency covers a nine-county Pennsylvania–New Jersey area. It is a service organization in which employment is predominantly white-collar professional and clerical.

The Commission departed from a fixed 8:30 A.M. to 5:00 P.M. work schedule in 1975 and started a flexitime program. Debit and credit hours were allowed within a week, but there were daily core hours and time accumulators were used. After only a few weeks, the flexitime program was cancelled and the work schedule became a fixed schedule of either 8:30 A.M. to 5:00 P.M. as before or 8:00 A.M. to 4:30 P.M., in accordance with the worker's choice (this might be called an employee-chosen staggered-hours schedule).

What went wrong? The presenting problem was timekeeping. Some people did not key out over their lunch period (either by oversight or deliberately). Others whose work took them to other offices were not able to record their working time correctly. Some professionals found the time accumulators to be a nuisance. The outcome was that the recorded time worked at the end of the week was not well related to the time actually worked.

If timekeeping, using time-accumulating machines, was the problem, why not eliminate the machines but continue flexitime with an alternative timekeeping method, such as sign-in/sign-out or the honor system? Indeed, the honor system would be just fine for professionals—they always had flexitime, in fact if not in name, and implicitly used the honor system. The agency's belief was that, in any event, output or job performance is what should count rather than time input.

Clerical workers and support staff were the source of the problem. On the one hand, most managers believed that clerical and support staff should be on the job predictably from 8:30 A.M. to 5:00 P.M. for job-performance reasons. They are needed during all of those hours. Yet this service agency does not face exacting demands from customers or the public, and intra-agency coverage problems could be worked out if flexitime were to continue. But these workers did not handle the time accumulators correctly, and an honor system would be hard to trust, based on the experience with time accumulators. Surely some time-keeping is necessary but, with flexible hours, how can it be done? Finally, even for support staff, it is desirable to look at output instead of input when evaluating employees, and so an intensive focus on time-keeping should be avoided. But measuring output for secretaries is hard to do and, in fact, is not done.

The upshot is that several complications combined to make flexitime not worth the trouble—managers who wanted secretaries there at all times, questions about how to record time, and ambivalence toward the importance of timekeeping. The company evidently did not consider flexitime important enough to try to solve these problems.

The PQR Company

PQR, a West Coast utility company, started flexible work hours in 1977 as a company-wide program. Today flexitime continues in some depart-ments but has been dropped in others. Even in the departments that continue to use flexitime, all is not well.

Where flexitime is used in the company, "it works great for the work-ers, but the supervisors are not thrilled," according to a member of the personnel staff. The problem that supervisors have is simply one of knowing who is where, when. Employees are not asked to post their planned work schedule in advance. To get around this problem, some supervisors make out daily work assignments for their employees. This is a way to transfer coverage, communication, and scheduling respon-sibilities to workers. The company has not increased the number of supervisors, nor has there been a noticeable increase in turnover. But supervisors perceive that their job is harder, although they tolerate it.

The company's word-processing unit discontinued flexitime. The problem was that each word-processing operator reported to several dif-ferent managers, all of whom traveled out of the office on an irregular schedule. Because both secretary and manager had variable work schedules that were not fully predictable in advance, and because they were often physically separated and unable to communicate closely, it was difficult to make sure that one would be available when needed by the other. The solution was to return the word-processing operators to a fixed schedule so that at least half of the equation would know what to expect from the other half.

The unit in the accounting department also dropped flexitime. This was a managerial accounting unit that analyzed information and made reports to management. The problem caused by flexitime in this work unit was missed deadlines. In one sense the failure of flexitime here is similar to the case of continuous-process assembly-line manufacturing units. In this kind of operation the workers are rigidly interdependent and individual flexitime usually cannot be used. Here there is also considerable interdependence—one worker is delayed if input from another is not ready on a timely basis. This case illustrates the importance of matching the work schedule to the work technology and, if the match is not good, taking management steps to (1) redesign the workplace to make the work technology suitable, (2) restrict the degree of individual flexibility in the flexitime program, or (3) transfer output responsibility from supervisors to workers, thus requiring them to find the right match between work schedules and job requirements.

Sercel Industries

Sercel Industries is a small manufacturing company that adopted flexitime when the company was founded in 1977. At that time the company operated a conventional semicontinuous two-shift assembly-line operation, in which the product was passed successively from worker to worker, each of whom did a single task. The flexitime program was very flexible and included debit and credit hours. Flexitime was adopted rather automatically because this kind of work schedule was used in the French parent company.

Flexitime was soon discontinued. There were two problems. First, there was excessive production downtime—time during which workers were idle because they had neither parts nor equipment to work with. Second, there was a high rate of absence and abuse of flexible hours. Some workers debited hours without crediting them back (time accumulators were not used). While these workers were not paid for the short hours, the company needed the work time.

Why did flexitime fail? Both the production system and the flexitime program had major design flaws. The production system was a conventional assembly line and so workers were interdependent on one another.

Yet there were few or no buffer stocks to permit individual schedule flexibility to succeed. Most workers were low-skill people and thus could not fill in for each other. The flexitime design flaws consisted of too much individual flexibility for the production system and too little time accountability. Employees did not understand either their privileges or responsibilities under flexitime.

This story has a happy ending. Flexitime was reinstituted coincident with a relocation to a new plant. Both the flexitime guidelines and the production system were changed. Now a fixed day length is required rather than debit or credit hours, and time accumulators are used. Workers are cross-trained and given a flexitime manual of rights and responsibilities. The factory was converted to a bench assembly operation with considerable worker independence. Production scheduling is done in advance, and buffer stocks are supplied.

The ABC Corporation

The ABC Corporation is a multi-billion-dollar multinational corporation in which a proposal to adopt flexitime in the headquarters office was rejected by senior management of the company. This case illustrates the failure of an attempt to use flexitime rather than a failure of the work schedule itself. The case is reported here because of the lessons in management it yields for people in companies who would seek to implement flexitime in a conservative business environment (see pages 180 to 185 for a full description of the projected flexitime program).

The flexitime idea came out of the corporate personnel director's office. Two serious operational problems were anticipated for the near future, both caused by the imminent move of the company headquarters to a new location. Those problems were commuting (the new location was not well served by public transportation) and labor supply (the company anticipated losing many employees because of the move and doubted that the labor market at the new location could absorb its demands on it).

The corporate personnel director managed the process of putting together a flexitime proposal. He assembled a study group of both personnel staff and operating managers from various divisions. An outside consultant was asked for advice and joined the study group. Study-group members visited companies in the area and in the industry that were already using flexitime and interviewed many people in their own company about their thoughts on flexitime. Possibilities for productivity gains as well as disruptions to business operations were checked out, and legal restrictions were identified. A needs assessment was also conducted, using outside data and simulation studies.

The study group favored the adoption of flexitime and sketched a brief proposal that included the major design features of the new work schedule. The plan was a genuine flexible-hours plan, but it was quite conservative. Called "controlled flexitime," it established long core hours, asked employees to give notice of their work-schedule plans a week in advance, and gave each work unit the power to modify flexitime to meet its own operating needs.

The flexitime proposal—recommended by the broad-based study group and endorsed by the vice-president for employee relations—was quickly and summarily rejected by senior management of the company. Fixed work hours of 8:00 A.M. to 4:30 P.M. with a 45-minute lunch break were prescribed for all employees by management.

Why was an apparently sound flexitime proposal so easily quashed? Here was a case of competent staff work and textbook management processes, and yet the recommendation was rejected. The essence of the answer is that there was a subtle and deeply held value position by top management that was at odds with their view of flexible work schedules. The senior management believed that the corporation's problem was lax work discipline and the toleration of laxity by managers. Flexitime was counter to the work ethic of senior management. They felt, subconsciously perhaps, that more flexibility in work schedules would mean only more laxity in work discipline. A perverse linkage was made between flexitime and the work ethic.

There was another reason for the management rejection of the flexitime proposal. The timing was bad. A recession was gathering just at the time the flexitime decision was being made. Although the corporation's profit results in the most recent quarter were at record levels, the outlook was uncertain. A defensive, draw-your-wagons-in-a-circle posture was taken. No changes of any kind were made that did not have to be made, even those with little direct cost or risk. Just as advertising budgets and training programs are the first to be reduced in order to shore up short-term operating results, so also was flexitime sacrificed in this climate of uncertainty. This is another dimension of the dilemma of trade-offs between the long run and the short run.

The lesson for implementing flexitime is that sound needs assessments and feasibility analyses can easily be overturned by opposition based on value stances. This means that perhaps a top-management endorsement of the concept of work-schedule flexibility is prudent before the schedule is designed. If a decision about flexitime is to be made at the top (it may not need top-management approval), the values and philosophy at the top should be made an early part of the flexitime study process.

NOTES

1. Andres Steinmetz and Gary Wydman are personnel managers at Corning Glass Works.
2. *Project JOIN Manual for Replication,* attachment II (Madison, Wis.: State Division of Human Resource Services, 1979).
3. "Job Sharing May Be Worth a Try," *Stanford University Manager,* November 1978, p. 1.
4. Gretl S. Meier, *Job Sharing* (Kalamazoo, Mich.: The W.E. Upjohn Institute, 1979), p. 147.
5. Telephone interview with Frances Kaufman, August 1980.
6. *Report to the Governor and the Legislature of the State of California: Final Report of the Part-Time Employment Pilot Program* (Sacramento, Calif.: Department of Motor Vehicles, 1979).
7. *Project JOIN Final Report* (Madison, Wis.: State Division of Human Resource Services, 1979), p. 15.
8. Meier, *Job Sharing,* p. 93.
9. "Job Sharing May Be Worth a Try," p. 83.
10. Meier, *Job Sharing,* p. 83.
11. "Job Sharing," *Good Housekeeping,* June 1979, p. 64.
12. *Project JOIN Final Report,* p. 1.
13. The 8 percent figure is from Stanley D. Nollen and Virginia H. Martin, *Alternative Work Schedules, Part 1: Flexitime* (New York: AMACOM, a division of American Management Associations, 1978) and is based on a sample of 211 one-time flexitime users. The earlier 3 percent figure is from Harriet Goldberg Weinstein, *A Comparison of Three Alternative Work Schedules: Flexible Work Hours, Compact Work Week, and Staggered Work Hours* (Philadelphia: University of Pennsylvania, The Wharton School, Industrial Research Unit, 1975), in which the sample was smaller.
14. The first three estimates are from Nollen and Martin, *Alternative Work Schedules, Part 1: Flexitime;* Weinstein, *A Comparison of Three Alternative Work Schedules;* and Virginia H. Martin, *Hours of Work When Workers Can Choose* (Washington, D.C.: Business and Professional Women's Foundation, 1975). The low 8 percent figure is from Kenneth Wheeler, Richard Gurman, and Dale Tarnowieski, *The Four-Day Week* (New York: American Management Associations, 1972), and the high 44 percent figure is from Haldi Associates, *Alternative Work Schedules: A Technology Assessment* (Washington, D.C.: National Science Foundation, 1977).

7.

Energy Savings and Transportation Efficiency from New Work Patterns

by Virginia Hider Martin

A. City-Wide Flexitime Programs

Transportation accounts for 53 percent of all petroleum consumed in the United States.[1] Clearly, there is a sizeable energy-saving potential from shifts to more energy-efficient modes of transportation as well as from conservation measures within each mode. The transportation system itself is sorely in need of efficiency and service improvements. To the extent that energy and transportation efficiency problems are linked to commuting to work, flexitime can help.

Quite a few cities already are including some version of flexible work hours in an energy emergency contingency plan or a transportation system management plan.[2] Other cities are considering or experimenting with area-wide flexible-work-hours programs of different types. These cities include Baltimore, Boise, Boston, Chicago, Cleveland, Kansas City, Knoxville, Milwaukee, New York City, Ottawa, Pittsburgh, Portland, Richmond, Sacramento, San Francisco, Seattle, Toronto, and Washington, D.C.

Flexitime's particular appeal as a transportation-management and energy-conservation strategy derives from its low cost. Area-wide flexitime programs require no capital investment, and their annual operating cost in a city of one million people is estimated to be $200,000 (five professionals at a cost of $40,000 each are needed to run such a program). In contrast, computerized traffic control in a city of one million people has a capital cost of 3 million dollars and an annual operating and maintenance cost of $300,000. Expanding local bus service by 200 buses requires a $14 million capital investment and an annual operating budget increase of $4.5 million.[3]

How do these transportation and energy savings come about? Flexitime can reduce energy consumption in two ways:

1. *Traffic flow characteristics.* Flexitime reduces congestion within and to and from major employment centers, especially central business districts, by spreading peak demand for highways and public transportation over a longer span of time. Vehicles that travel outside the rush hour consume less fuel because they move at a steadier and faster pace. Elimination of stop-and-go driving similarly reduces the emission of air pollutants.

2. *Commuting mode shift.* Ride sharing and public transportation become more attractive alternatives to driving alone. Car pools and van pools are facilitated when workers choose their own schedules because spouses in two-worker families can ride together and workers with different employers can form pools. Workers who are free to commute before or after rush hour find that the quality of mass transit improves—trips are faster, seats are available, and the fear of tardiness caused by unreliable schedules is removed. Moreover, when working hours can be matched to transit schedules, personal time need not be wasted in waiting to start work.

Transportation efficiency can be improved by flexitime because both capital needs and labor costs can be reduced:

1. *Capacity-load match.* New capital outlays for constructing highways and purchasing additional rolling stock can be reduced by transferring peak demand to periods immediately preceding and following the rush hour, when spare capacity usually exists.

2. *Labor costs.* Bus drivers who normally make only one trip each rush hour can make two, or even three, trips per morning or evening when flexitime shifts a significant number of commuters to earlier or later travel times. Thus, idle time at off-peak periods and use of split shifts, with attendant wage premiums, can be reduced.

Some transportation planners favor the certainty of staggered hours as a strategy to disperse congestion rather than the uncertainty of an individually voluntary flexitime program. Many people fear that flexitime will break up car pools and encourage workers to drive alone. Others argue that flexitime is better than staggered hours precisely because of the freedom it gives commuters to select mutually agreeable work schedules and form multiemployer car pools or van pools. Moreover, flexitime is likely to give a much broader spread of travel times than staggered hours. Whereas most employers are reluctant to shift their business hours much more than a half hour earlier or later, apparently a significant number of employees will choose to begin work as early as 6:30 A.M. or 7:30 A.M. if they are given the opportunity to do so.

Flexitime is a self-adjusting strategy that lets employees accommodate to public transportation schedules and to work schedules among different employers. Flexitime takes less, not more, government planning. Perhaps most important in the long run, company management and employee benefits are thought to accrue from the use of flexitime.

There is one potential energy drawback to flexitime. If offices and factories have to be open longer because some workers on flexitime come in earlier and some stay later, then building utilities costs (heating, cooling, ventilating, lighting, equipment operation) will go up. Of course, companies can establish earliest and latest work times (e.g., 6:30 A.M. and 7:00 P.M.) to minimize this added cost, or buildings may already be open during such a band width because maintenance people are there. New buildings with decentralized heating and cooling controls, can accommodate flexitime less expensively.

The objective of this chapter is to learn whether flexitime actually does spread rush-hour commuting, speed work trips, bring about conversions to more energy-efficient modes of transportation, and improve transit efficiency. Findings from recent research and from case studies of four area-wide flexible work hours programs are presented, along with a discussion of the transferability of the good results.

The four case studies that follow describe area-wide flexitime programs in Seattle, San Francisco, Boston, and Kansas City. These are all examples of government–business cooperation in organized efforts to persuade a group of employers to adopt flexitime for their employees. In each case energy and transportation savings were the objective. These cities were selected because of their diversity in population make-up and density, geography, transit systems, industrial mix, and political approach to area-wide flexitime. The focus of these case studies is on how the area-wide flexitime program was handled, and on its effect on energy and transportation.

THE CASE OF THE SEATTLE FLEXIBLE WORKING HOURS PROGRAM[4]

Seattle, a medium-sized city located on Puget Sound, is a port and the center of a four-county metropolitan area. It has no rapid rail system, but the downtown area is well served by the local bus system, METRO. About 40 percent of those who work in the central business district commuted via public transit before the flexible working hours program commenced. Traffic congestion occurs at the bridges leading into the city. In the suburbs, particularly the fast-growing eastern area, bus service is poor and congestion problems on roadways can be severe. Seattle enjoys a strong economy and a low unemployment rate. Known as an aerospace, banking, and insurance center, it also is the home of a booming computer industry, several universities, and a number of government offices, since Seattle is a federal regional center.

Why City-Wide Flexitime?

Several studies made in Seattle recommended the use of a work rescheduling strategy to relieve present and projected traffic and transit congestion problems:

- Traffic counts conducted by the Traffic and Transportation Division of the Seattle Engineering Department in 1977 showed that the city suffered from severe "peaking," evidenced by a maximum rate of traffic flow during a time period preceded and followed by a period of reduced traffic flow.
- A forecast of peak-hour traffic demand for the year 1990 by the Puget Sound Council of Government Transportation Systems Plan identified 24 locations at which roadway capacity would be exceeded, with the degree of overload ranging as high as 218 percent.
- METRO advocated alternative work schedules in its Energy Crisis Contingency Plan as a means of increasing miles and hours of service without the need for additional buses or drivers. Though

transit overloads occurred during the morning and evening peaks, substantial reserve seat capacity existed during times immediately adjacent to the peak.

Feasibility Studies

The feasibility of an area-wide alternative work schedules program for Seattle was explored through a two-step process. First, the Seattle/King County Commuter Pool (the local ride-sharing program), in cooperation with the Downtown Seattle Development Association and the Seattle Chamber of Commerce, surveyed the work hours of major employers located in the central business district and in the King County area. Start and stop times were found to be concentrated within peak-hour and half-hour periods that correlated strongly with demonstrated traffic-congestion problems. Thirty percent of responding businesses requested information on altering their work schedules.

Second, the Commuter Pool sponsored a study to investigate other cities' and employers' experiences with variable work hours. The study determined the advantages and disadvantages of flexible, staggered, and compressed work schedules from transportation, energy, business management, and trade-union perspectives. The report issued in November 1977 recommended the adoption of an area-wide flexible working hours program. Though minimal technical assistance and information also would be offered on staggered hours and compressed workweeks, the report urged concentration on flexitime because this schedule appeared to offer at least as much peak-hour congestion relief as the other two systems and was free of their disadvantages. (The compressed workweek encountered substantial union resistance in this study. It also would have reduced transit revenues, since workers would commute fewer days per week. Compressed and staggered schedules were thought to disrupt car pools and require travel at hours when public transportation was unavailable.) Moreover, flexitime appeared to be most saleable to employers because it provided the largest number of potential benefits to management and employees.

A rough assessment indicated that flexible scheduling was compatible with the work processes of a large number of local industries. Several local companies were already using flexitime.

How the Program Got Started

In November 1977 the Puget Sound Council of Governments authorized a one-year (subsequently extended) flexible working hours program for Seattle and surrounding suburban areas. Authority to begin the program was secured with relative ease inasmuch as federal financial assistance (a $100,000 Urban Mass Transit Administration grant) was available to carry it out, and the role of the program's other two sponsors, METRO and the Washington State Department of Transportation, was largely signatory and advisory. Institutionally, the flexible work hours program was located in Seattle city government as an addition to the Commuter Pool.

Program Objectives

Seattle's program had these objectives:

Primary
- Reduce rush-hour traffic congestion.
- Increase transit efficiency by shifting peak-hour demand to adjacent time periods.
- Increase car-pooling.

Secondary
- Conserve fuel.
- Reduce air pollution.
- Improve the quality of commuting.

Program Activities and Experiences

Basing its decision on the experience of New York City's staggered work hours program, Seattle emphasized marketing and promotion as the keys to a successful flexitime program. A multifaceted campaign was launched with help from all sectors.

Executives of local companies that used flexitime became the program's best sales force. They were asked to speak at a series of informational breakfasts for the chief executive officers of Seattle's largest companies. They also accompanied Commuter Pool staff to give presentations to other firms interested in implementing flexitime. Particularly convincing to other business leaders were manager–users who themselves had opposed the concept of flexible work hours originally, expressed their fears, and reported how pleasantly surprised they had been about the success of their own company's flexitime program.

The Seattle program staff found that the best approach to employers was one that emphasized management and employee benefits of flexitime rather than transportation and energy advantages. Consequently, various newsletters and promotional brochures distributed by the program stressed decreased absenteeism and turnover, improved morale, quicker and more comfortable commuting, and better integration of work and personal life.

Other marketing strategies were also utilized in Seattle. A speakers' bureau was established, and presentations were given to community organizations. Several lively public service announcement television spots were produced and aired to gain grass-roots familiarity and interest in flexitime. They brought the program $100,000 worth of free publicity. The staff worked with the education director of the Washington State Labor Council to put on a seminar for labor leaders. A seminar on flexitime was also cosponsored with the Seattle Region Federal Executive Board.

The program coordinators spent a great deal of their own time providing consulting services to employers who were considering or implementing flexitime programs. Because no transportation publications and few other materials were available to guide staff efforts, they engaged a management consultant to share expertise with staff members and contribute materials for a staff-produced flexitime implementation kit to give employers. The kit was later expanded into an attractively designed, book-length manual. The staff placed emphasis on professional, top-quality written materials.

The program staff found that company-level flexitime applications proceeded more smoothly when top management gave the program strong support and a personnel administrator was given responsibility for actual implementation.

In 1981, the use of flexitime is continuing to grow in Seattle's downtown and suburban areas, though it tends to be concentrated in the computer, insurance, and banking industries. In addition to the 90 or so organizations to whom the program gave technical assistance in the implementation of flexitime, numerous others have converted on their own as a consequence of media attention given to some of the more prominent flexitime successes in local firms. Some federal agencies have adopted either flexible or compressed workweek schedules as participants in the Federal Alternative Work Schedules Experiment.

Only half of the program coordinator's time is presently devoted to flexitime, with the balance spent on program development and promotion of Commuter Pool's newer transportation services, which include van pools, bus pools, parking management, and an employer-subsidized transit-pass program.

In 1981, Commuter Pool staff will work more closely with METRO, which is considering two new services: (1) a "flexitime pass," or transit pass, sold at a reduced rate through employers who have adopted flexitime, and (2) a reduced-rate subscription bus service, if such service can be contracted for at off-peak hours. A slide presentation that companies can use to orient their employees to flexitime is also being prepared.

Problems

The program's greatest failure has been its inability to persuade its financial sponsors, King County and the City of Seattle, to adopt flexitime for their own employees, even though they are two of the area's largest employers. This situation has made the program vulnerable to criticism from a sometimes wary private sector. Active trade-union support has also been difficult to obtain, despite women members' advocacy of flexible working hours.

Evaluation of Transportation and Energy Effects

Some 1200 employees of eight downtown Seattle firms that converted to flexitime were surveyed on the results of the area-wide program in regard to energy and transportation. These were the responses of the 626 employees who took part:[5]

● Rush-hour commuting peaks were spread out. The proportion of flexitime employees who commuted during the previous morning peak hour of 7:30 A.M. to 8:30 A.M. decreased from 75 percent before area-wide flexitime to 42 percent afterwards; in the evening peak hour the proportion decreased from 77 percent to 57 percent.

- Commuting times of flexitime employees shifted to earlier hours. The morning peak hour is no longer 7:30 A.M. to 8:30 A.M. Now it is 7:00 A.M. to 8:00 A.M. (Fifty-nine percent of all arrivals at work are during this hour.)
- Avoiding rush-hour traffic and having more time at home to spend with family and friends were the two most important reasons influencing flexitime employees' choice of work start time.
- Travel time was reduced for most flexitime employees. Thirty percent of these employees saved more than ten minutes per trip, and 43 percent saved six or more minutes per trip.
- Commuting modes shifted to more energy-efficient modes. Driving alone decreased from 24 percent to 14 percent of flexitime employees, while ride sharing and public-transit usage both increased.

A similar survey is presently under way in suburban firms that use flexitime.

THE CASE OF THE DOWNTOWN SAN FRANCISCO FLEX-TIME DEMONSTRATION PROJECT[6]

San Francisco, the center of a nine-county industrialized metropolitan area that rings San Francisco Bay, has the third densest transit system in the United States. About half the downtown work force commuted by public transit at the time the demonstration project was initiated. Public transportation is provided by a heavy rail system, Bay Area Rapid Transit (BART); a commuter railway, the Southern Pacific Commuter; San Francisco Municipal Railway (MUNI), which operates buses, trolleys, and cable cars within the city; and three suburban bus companies that provide commuter service. City housing costs are high, with the result that a large number of downtown workers commute long distances from far-off suburbs. Traffic congestion is severe on the Bay and Golden Gate bridges.

The major industries located in the central business district are banks, insurance companies, brokerage houses, and corporate headquarters. Of the 250,000 people who work in downtown San Francisco, 50,000 are public employees who are concentrated in the Civic Center area. The economy is strong, and unemployment is not a serious problem.

Motivation for the Flexitime Project

San Francisco's Flex-Time Demonstration Project, which concentrates
on the downtown area, is part of an ongoing, statewide research effort
that is funded by the California Department of Transportation
(CALTRANS) and the U.S. Department of Transportation's Urban
Mass Transportation Administration (UMTA) and conducted by a
team led by David Jones at the University of California's Institute of
Transportation Studies (ITS). The San Francisco city-wide demonstration project was conceived when surveys of employees' commuting
behavior after the adoption of flexitime at the California Department
of Water Resources in Sacramento and the California State Automobile Association headquarters in downtown San Francisco showed
transportation benefits. Simulation studies based upon these surveys
and on road and rail characteristics showed that a half-hour shift in
travel time by 20,000 commuters could reduce delay on the Bay Bridge
by 10 percent and reduce fuel usage by 8 percent. Jones proposed a
demonstration project to allow commuters to use transit when seats
were available and highways when traffic was light. Flexitime would
enable commuters to avoid peak-load periods and absorb the problems
of BART schedule failures.

The knowledge that 50,000 additional employees would be working
in downtown San Francisco by 1985 as the result of construction of new
high-rise office buildings provided further impetus for a demonstration
project. Travel by the one-quarter of these new employees who were
expected to drive to work was projected to cause congestion on all the
major bridges and freeways leading into the city so severe that traffic
levels would exceed maximum design capacity by 10 percent. Though
increased office-building construction clearly had a favorable economic
impact on San Francisco, the business community realized that traffic
of that projected magnitude would impair the effective functioning of
business and could also create public demand either to freeze further
office growth or to impose high business taxes to finance more costly
solutions to the congestion problem. Individual taxpayer unwillingness
to finance additional public works had recently been demonstrated by
passage of Proposition 13.

Growing concern about gasoline shortages also increased public
interest in alternative work schedules as an energy-conservation
measure.

The researchers at ITS recommended a flexible rather than a staggered-hours program partly because of the weblike nature of San Francisco's transit and freeway networks. Whereas staggered work hours had proved successful in relieving crush platform loads on New York City's linear subway system, an alternative work schedule that did not allow self-adjustment on the part of individual commuters was thought likely only to shift congestion from one link to the next in a weblike system. Noting the positive reactions of both managers and employees to flexitime at the Department of Water Resources and the California State Automobile Association, they also felt that flexitime was more likely than staggered hours to engender a high enough rate of employer participation to relieve congestion at the network scale.

Feasibility Studies

Several bits of concrete feasibility data were collected, beyond the transit projections and previous case studies. San Francisco's Metropolitan Transportation Commission conducted a work-arrival-time study of downtown employees and found that most were scheduled to begin work during the same one-hour period. ITS surveyed San Francisco-based firms with a work force of more than 750 employees. Twenty-six firms with 32,000 employees responded, indicating that only a few were using flexible or staggered work hours. Only a few thought adoption of one of these work schedules would be impossible for them (these were firms with blue-collar shift operations). BART and CALTRANS data showed that spare capacity existed on transit systems outside the rush hour.

How the Demonstration Project Got Started

ITS then requested a CALTRANS grant to carry out a flexitime demonstration project in downtown San Francisco and received $82,000 in June 1978. The grant was enlarged to $160,000 the following year. Jones attributes the institute's success in obtaining the grant to CALTRANS' confidence in the researchers, which had been built up over a three-year working relationship, and the promise of flexitime indicated by ITS's earlier study at the Department of Water Resources.

The fact that a research unit of the University of California conducted the demonstration was good insofar as the people who were responsible had substantial knowledge about flexitime. They could take advantage of other cities' and companies' experience, and they knew how to evaluate the project. However, Jones believes that locating the project in the mayor's office would have speeded the implementation.

Program Objectives

The project's objectives were to:

1. Improve travel circumstances for workers so they could travel more comfortably and coordinate commuting needs with personal needs.
2. Reduce congestion and traffic delay.
3. Encourage transit use by allowing employees to ride when seating was available and to match work schedules to transit timetables.
4. Encourage car pools by allowing employees from different firms and work groups to coordinate their schedules, and by allowing family members to coordinate their work/school schedules.

The project's operating goal was to get 20,000 or more additional downtown employees on flexitime, the number estimated to be necessary to reduce Bay Bridge traffic delays by 10 percent. Before the demonstration project began, the downtown work force of 250,000 employees had a 15 percent flexitime usage rate, or 30,000 employees on flexitime; the desired increase was to a 25 percent usage rate, or 50,000 employees on flexitime. This goal could be reached only if 15 major employers adopted flexitime.

Project Activities and Experiences

San Francisco's demonstration project has proceeded according to the action plan shown in table 7-1.

Business associations—the San Francisco Planning and Urban Research Association (SPUR), the Bay Area Council, and the Blyth-Zellerbach Committee (chief executives of 18 large corporations headquartered in San Francisco)—played a key role in getting the program off the ground and opening corporate doors to the project staff. The San Francisco Chamber of Commerce hosted a workshop at which companies placed on flexitime by the project staff briefed companies considering the use of flexitime. Two insurance companies permitted distribution of case studies describing their flexitime experience.

Table 7-1.   San Francisco Demonstration Project Action Plan

1. DIAGNOSE AND PRESCRIBE
    a. Document the degree of peaking and current concentration of work-start times
    b. Identify firms with conventional schedules and flex-time–compatible operations
    c. Assess the availability of unused capacity in the shoulder of the peak
    d. Predict the impact of flex-time on time and mode of travel, based on the experience of
       firms that have already adopted flex-time
    e. Present results in a communicable format
2. ENDORSE
    Seek project endorsements necessary to legitimize the effort:
       • Business associations: Bay Area Council, SPUR, San Francisco Chamber
       • City and County of San Francisco: The Transportation Policy Group
       • Civil associations: League of Women Voters
       • Transit operators: BART, AC, Golden Gate, Muni, SamTrans
       • Regional agencies: MTC, RIDES
3. UNVEIL
    a. Stage press conference announcing project
    b. Develop media materials explaining the project
4. INVITE PARTICIPATION
    Letter to chief executive officer of 50 large firms with conventional schedule and flex-time
    compatible operations
       • Request CEO to assign senior executive to explore feasibility of flex-time
       • Invite to participate in workshops where executives of firms which have adopted flex-
         time will brief others on its pros and cons
5. COMMIT
    a. Host workshops
    b. Offer no-cost consulting services: personnel management consultant will develop
       customized flex-time plan for each participating company (up to 15 companies)
6. SNOWBALL
    Media campaign designed to create broad public awareness and employee interest in flex-
    time
       • Bridge fliers
       • Public-service announcements
       • Bus ads
       • BART message board
       • Talk show appearances
       • Editorial endorsements
7. ASSESS
    a. Measurement of "before" loads and delays on highway and transit systems
    b. Survey of employees of companies which adopt flex-time
    c. Measurement of "after" conditions on system

Source: San Francisco Flex-time Demonstration Project, Institute of Transportation Studies, University of
California at Berkeley, 1979.

Endorsements were sought and received separately from the boards of each transit operator. The Regional Transit Association announced its support for the project through a front-page story in the *San Francisco Examiner*.

Providing free technical assistance to firms for the design and implementation of customized flexitime programs was a key element in the project's strategy for gaining employer participation. A large portion of the project's CALTRANS grant was spent to engage a local flexitime consultant to provide this no-charge service to companies. (The consultant also sold the special time-accumulating devices used in some flexitime applications to those firms that wished to use them.) From the project's standpoint, the advantage of employing the consultant was that his availability provided an opportunity for follow-up with employers. After companies were introduced to flexitime at a project-sponsored workshop, the project staff telephoned participants to offer the free consulting services. Most companies used the consultant to advise their own personnel people rather than to provide direct design and implementation services.

Conversion to flexitime in government agencies has been slow. Though flexitime usage is permitted in state government, the project's sponsor, CALTRANS, adopted only a restricted form of flexitime and took a year to implement it. The City and County of San Francisco, which employs 27,000 people, took two years to authorize flexitime. It currently has three pilot units on flexitime and has promised to expand its programs to all other units where it is suitable.

One union leader, Dennis P. Bouey of the International Federation of Professional and Technical Engineers, Local 21, has given strong support to the project. He himself had been negotiating flexitime contracts for several years prior to the commencement of the project. Target employers, however, tend to be nonunion (e.g., the corporate headquarters of companies), and hence unions were not integral to the project.

Though the San Francisco project has only a limited public-relations budget, the media have played an important role in the demonstration project by inviting staff to appear on talk shows, interviewing them for news shows, publishing staff-written articles, and publicizing successful projects. Care was taken to steer reporters to permanent programs, since companies were reluctant to have attention drawn to their flexitime programs while they were still in the experimental stage.

The Metropolitan Transit Commission sponsored, and project staff took the lead in developing, a "how to" manual and training courses for company transportation coordinators who will be responsible for distributing transit and ride-sharing information within their organization, developing internal flexible work hours programs, and setting up company and intercompany van pools. The training was scheduled for four different locations in the Bay Area in fall 1980 and spring 1980. The manual also serves as a resource for company flexitime coordinators who are unable to attend a training session.

To date, the project has placed eight companies on flexitime, with pilot programs involving 6,000 employees. If these company programs expand as expected, the project will be only 4,000 people short of its goal of placing 20,000 downtown employees on flexible hours.

The demonstration project is already having ripple effects around the state. Sacramento has recently initiated an area-wide flexible work hours program. Branches of some San Francisco banks are following the lead of their headquarters and adopting flexitime in Los Angeles and other cities. More than 500 companies located throughout the state have asked the project staff for guidance. CALTRANS seems ready to sponsor a statewide flexitime program.

Problems

San Francisco's mayor was assassinated early in the project's life, causing delay in the new mayor's agreement to endorse the project and host a planned meeting with business leaders. Separation of the project from City Hall exacerbated the delay. Corporate conservatism also slowed the pace of company conversions. A duality of attitudes at CALTRANS complicated relations between the project and its financial sponsor; while flexitime was regarded favorably as a transportation management strategy, some who perceived a need for CALTRANS to adopt flexible scheduling for its own employees were dubious from a managerial perspective.

Evaluation of Transportation and Energy Effects

The project will be evaluated when it is complete by means of:

● Employee surveys to determine shifts in time of travel, travel duration, and mode of travel.

- Simulation of transportation impact on selected routes, using survey data as input.
- Estimate of "growth absorption value" of the project (that is, the value of transit and highway investment that is not needed).

Data collection for these evaluations is currently under way.

THE CASE OF THE BOSTON AREA VARIABLE WORK HOURS PROGRAM[7]

Boston is a port located on Massachusetts Bay at the convergence of the Charles, Mystic, and Chelsea rivers. The downtown area, where approximately 300,000 people work, is served by a dense public transportation network that includes commuter rail, rapid rail, bus, trolley, and ferry systems, collectively operated by the Massachusetts Bay Transportation Authority (MBTA). MBTA transports almost 500,000 passengers daily.

The city has a diverse industrial base and a stable economy. It is the financial center of New England. Industries located in the downtown area include banking, finance, insurance, advertising, publishing, corporate headquarters, retail trade, and manufacturing. A booming electronics industry is situated outside Boston along Route 128. Several large universities and smaller colleges are located in the metropolitan area. Boston is a federal regional center as well as the capital of Massachusetts, with most public employment concentrated downtown in the Government Center area.

Why the Variable Work Hours Program Was Initiated

During the winter of 1977–78, Boston suffered a severe snowstorm that brought automobile travel to a standstill. Governor Michael S. Dukakis imposed an emergency staggered work hours program that proved to be extraordinarily effective in expanding the capacity of the public transit system to carry the city's work force while all roads were closed to automobile travel. The success of the emergency program encouraged the governor to organize a permanent variable work hours program as a cost-effective alternative to capital investment in rolling stock and highways needed to accommodate anticipated growth in commuting.

New England's cold climate and reliance on imported petroleum created a particularly strong public awareness of the need for energy conservation, including use of public transportation and more efficient operation of transit systems.

In June 1977, MBTA conducted rapid-rail ridership surveys indicating that demand exceeded capacity during a 45-minute evening period. Rush-hour congestion was most severe at four subway stations: Park Street, State Street, Arlington Street, and South Station. Park Street is located close to the State House and other state office buildings. State Street is in the heart of the banking and financial district. Arlington Street is in close proximity to large advertising agencies, insurance companies, and specialty stores. South Station serves engineering and manufacturing areas.

A household survey made by MBTA found that 50 percent of respondents felt that overcrowding was the most serious problem of transit service. Overcrowded platforms during the peak period compounded rider frustration by increasing the time trains had to spend in stations loading and unloading passengers. As this dwell time increased, other trains fell behind schedule waiting for clearance to enter the station. Eventually the whole line became involved, and inordinate delays resulted.

Initially MBTA favored an area-wide staggered work hours program to spread peak-period demand for service. Findings from research conducted by Boston's independent Association for Public Transportation, Inc., on other cities' experience with alternative work schedules in the central business district, however, convinced planners of the wider acceptability of a variable work hours program, which encouraged employers to adopt either a staggered or flexible work schedule.

How the Program Got Started

Implementation of the Boston Area Variable Work Hours Program was made possible in March 1978 when six public agencies authorized the project. These agencies were MBTA, the Executive Office of Transportation and Construction, the Metropolitan Area Planning Council, the MBTA Advisory Board, the Massachusetts Department of Public Works, and Massport. MBTA was later designated as the lead public agency. It successfully solicited cosponsorship by the Greater Boston Chamber of Commerce as a private-sector representative. The Association for Public Transportation, a nonprofit organization, was hired by MBTA to coordinate activities. Technical assistance on organization of the area-wide program and implementation of firm-level programs has been provided by Gordon Lewin of the Association.

Funding for the Boston area's program's budget was provided by the public agencies, utilizing, in part, federal transportation planning funds. Suburban cities, as well as downtown Boston, are included in the program.

Program Objectives

The program's objective was to improve utilization of public transportation, thereby:

- Reducing peak-period congestion.
- Encouraging shifts from solo driving to public transit.
- Increasing the operational and cost efficiency of MBTA.
- Creating speedier work trips and more pleasant commuting conditions for riders.

Its operational goal was to spread peak subway loadings at key stations by 25 percent.

Program Activities and Experiences

The Boston staff sought advice from directors of the New York, Seattle, and nascent San Francisco area-wide alternative work schedule programs and followed their recommendations to use a "soft sell," asking employers for voluntary participation and stressing management and employee advantages.

The Boston program was publicly launched with a Conference on Variable Work Hours held in June 1978 and attended by 160 managers and executives from local businesses and government agencies. Speakers included the governor, the president of the Greater Boston Chamber of Commerce, the manager of New York City's Staggered Work Hours Program, and the president of the Downtown–Lower Manhattan Association (an employers' association that had been instrumental in organizing the New York staggered hours project). Workshops provided guidance to participants on planning a schedule suited to their own needs, working with unions, and preparing first-line supervisors. Company and agency representatives presented case studies on white-collar, manufacturing, and government applications of flexitime. A published conference report later became a sales tool for the variable work hours program as well as a resource for companies interested in adopting a new work schedule.

At the time that the Boston variable hours program was being planned, the president of a large insurance company that used flexitime was also president of the Greater Boston Chamber of Commerce. His personal enthusiasm for flexitime, dedication of Chamber resources, and willingness to cooperate with the governor contributed immeasurably to the successful organization of the project.

Local employers responded positively to Chamber of Commerce appeals to consider new work schedules. Most personnel managers were well acquainted with the flexitime concept. Public policy considerations provided impetus for conversion.

Several government agencies have adopted flexitime as participants in state and federal alternative work schedule programs. City government has 700 employees on staggered hours. Overall, however, the impact of the public sector on the program has been only moderate. Only 10 percent of all state employees are on flexitime, whereas a 25 percent participation had been called for.

Unions have maintained a neutral position toward the variable work hours program.

The Metropolitan Area Planning Council, an organization composed of 101 cities and towns in the region, has contributed to the program by opening a Variable Work Hours Resource Center and funding production of radio and television spot announcements.

The Boston project gained strong media support. The editorial director of one television station promoted both the variable work hours program and public transit extensively through interviews and editorials.

MBTA and the Association for Public Transportation also promote a transit-pass program. Each month 50,000 to 60,000 transit passes are sold, largely through employers.

By October 1979, 250 organizations, with almost 85,000 employees (14 percent of the downtown Boston work force), had adopted flexible or staggered work hours.

In the future MBTA will distribute to local employers a flexitime implementation guide that has been prepared by the Association for Public Transportation. It also will advertise variable hours on subways and buses.

Evaluation of Transportation and Energy Effects

A report issued two years after the Boston program was launched concluded that:

- Utilization of public transit improved, with substantial benefit to the transit authority, its riders, and the community.
- Peak-period demand at the four most congested subway stations was reduced by 21 percent, 22 percent, 30 percent, and 46 percent, respectively. Subway usage just before and directly after the peak period increased. In most cases, employees on flexitime chose to commute outside MBTA peaks.
- Employees in 12 state agencies saved two hours per week in commuting time on the average, and 83 percent found commuting easier.
- Auto ownership decreased 13 percent among state employees on flexitime.
- Commuting by driving alone decreased from 15 to 8 percent of all state employees on flexitime, while public transit use increased from 71 to 77 percent among the state employees. Car pooling increased by one percent.

THE CASE OF THE KANSAS CITY VARIABLE WORK SCHEDULE PROGRAM[8]

The Kansas City Metropolitan Region, populated by 1.34 million people, includes eight counties and 114 cities located in two states. The two medium-sized cities of Kansas City, Kansas, and Kansas City, Missouri, lie across from each other at the confluence of the Missouri and Kansas rivers. About 55,000 people work in downtown Kansas City, Missouri, and about 7,000 in the downtown area of Kansas City, Kansas.

The region is heavily dependent on the private automobile for transport. In 1976, approximately 92 percent of all work trips were made by auto or truck. Only 4 percent were made by bus, as compared with 17 percent for the 33 largest Standard Metropolitan Statistical Areas in the United States. The metropolitan region is characterized by a low population density and a commuting distance that is longer than most areas of comparable population size.

Employment centers are spread out, and consequently traffic congestion is not a serious problem. The major sectors of employment are services, manufacturing, retail trade, and government and government enterprises.[9] Employment within these sectors is predominantly white collar.

Motivation for the Variable Work Schedule Program

During the 1979 energy crisis, the Mid-America Regional Council (MARC), which is composed of representatives of the local governments in the Kansas City Metropolitan Region, received a $75,000 grant from the Urban Mass Transportation Administration to develop a Transportation Energy Contingency Plan (TECP). The purpose of the plan was to recommend strategies for providing energy-efficient alternatives for traveling to work during a transportation fuel crisis. The Chamber of Commerce of Greater Kansas City and the Federal Executive Board, as well as MARC energy, transportation, and citizen advisory committees participated in the development of the TECP.

Feasibility Study

As a start in preparing the TECP, an analysis was made of travel behavior in the region during the 1979 fuel shortage. Traffic counts showed that travel declined by 5 to 7 percent, with most reductions occurring in nonwork and weekend trips. An auto-occupancy study indicated no increase in car pools.

Variable work scheduling was one of some 50 strategies considered for maintaining essential transportation services while reducing overall transportation fuel demand. Each proposed strategy was evaluated on the basis of its institutional feasibility (legally, politically, and in terms of resource availability and implementation time); its costs; and its travel, energy, air quality, noise, safety, economic, and geographic distribution impacts. The ten strategies finally recommended included both variable work schedules (flexible and staggered hours) and promotion of a four-day workweek if fuel shortage or price reduced discretionary travel by 20 to 30 percent.

How the Program Got Started

MARC adopted a variable work schedules policy in July 1979. Agreement by the Chamber of Commerce to cosponsor the program was quickly obtained because of a long history of cooperation on regional problem solving and because both elected officials and business leaders were eager to take positive action in response to the energy crisis. The program extended throughout the region and was financed out of the two organizations' existing operating funds. Progress towards implementing the variable work schedules program was reviewed by both MARC and the Chamber. At the same time, MARC began advance planning to increase peak period transit capacity, organize a regional car-pooling program, and improve transit feeder service.

Program Objectives

Energy conservation was the prime objective of the Kansas City work-scheduling program. Greater emphasis was placed on flexible hours than on staggered hours as flexitime was perceived to have a larger potential for promoting more energy-efficient travel to work by:

- Enabling commuters to use transit when seats were available.
- Permitting employees to match their work hours to transit schedules.
- Making ride sharing easier to arrange.
- Alleviating gas-pump congestion.
- Reducing rush-hour traffic congestion, thus allowing vehicles to move at faster and steadier speeds.

There were no specific operational goals set for the program.

Program Activities and Experience

The variable hours program was announced in August 1979 when MARC and the Chamber of Commerce jointly issued a brochure describing the benefits of flexitime. MARC handled logistics and provided technical assistance on program organization as well as firm-level application of new work schedules. Various users were contacted to learn more about the costs and benefits of each schedule. The Chamber assumed prime responsibility for publicizing the program and persuading employers to adopt new work schedules. The prestige and power of the Chamber were vitally important in winning acceptance of alternative work schedules in a conservative business community. Previous flexitime use had been confined to local branches of national organizations.

Another business group, Downtown, Inc., representing businesses located in downtown Kansas City, Missouri, also promoted variable work schedule usage among its members. The Federal Executive Board agreed to promote flexible scheduling within government agencies, but did not launch an active campaign. City and county governments have endorsed the concept of variable work scheduling as members of MARC. However, local governments have been slow to adopt these programs for their employees.

The local media frequently reported on variable work scheduling programs during 1979 and 1980. Their coverage tended, however, to be of national rather than local applications of flexitime because MARC and the Chamber of Commerce did not actively promote the program in this way. The Kansas City media were generally very cooperative in publicizing and promoting energy issues.

Since employment in the Kansas City area occurs primarily within services, retail trade, and government, most employees are not organized and trade unions had little impact on the program. The Central Labor Council was asked to review and comment on program plans, but displayed little interest in it.

In December 1979, MARC and the Chamber jointly conducted a survey of 114 private-sector firms in the Kansas City area employing 250 or more persons in order to learn how extensively flexible, staggered, and compressed work schedules were being used and what their benefits and costs were for employers and employees. Of the 43 respondents, 13 were using either assigned or employee-chosen staggered hours, nine were using three- or four-day workweeks, and two were using true flexitime. The favorable impacts reported for all three schedules led to combined MARC and Chamber of Commerce adoption in February 1980 of a policy encouraging the use of all forms of alternative work schedules. Transit revenue losses from use of compressed work schedules were of little concern, since the local transit authority has been unable to accommodate the ridership demand since the 1979 energy crisis. Program materials are being developed by MARC and disseminated by the Chamber and an active alternative work schedule promotion is being carried out in fall 1980.

MARC has also contracted with the city of Kansas City, Missouri, to institute a ride-sharing program. Variable work scheduling is promoted as a component of the ride-sharing program to major area corporations.

Problems

The long-standing working relationship that existed between MARC and the Chamber of Commerce made implementation of a work rescheduling program easy in Kansas City's private sector, but participation by federal agencies has been less than anticipated. Scarcity of data on the transportation and energy costs and the benefits of various alternative work schedules has been the program's major problem.

Evaluation of Transportation and Energy Effects

No formal evaluation of the program has been made so far, but measurement of its transportation and air-quality impacts, as well as its energy effects, is planned.

THE CASE OF THE PORT AUTHORITY OF NEW YORK AND NEW JERSEY: PIONEERS IN CITY-WIDE EFFORTS TO INCREASE TRANSPORTATION EFFICIENCY

The original effort to use alternative work schedules to save energy and improve transportation was the staggered work hours experiment of the Port Authority of New York and New Jersey. This effort is only briefly noted here because staggered hours appear less promising than flexitime to achieve these goals. The New York project, which was partially financed by UMTA, is fully documented in a three-volume report (executive summary, technical report, and manual)[10] that has been studied by countless others interested in work-schedule change as a mechanism for relieving transit and roadway congestion. The program's original directors, Brendan O'Malley and Carl Selinger, have given generously of their time as informed consultants to other cities. Thus New York's basic program design and strategies have been replicated by the organizers of subsequent area-wide alternative work schedule programs nationwide.

When the New York project was launched in 1970, flexitime was unknown in the United States. As the merits of this newer alternative work schedule became better known, the Port Authority experimented with flexitime in its own headquarters. Convinced that the newer schedule was not only as effective as staggered work hours in dispersing rush-hour congestion, but also superior in terms of human benefits, the staff began to advocate adoption of either flexible or staggered hours. They continued, however, to place greater emphasis on staggered work hours, which they felt was the more readily accepted concept for quick implementation. It does not involve fundamental change in an organization's operations, and a significant amount of informally staggered scheduling is already practiced in the business community. It is usually noncontroversial. They also noted that many firms that first adopt staggered hours evolve toward flexitime.

The results of the New York project are impressive. Major employers were invited to a series of breakfast meetings to learn more about alternative work schedules, and some 400 companies with 300,000 employees subsequently adopted either staggered or flexible hours. Numerous measures, such as subway line and station counts, bus and train travel times, pedestrian counts on sidewalks and in building lobbies, and vehicle counts at tunnels and bridges were taken to assess the effect of the program on transportation systems. Staggered hours proved most effective in relieving congestion on rapid-rail systems and elevators, where the problem was due to peaking of demand rather than capacity constraints. Staggering work hours could do nothing about congestion at vehicular access/egress points where automobile facilities operated above capacity for almost three hours in both the morning and evening.

TRANSFERABILITY OF RESULTS

The quick look we have had at area-wide flexitime programs so far suggests they are a sound strategy for temporally dispersing transportation demand and fostering faster, more efficient travel. Load leveling allows public transportation to operate more efficiently. Small, but significant, mode shifts away from solo driving and toward ride sharing and public transit take place. Individual company results reported here support these conclusions.

But can good results achieved in one major city be transferred to another city? Should small and middle-sized cities consider area-wide flexitime programs, or is this traffic-management strategy suited only to large cities with bottlenecks at bridges and subway entrances? How is feasibility to be determined?

Several factors, including population size, transit-system density, geography, and industry mix, affect the manner in which and the extent to which an area-wide work-rescheduling program can increase energy and transportation efficiency. They influence one another and cumulatively affect flexitime's contribution to the solution of a particular energy or transportation problem.

Population.   Large cities have the worst congestion problem, and so they are the first to seek relief through work-schedule manipulation. Medium-sized cities and suburban employment centers, however, may experience more noticeable benefits from a flexitime program.

Peak periods usually are of shorter duration in smaller cities than in larger ones; therefore a shift to a slightly earlier or later schedule can result in a dramatically improved commute. In larger cities, a more substantial shift is needed to avoid rush-hour congestion. In very large cities, a transit or highway system may already be operating beyond capacity for two or more hours each workday morning and evening. Though flexitime can solve distribution problems, it cannot solve this kind of capacity problem.

In large cities where downtown parking is expensive and a large proportion of the work force already uses public transportation, there also is less opportunity for flexitime to induce use of transit by increasing its relative attractiveness. Smaller cities are likely to find area-wide programs easier to initiate because fewer governments and less complex bureaucracies are involved.

Transit Density.   While flexitime spreads peak-period demand in cities with dense public transportation systems, in areas less well served by mass transit, its chief advantage is more often that it encourages mode shifts to transit or ride sharing. Fixed work schedules are especially frustrating to commuters when buses run infrequently and waits to make transfers are long or of uncertain length. Suburban work sites with free parking and poor transit service have traditionally encouraged solo driving. Ride sharing is becoming a necessity for employees, however, as the price of gasoline continues to rise and flexitime is beginning to be used to facilitate formation of multiemployer car pools, van pools, and bus pools to serve suburban employment centers.

Geography.   The same rivers and harbors that account for the growth of a city into an important center of commerce and industry may later produce some of its worst traffic bottlenecks. Bridges and tunnel entrances are the funnels through which suburbanites must pour in order to reach their downtown workplaces. It is not surprising, therefore, that seaports as well as inland metropolitan centers located on rivers have been early adopters of flexitime. Other cities with geography-related congestion problems, including bottlenecks at freeway entrances and exits, should consider flexitime.

The geographic distribution of the residences of a metropolitan area's labor force may also recommend flexitime. In San Francisco, for example, housing costs are high within the city; therefore many workers travel long distances to their jobs. If flexitime permits them to save gasoline by ride sharing, avoiding stop-and-go driving conditions, or switching to public transit for all or a portion of their trip, the individual saves money, the employer retains an employee who otherwise might have been forced to quit by escalating travel costs, and the public interest is served.

Industry Mix. Fortunately, many of the same kinds of industries that typically locate in a central business district also find that flexitime is suited to their work technologies. Banks, insurance companies, brokerage houses, corporate headquarters, and government agencies all employ large numbers of white-collar workers whose tasks generally are not disrupted if their colleagues follow slightly different work schedules. Two other industries frequently located in downtown areas, retail stores and hospitals, are less able to use flexitime because of the fixed-hours coverage they must maintain. Since their employees often work staggered, part-time, or shift schedules, however, these industries are lesser contributors to rush-hour congestion. High-technology industries, such as electronics and research and development, often cluster along a particular corridor leading into a large city, as for example, Route 128 in Boston. These industries also find flexitime suited to their work processes and can use the system to relieve congestion problems at entrances to industrial parks or parking lots.

Determining Feasibility. Bringing about significant shifts in commuting patterns requires cooperation among employers, employees, transit operators, and government officials. Consequently, the concerns of all these groups should be taken into account in determining the feasibility of an area-wide flexitime program. Questions to answer include:

● Does peaking occur? Does spare capacity exist before and after rush hour on one or more congested transportation systems, such as bridges, buses, rapid rail lines, freeway ramps, or plant entrances?

● Is demand expected to increase on one or more transportation systems in the future?

● What are the present work schedules of major employers? Do they coincide with peaks occurring on transportation systems?

● If they do coincide, are the work technologies of these employers compatible with flexitime? If not, could staggered or compressed work schedules for some or all employees be instituted as an alternative?

● Would target employers consider use of alternative work schedules?

● Are any employers already using flexitime? Has their experience been favorable? Do employers and leaders of employer organizations perceive a need to reduce congestion?

● What is the attitude of key public officials toward area-wide flexitime and use of flexible hours in public agencies?

● What is the attitude of union leaders toward an area-wide flexitime program?

B. Commuting Changes by Flexitime Employees

Empirical data to show the desirability of flexible work hours to save energy and improve transportation efficiency are scarce. Some results from city-wide flexitime programs are in, and they look good. Several individual employers have done case studies that indicate favorable energy and commuting outcomes experienced by their own employees after a switch to flexitime. Few of these studies are published, and their results are not widely known. Yet the interest is there. For example, during 1980 hearings held by the U.S. Congress in three different parts of the country to find ways to obtain more efficiency and productivity from existing transit equipment, facilities, and capital investments, flexible work schedules were mentioned several times. Yet witnesses representing cities where area-wide flexitime programs were in effect did not have information about their outcomes.[11] Forthcoming econometric and case-study research on the energy, transportation, and economic effects of alternative work schedules, sponsored by the U.S. Department of Energy and conducted by Jack Faucett Associates, should help out, as should the reports on the Federal Alternative Work Schedule Program which the U.S. Office of Personnel Management is to issue in 1981 and 1982.

In this section, the key energy and transportation results from company-conducted case studies are described, along with the results of city-wide flexitime programs.

Effects of Flexitime on Rush-Hour Congestion

A host of company studies, as well as area-wide surveys, indicate that employees who are given a choice of schedule elect to commute outside the rush hour. Most select an earlier start time, but a few prefer later-than-normal hours, as is shown in table 7-2. Corroborating evidence of flexitime's power to disperse peak-period commuting is provided by evaluations recently made of several area-wide flexible work hours programs (see pp. 212–239, this chapter). The results in Seattle and Boston were reported above. Here are others:

- When federal employees in Ottawa were placed on flexible hours, the number of work starts occurring during the morning peak 30 minutes dropped from 78 to 40 percent, and the number of work stops from 68 to 33 percent during the evening peak.[12]
- A year after Toronto's Variable Work Hours Project was launched, 34 percent of the 55,000 employees working in downtown Toronto were on flexible or staggered hours, and almost half of these people chose to travel outside the peak hour in the morning.[13] In Toronto's government complex, Queen's Park, peak fifteen-minute subway use was halved during the morning peak and reduced by one-fourth during the evening peak.[14]
- In Richmond, Virginia, when employee-chosen staggered hours were instituted for state employees (only 17 percent of whom use public transit), traffic counts in the Capitol Square area revealed significant reductions in peak-period congestion at heavily traveled intersections, freeway ramps, and parking-lot entrances and exits. Forced-flow conditions at intersections were reduced in both frequency and duration (from 15 to 5 minutes).[15]

The reason that flexitime promotes a wider dispersal of work start and stop times than do staggered hours is because employees choose

Table 7-2.   Distribution of Arrival Times of Employees on Flexitime: Summary of Survey Research

	Arrival Time	Before 7:00 A.M.	7:00 A.M. to 7:30 A.M.	7:30 A.M. to 8:00 A.M.	8:00 A.M. to 8:30 A.M.	8:30 A.M. to 9:00 A.M.	After 9:00 A.M.
				Percent of Employees*			
Metropolitan Life Insurance Co.	NYC Headquarters[1]			29	27	30	14
	Southeast Home Office[1]	37	22	21	12	4	4
	San Francisco[2]		53	24	14	6	3
California State Automobile Association[2]			16**	31	40	7	6
Fireman's Fund[2]			31	34	20	10	5
N.Y. Division of Motor Vehicles[3]			55	26	16	2	
Transportation Systems Center[4]		7	11	40	22	15	5
Virginia state employees[5]			23	38	32	3	
Downtown Toronto employees[6]			1	46	34	13	6
Downtown Seattle employees[7]		21	34	25	17	4	

Notes:
*Some totals vary from 100 percent due to rounding.
**However, 28 percent said that they would begin by 7:00 A.M. if given the option.
Sources:
[1]Port Authority of New York and New Jersey. *Flexible Work Hours Experiment at the Port Authority of New York and New Jersey,* vol. II (New York: Port Authority of New York and New Jersey, Planning and Development Department, 1975), p. 140.
[2]Frances Harrison, David Jones, and Paul Jovanis, *Flex-Time and Commuting Behavior in San Francisco: Some Preliminary Findings. Summary Report,* UCB-ITS-RR-79-12 (Berkeley, Calif.: University of California, Institute of Transportation Studies, 1979), p. 1.
[3]New York State Department of Motor Vehicles, "Department of Motor Vehicles Work-Hours Program: Attendance Survey, January 1972" (Albany, N.Y.: New York State Department of Motor Vehicles, 1972), p. 3.
[4]Marian Ott, Howard Slavin, and Donald Ward, *The Behavioral Impacts of Flexible Working Hours.* Final Report. 600-446-437 (Washington, D.C.: Government Printing Office, 1980), p. 6.
[5]Virginia Department of Highways and Transportation, Public Transportation Division, "The Impact of the State Employee Adjustable Work Schedule Program in the 'Capitol Square' Area of Richmond" (Richmond, Va.: Virginia Department of Highways and Transportation, 1979), p. 18.
[6]Toronto Variable Work Hours Project, *Variable Work Hours in Downtown Toronto* (Toronto, Canada: Metropolitan Toronto Planning Department, 1975), p. 22.
[7]Frances D. Harrison, Paul Jovanis, David Jones, and Jane Walczak, "Hours and Commuting Choices: Survey Results from Downtown Seattle" (Seattle: Seattle/King County Commuter Pool, 1980), p. 7.

much earlier start times than an employer would normally assign to any group of workers.[16] The Port Authority of New York and New Jersey reports that building lobby counts showed that when employees who had previously been on staggered hours were placed on flexitime, arrival and departure times remained spread out, but became earlier.[17]

However, congestion relief does not extend far beyond the vicinity of geographically limited flexitime applications. A traffic assignment model estimated a small impact from a 28.4 percent reduction in peak-period arrival times on the streets surrounding the State Campus in Albany, New York (an enclave of 10,000 government employees located in an otherwise residential area). Only a 9.4 percent improvement in traffic volume on expressways and a 3.9 percent improvement on arterials was calculated.[18]

While flexitime clearly encourages off-peak commuting, a worker's choice of schedule is influenced by several factors in addition to avoiding congestion. Whereas matching workday to office needs was regarded as important by the largest number of employees at the California State Automobile Association (81 percent), among members of car pools the ability to coordinate schedules with other participants was of prime importance.[19] Having more time at home and avoiding the rush hour were major schedule determinants to most people on flexitime in Seattle (75 and 70 percent, respectively), but matching commuting times with transit schedules was even more important to those who used public transportation.[20] Important considerations to employees at the Transportation Systems Center in Cambridge, Massachusetts, were after-work activities (72 percent), avoiding traffic congestion (69 percent), schedules of other household members (39 percent), and sleep patterns (38 percent).[21] At the New York State Department of Transportation in Albany, the desire for flexibility in work and family schedules was a more important factor than avoiding congestion,[22] but in New York City, 73 percent of employees on flexitime at the Port Authority tried to travel outside the most congested periods. Those who did not, cited car-pool commitments and the scarcity of trains outside the peaks as constraints.[23]

The work time an employee selects is a function of several variables, including occupation, life stage, residence location, and travel mode. At the Transportation Systems Center, mean arrival times were later for employees who used transit, had higher salaries, and had longer travel times. They were earlier for those who had larger numbers of children and other household members, had children under five years, and who were themselves in an older age group.[24] Similarly, managers at the California State Automobile Association were inclined to arrive either very early or very late. Suburbanites, especially managers, arrived earlier than their urban counterparts. Those with family concerns were also more likely to arrive early. People in car pools most often arrived early, followed by solo drivers. Transit users arrived latest, suggesting that transit schedules limit schedule choices.[25]

Effects of Flexitime on Vehicle Fuel Consumption

Relieving the stop-and-go driving conditions that characterize rush hour should lead to energy conservation, since buses and private vehicles that travel at a faster and steadier pace consume less fuel. Looking at individual flexitime workers' commuting experience suggests that gasoline savings do occur.

Time savings of at least ten minutes per trip are frequent in both urban and suburban work settings (see table 7-3).

Wagner and Gilbert estimate that 20 percent participation of central business district employees in an area-wide flexitime program will yield an area reduction in work travel time of 0.5 percent.[26]

At the Transportation Systems Center, fuel efficiency was estimated to have improved 11.7 percent (from 14.9 miles per gallon to 16.6 miles per gallon) for drivers who experienced savings in travel time after the introduction of flexitime, and 7.6 percent for drivers overall. Fuel consumption was estimated to have dropped 9 percent (from one gallon per trip to .9 gallon per trip) for those with improvements in travel time, and 5.8 percent for drivers overall.[27]

Many Geological Survey employees also reported decreases in gasoline consumption due to off-peak commuting—54 percent of those who worked in suburban Reston, Virginia, and 23 percent of those who worked in downtown Washington, D.C.[28]

Effects of Flexitime on Mode of Travel

When flexitime arrived on American shores in the early 1970s, some transportation planners welcomed the new work schedule as a "better mousetrap"—a system that overcame the tendency of staggered hours to disrupt car pools and convert transit users to solo driving if service

Table 7-3.   Travel-Time Savings for Employees on Flexitime

Case	Amount of Savings	
	Minutes per Trip	Percent of Employees
California State Automobile Association[1]	0–5	56
	6–10	13
	10+	31
Eight downtown Seattle firms[2]	0–5	45
	6–10	13
	10+	30
U.S. Geological Survey:[3]		
Reston, Va.	0–5	13
	6–10	21
	10+	21
Washington, D.C.	0–5	—
	6–10	12
	10+	25
State employees in Boston[4]	Average savings of 2 hours per week or 12 minutes per trip.	
State employees in Richmond[5]	Quicker work trips reported by 67 percent. Subsample reported savings of 2 to 10 minutes, representing 10 to 20 percent time savings. Time savings greatest for intermediate-length trips of 5 to 10 miles.	

Case	Average savings per trip for those who:	
Transportation Systems Center[6]	Did Not Change Mode	Did Change Mode
Solo drivers	14 minutes	18 minutes
	11 minutes	13 minutes
	11 minutes	11 minutes

Sources:

[1] Frances Harrison, David Jones, and Paul Jovanis, *Flex-Time and Commuting Behavior in San Francisco: Some Preliminary Findings. Summary Report,* UCB-ITS-RR-79-12 (Berkeley, Calif.: University of California, Institute of Transportation Studies, 1979), p. 13.

[2] Frances D. Harrison, Paul Jovanis, David Jones, and Jane Walczak, "Hours and Commuting Choices: Survey Results from Downtown Seattle" (Seattle: Seattle/King County Commuter Pool, 1980), p. 11.

[3] U.S. Geological Survey, "Comprehensive Report of a One-Year Experiment with Flexitime at the U.S. Geological Survey" (Reston, Va.: U.S. Geological Survey, Branch of Management Analysis, 1977), p. 42.

[4] Association for Public Transportation, *The Variable Work Hours Program: Final Report,* prepared by Gordon Lewin for the Massachusetts Bay Transit Authority, June 1980, p. 19.

[5] Virginia Department of Highways and Transportation, Public Transportation Division, "The Impact of the State Employee Adjustable Work Schedule Program in the 'Capitol Square' Area of Richmond" (Richmond, Va.: Virginia Department of Highways and Transportation, 1979), pp. 21–22.

[6] Marian Ott, Howard Slavin, and Donald Ward, *The Behavioral Impacts of Flexible Working Hours.* Final Report. 600-446-437 (Washington, D.C.: Government Printing Office, 1980), p. 20.

were less available at their new hours. They thought that flexitime provided an incentive to use public transportation, since work hours could be matched to transit schedules. They also thought flexitime facilitated car-pool formation among household members or neighbors with different employers. Other transportation authorities feared that flexitime and employee desire to enjoy as much schedule variability as possible would cause shifts from ride sharing and transit use to driving alone.

This important policy question has been answered conclusively by recent research. Commuters who are given schedule choice do not desert ride sharing and transit. Though a few shifts in mode of travel did occur, changes are far more likely to be toward more energy-efficient forms of transportation than away from them. For example, only 11 percent of employees at the California Department of Water Resources changed their mode of transportation after flexitime was adopted. Of those who changed, 26 shifted from car to bus, while only three shifted from bus to car. Ten went from car to car pool, while only three went from car pool to car. The net effect of these mode shifts was a 15 percent increase in transit use, a 9 percent increase in the use of car pools, and a 20 percent decline in solo driving.[29]

The preponderance of positive over negative shifts is clear from findings of 11 other studies presented in table 7-4. The most pronounced shift is from driving alone toward participating in a car pool. Shifts toward transit also occur, but happen less frequently. When transit defections occur, they are toward ride sharing rather than solo driving.

Were these shifts to more energy-efficient modes of transportation caused by flexitime or by rising gasoline prices? Researchers addressed this question specifically in their survey of employees on flexitime in eight firms in Seattle and concluded that the escalating price of gasoline *motivated* increased use of car pools and transit, while flexitime *facilitated* the change. Virtually all converts from solo driving and ride sharing to transit indicated that saving money on gasoline was an important reason for their mode change. Also important to most was the ability to cope with unreliable transit service (85 percent of former solo drivers and 90 percent of former ride sharers), to meet transit schedules (83 percent and 90 percent), and to get a seat (77 percent and 80 percent). Being able to adjust schedules to form car pools was important to both those who previously drove alone (76 percent) and those who formerly used transit (61 percent). While the first group usually wanted to save money on gasoline (68 percent), half of those who shifted from transit

Table 7-4.   Effects of Flexitime on Travel Mode: Research Summary

Sample	Mode	Percentage of Employees Using Mode		Change in Percentage
		Before	After	
Lawrence Berkeley Laboratory[1]	Drive alone	50	45	− 5
San Francisco	Shared ride	22	26	+ 4
	Transit	13	14	+ 1
	Other	15	15	0
CALTRANS[1]	Drive alone	27	20	− 7
San Francisco	Shared ride	43	55	+ 12
	Transit	28	23	− 5
	Other	2	2	0
Chubb–Pacific Indemnity[1]	Drive alone	3	1	− 2
San Francisco	Shared ride	71	72	+ 1
	Transit	20	21	+ 1
	Other	6	6	0
Standard Oil[1]	Drive alone	2	1	− 1
San Francisco	Shared ride	15	17	+ 2
	Transit	80	78	− 2
	Other	3	4	+ 1
Metropolitan Life[1]	Drive alone	6	3	− 3
San Francisco	Shared ride	17	18	+ 1
	Transit	75	77	+ 2
	Other	2	2	0
California State Automobile Association[1]	Drive alone	—	—	− 3
San Francisco	Shared ride	—	—	+ 4
	Transit	—	—	− 2
Eight downtown[2]	Drive alone	24	14	− 10
Seattle firms	Shared ride	19	23	+ 5
	Transit	56	61	+ 5
	Other	1	1	0
State employees[3]	Drive alone	15	8	− 7
Boston	Shared ride	9	10	+ 1
	Transit	71	77	+ 6
State employees[4]	Drive alone	37	38	+ 1
Richmond	Shared ride	40	39	− 1
	Transit	17	17	0
Federal Energy Administration[5]	Drive alone	—	—	− 10
Seattle	Shared ride	—	—	+ 4
	Transit	—	—	+ 17
Transportation Systems Center[6]	Drive alone	—	—	− 3
Cambridge	Shared ride	—	—	+ 2
	Transit	—	—	+ 1

to ride sharing cited the ability to adjust schedules to ride with family members as an important factor in their decision to change.[30]

One unexpected and encouraging effect of flexitime on travel behavior was discovered among federal employees at the Transportation Systems Center in Cambridge, Massachusetts, and among state employees in Boston. Auto ownership declined, apparently as the result of increased opportunity for family members to travel together and enhanced public transportation options. Six percent of the federal employees changed the number of automobiles they owned, with most decreasing ownership.[31] Only one percent of the state employees acquired additional cars after going on flexitime, while 14 percent divested themselves of an automobile.[32]

Effects of Flexitime on Transit Efficiency

Does temporal dispersement of work schedules, improved traffic flows, and increased transit ridership brought about by flexitime combine to reduce the subsidies required to furnish public transportation? To date, conclusive evidence on the effects of flexitime on transit operating costs is not available in the American cities that have instituted area-wide flexitime programs. The experience of Ottawa, Canada, however, is encouraging.

Faced with the prospect of a major capital investment in additional buses, the city's transit commission secured federal government agreement to experiment with flexible hours as an alternative to purchase of rolling stock. After federal employees were placed on flexitime in 1974,

---

Sources:
[1]Frances Harrison, David Jones, and Paul Jovanis, *Flex-Time and Commuting Behavior in San Francisco: Some Preliminary Findings. Summary Report,* UCB-ITS-RR-79-12 (Berkeley, Calif.: University of California, Institute of Transportation Studies, 1979), pp. 10–11.

[2]Frances D. Harrison, Paul Jovanis, David Jones, and Jane Walczak, "Flexible Work Hours and Commuting Choices: Survey Results from Downtown Seattle" (Seattle: Seattle/King County Commuter Pool, 1980), p. 11.

[3]Association for Public Transportation, *The Variable Work Hours Program: Final Report,* prepared by Gordon Lewin for the Massachusetts Bay Transit Authority, pp. 19–20.

[4]Virginia Department of Highways and Transportation, Public Transportation Division, "The Impact of the State Employee Adjustable Work Schedule Program in the 'Capital Square' area of Richmond" (Richmond, Va.: Virginia Department of Highways and Transportation, 1979), p. 20.

[5]Quoted in Sharon M. Bronte, Draft Report on Variable Work Hours (Seattle: Commuter Pool, 1977), p. 42.

[6]Marian Ott, Howard Slavin, and Donald Ward, *The Behavioral Impacts of Flexible Working Hours.* Final Report. 600-446-437 (Washington, D.C.: Government Printing Office, 1980), p. 19.

peak half-hour ridership dropped 10 percent in the morning and 14 percent in the evening at the same time that *total* ridership increased 8 percent (by 7000 passengers). Growth in the number of commuters who traveled outside the peak period allowed the transit commission to lengthen the period over which peak-schedule frequency of buses could be operated, from 45 to 75 minutes in the morning and from 45 to 105 minutes in the evening. This lengthening of the peak-schedule period produced a 24 percent improvement in work-force utilization, since drivers who previously had been able to make only one trip per rush-hour period were now able to turn around and make one or two additional trips each morning and evening. Operator cost was reduced from 44 to 43 cents per mile, and the cost of adding an extra mile of service was reduced from 46 to 30 cents per mile. Reduced road congestion and passenger boarding time permitted a rescheduling of several routes and a reduction in the number of buses that had to be assigned to them.[33]

NOTES

1. U.S. Department of Transportation. *Energy Conservation in Transportation* (Washington, D.C.: U.S. Department of Transportation, Technology Sharing Office, 1979), p. ii.
2. The Urban Mass Transportation Administration and the Federal Highway Administration, in anticipation of a severe future gasoline shortage, have requested each region to develop an energy emergency contingency plan outlining realistic and practical courses of action that could be implemented within a two- to three-week period.

   All urban areas with populations greater than 50,000 are required by the U.S. Department of Transportation to develop a transportation system management plan that documents its strategies for improving air quality, conserving energy, and increasing the efficiency of the overall transportation system. Similar state implementation plans are mandated by the U.S. Environmental Protection Agency, pursuant to the Clean Air Act.
3. Fred A. Wagner and Keith Gilbert, *Transportation System Management: An Assessment of Impacts* (Washington, D.C.: U.S. Department of Transportation, 1978), p. 35.
4. Information for this case study is from:

   Sharon Bronte, *Draft Report on Variable Work Hours* (Seattle: Commuter Pool, 1977).
   Commuter Pool Progress Report (Seattle: Commuter Pool, n.d.).
   "Labor Letter," *Wall Street Journal,* 13 May 1980, p. 1.
   Correspondence and telephone interviews with Sharon Bronte, John Shadoff, and Candace Carlson of the program staff, between January 1978 and October 1980.
5. Frances D. Harrison, Paul Jovanis, David Jones, and Jane Walczak, "Flexible Work Hours and Commuting Choices: Survey Results from Downtown Seattle" (Seattle: Seattle/King County Commuter Pool, 1980), p. 7.
6. Data for this case study are from the following sources:

   "Downtown San Francisco Flex-Time Demonstration Project," Flextime Demonstration Project, San Francisco, n.d.
   David W. Jones, Jr., "Downtown San Francisco Flex-Time Demonstration Project: Pros-

pectus and Progress Report," Flex-Time Demonstration Project, San Francisco, October 1978.

David W. Jones, Jr., Frances D. Harrison, and Paul P. Jovanis, "Work Rescheduling and Traffic Relief: The Potential for Flex-Time," Public Affairs Report, Bulletin of the Institute of Governmental Studies, University of California at Berkeley, February 1980.

David W. Jones, Jr., Takuya Nakamoto, and Matthys P. Cilliers, *Flexible Work Hours: Implications for Travel Behavior and Transport Investment Policy,* PB-292 448 (Springfield, Va.: U.S. Department of Commerce, National Technical Information Services, 1978).

Paul P. Jovanis and Adolf May, *Flextime Travel: Research Framework and Preliminary Findings.* Working Papers UCB-ITS-WP-79-8 (Berkeley: University of California, Institute of Transportation Studies, 1979).

A series of telephone and personal interviews with David Jones, March 1980–October 1980.

7. Data for this case study are from the following sources:

Association for Public Transportation, *The Variable Work Hours Program: Final Report.* Prepared by Gordon Lewin for the Massachusetts Bay Transit Authority, June 1980.

Boston Area Variable Work Hours Project, *Conference Report 1978* (Boston: Greater Boston Chamber of Commerce, 1978).

Massachusetts Bay Transit Authority, *Spred-Sked: A Work Rescheduling Program for Boston* (Boston: Massachusetts Bay Transit Authority, 1977).

Personal participation in the Boston Area Variable Work Hours Project Conference.

Telephone interviews with Gordon Lewin of the Association for Public Transportation, from April 1978 to August 1980.

8. Data for this case study are from Mid-America Regional Council (MARC), *Transportation Energy Contingency Plan for the Kansas City Metropolitan Region* (Kansas City, Mo.: Mid-America Regional Council, 1980) and from correspondence and telephone interviews conducted from July 1980 to December 1980.

9. This information was compiled by the Mid-America Regional Council in April 1980 with data from the Bureau of Economic Analysis, U.S. Department of Commerce.

10. Port Authority of New York and New Jersey, *Staggered Work Hours Study, Phase 1: Final Report,* Federal Project No. IT-09-0023/34, TS No. A520 (New York: Port Authority of New York and New Jersey, 1977).

11. U.S. Congress, House of Representatives, Committee on Public Works and Transportation, *Mobility for Americans in an Era of Increasing Energy, Environmental, and Financial Constraints.* Hearings before the Subcommittee on Oversight and Review, 96th Congress, 2nd session, 1980.

12. John A. Bonsall, "Flexible Hours and Public Transit in Ottawa," a paper presented at the Annual Conference of the Roads and Transportation Association of Canada, Toronto, 23–26 September 1974, p. 11.

13. Toronto Variable Work Hours Project, *Variable Work Hours in Downtown Toronto* (Toronto, Canada: Metropolitan Toronto Planning Department, 1975).

14. Wagner and Gilbert, *Transportation System Management,* p. 107.

15. Virginia Department of Highways and Transportation, Public Transportation Division, *The Impact of the State Employee Adjustable Work Schedule Program in the "Capitol Square" Area of Richmond* (Richmond, Va.: Virginia Department of Highways and Transportation, 1979), pp. 5–6, 10, 14.

16. Jones, Harrison, and Jovanis, "Work Rescheduling and Traffic Relief: The Potential of Flex-Time," p. 2.

17. Port Authority of New York and New Jersey, *Staggered Work Hours Study,* pp. 11–12.

18. Anis A. Tannir and David T. Hartgen, "Traffic Impacts of Work! Schedule Changes in Medium-Sized Urban Areas," *Transportation Research Record,* no. 677, pp. 58–61.

19. Jones, Harrison, and Jovanis, *Work Scheduling and Traffic Relief.*
20. Harrison, Jovanis, Jones, and Walczak, "Flexible Work Hours and Commuting Choices," pp. 8–9.
21. Marian Ott, Howard Slavin, and Donald Ward. *The Behavioral Impacts of Flexible Working Hours.* Final Report. 600-446-437. (Washington, D.C.: U.S. Government Printing Office, 1980), p. 9.
22. Anis A. Tannir and David T. Hartgen, "Who Favors Work-Schedule Changes and Why," *Transportation Research Record,* no. 677, pp. 53–55.
23. Port Authority of New York and New Jersey, *Flexible Work Hours,* p. 11.
24. Ott, Slavin, and Ward. *The Behavioral Impacts of Flexible Working Hours,* p. 12.
25. Jovanis and May, *Flex-Time Travel,* pp. 61–79.
26. Wagner and Gilbert, *Transportation System Management,* p. 16.
27. Ott, Slavin, and Ward, *The Behavioral Impacts of Flexible Working Hours,* p. 12.
28. U.S. Geological Survey, *Comprehensive Report of a One-Year Experiment with Flexitime at the U.S. Geological Survey* (Reston, Va.: U.S. Geological Survey, Branch of Management Analysis, 1977), p. 42.
29. David W. Jones, Jr., Takuya Nakamoto, and Matthys P. Cilliers, *Flexible Work Hours: Implications for Travel Behavior and Transport Investment Policy,* PB-292 448 (Springfield, Va.: U.S. Department of Commerce, National Technical Information Services, 1978), p. 25.
30. Harrison, Jovanis, Jones, and Walczak, "Flexible Work Hours and Commuting Choices," p. 12.
31. Ott, Slavin, and Ward, *The Behavioral Impacts of Flexible Working Hours,* p. 19.
32. Association for Public Transportation, *The Variable Work Hours Program. Final Report,* p. 20.
33. Bonsall, "Flexible Hours and Public Transit in Ottawa," pp. 2, 12–21.

Appendix

DOCUMENT A-1. EXCERPTS FROM COMPRESSED WORKWEEK EXPERIMENT MANUAL, BOARD OF GOVERNORS, FEDERAL RESERVE SYSTEM

A. *Purpose of the Manual.*

This manual describes the provisions of the Board's Compressed Workweek Experiment. It provides guidelines and a general framework for the authorized six-month experimental program. The information contained in the manual answers some of the basic questions about the experiment; however, it does not cover every possible detail about the program. Some decisions will have to be made by supervisors and managers just as they are now in various situations.

B. *General Background.*

A six-month experiment with a compressed workweek will be conducted using the so-called 5/4–9 plan. Under the 5/4–9 plan, an employee who is approved to engage in the experiment will work a nine-and-one-half-hour day, inclusive of lunch, five days one week and four days the next or vice versa during a two-week period.

Some major features of the approved program are:

The Program Is an Experiment. The compressed workweek arrangement is not permanent and would not be made so unless and until data collected during the six-month experiment clearly demonstrate that operating efficiency is not reduced and that there are few, if any, abuses. The program is strictly experimental. The data to be collected and analyzed during the six-month period are for the purpose of measuring its effects. A report to the Board will be developed at the end of the experiment which will contain recommendations for its continuation or dissolution.

Program Participation Is Voluntary. Supervisors or managers may not require employees to work compressed workweek schedules.

Program Participation Is at the Discretion of Division Directors. Professional as well as nonprofessional staff members are permitted to experiment only to the extent that their work priorities in no way conflict with their work schedules. Strict work schedules are not required under a compressed workweek arrangement any more than existing work schedules are under the present traditional eight-hour/

five-day workweek. However, the demands of the job are paramount and all participants will continue to be held responsible for ensuring that participation in the program in no way diminishes their obligation to meet these demands. If time away from the job is not compatible with the Board's needs, then staff members would not be permitted to participate. In any case where results, timeliness, or safety are degraded as a result of participation, such participation may be immediately terminated by the participant's supervisor or division director. Of course, there may be some staff members who could not participate in the experiment because their job demands do not lend themselves to the program. Those decisions are to be made by each division director.

Participation May Take Various Forms. It is not required that participation be for the entire six-month period. Participation may be on an intermittent basis, permitting some individuals to go on and off the program as time constraints and work demands dictate. In all cases, participation must be for an entire pay period.

C. *Basic Work Requirement.*

The basic work requirement for a full-time employee is a nine-and-one-half-hour day inclusive of the lunch period (approximately 37 minutes long) but exclusive of breakfast and other nonwork activities. During a two-week pay period, nine of these basic workdays would be required. Starting times for participants may be as early as 7:30 A.M. and as late as 8:30 A.M. with commensurate departure times between 5:00 P.M. and 6:00 P.M. Starting times and departure times once set are to remain set as they are under the present gliding hours program. Individuals are not permitted to work more than the nine-and-one-half-hour workday for the purpose of varying the length of subsequent days within the pay period. In addition, individuals are not permitted to work more than nine of these workdays during a pay period nor on weekends, nor on holidays in order to reduce the number of days to be worked in a subsequent pay period. This in no way prohibits an employee from working overtime when required, but such work must be requested by the employee's supervisor.

In deciding which one of the ten normal working days an individual participant may take off, division management has the final authority and would be guided by job demands when these conflict with employee preferences. As in the case of starting and departure times, the day off may only be changed at very infrequent intervals.

D. *Sign-in/Sign-out Provisions.*

Individuals participating in the experiment will be required to sign-in/sign-out, using a new Board form designed for this purpose. Specifically, individuals will log in at the start of the workday, log out for any annual or sick leave taken during the course of the workday, log in on their return to work and log out at the end of the workday. The log sheets will be used to monitor the experiment and to analyze experimental data.*

*The sign-in/sign-out rule was eliminated at the six-month point of the experiment by majority vote of the 11 division directors; both workers and supervisors asked for it (76 percent of the supervisors said they did not need it).

E. *Premium Pay Provisions.*

Overtime Pay. Work requested and performed outside an employee's compressed work schedule *and* in excess of the nine-and-one-half-hour basic daily work requirement (lunch time included), or a biweekly work requirement of eighty hours (exclusive of lunches) is overtime work. An employee is entitled to overtime pay for overtime work. Compensatory leave may be requested by employees on compressed workweek schedules in lieu of overtime pay.

Night, Holiday, and Sunday Pay. An employee is entitled to night pay for regularly scheduled night work performed between the hours of 6:00 P.M. and 6:00 A.M. A full-time employee who performs nonovertime work on a holiday (or a day designated in lieu of a holiday) is entitled to premium pay. A full-time employee who performs nonovertime work during a period of service, a part of which is performed on Sunday, is entitled to premium pay for that period of work.

F. *Leave Accounting.*

When an employee is off for an entire day he/she is charged for nine hours of leave. For less than a full day off, the number of hours of leave charged will be the difference between nine hours and the number of hours the employee actually works (exclusive of any lunch period). If an employee is absent for an entire pay period, he/she is charged for eighty hours of the appropriate categories of leave.

Statutory provisions relating to sick, annual, and military leave and, in some cases, creditable service for retirement purposes, are framed in terms of "days," meaning eight hours. It is not the intent of the experiment either to decrease or increase any employee's existing entitlement to hours of leave or recreditable service for retirement purposes.

G. *Data Reporting.*

Because the Compressed Workweek Experiment must be evaluated, individuals participating will be requested to submit data of various types. These data will include (1) commuting time and energy usage before and after the 5/4–9 schedules, (2) sign-in/sign-out reporting to determine leave-time usage and days off, (3) a transition impact questionnaire to determine initial effects of the 5/4–9 schedule after four weeks of usage, (4) productivity measures that will be unique to each division, (5) a midpoint questionnaire after six months, and (6) an end of experiment questionnaire after one year.

H. *Miscellaneous Provisions.*

Limitations. The provisions outlined in this manual are applicable *only* to approved participants in the compressed workweek schedule experiment.

Official Office Hours. The official office hours of the Board will continue to be 8:45 A.M. to 5:15 P.M., Monday through Friday. Every organizational unit is responsible for providing coverage and services during these hours.

Suspension and Termination. If deemed necessary for operational reasons, participation in experimental compressed workweek schedules may be temporarily suspended or terminated by a unit, section, division, or the Board.

Employee Responsibility. Employees must accept any increased individual responsibility associated with compressed workweek schedules and must be willing to adjust their work schedules when necessary to meet job requirements.

Holidays. An employee working a compressed workweek schedule is entitled to nine hours pay with respect to each day designated as an official holiday.

Should the holiday fall on the employee's approved day off, employee will be excused the day before or after the holiday.

Source: Board of Governors, Federal Reserve System

DOCUMENT A-2. FLEXITIME PROVISIONS IN THE LABOR AGREEMENT BETWEEN COUNTY OF ALAMEDA AND LOCAL 21, INTERNATIONAL FEDERATION OF PROFESSIONAL AND TECHNICAL ENGINEERS

SECTION 6. HOURS OF WORK: SCHEDULES AND SHIFTS: REST PERIODS

a. HOURS OF WORK DEFINED. Hours worked, including all hours suffered to be worked, shall include all time not under the control of the employee whether such hours are worked in the County's workplace, or in some other place where the employee is carrying out the duties of the County.

b. PAY PERIOD. The normal pay period shall be 80 hours.

c. WORK SCHEDULES. Employees may work flexible daily work schedules provided that:

   1. A total of 80 hours is accumulated during the daily hours of 7:00 A.M. to 6:00 P.M. each normal pay period except that on the last official day of work of the pay period, time shall be accumulated between the hours of 7:00 A.M. to 5:00 P.M.

   2. Employees are present at their job assignment during the "core time" established by the Director of Public Works Agency. (9:30 A.M. to 11:30 A.M. and 1:30 P.M. to 3:30 P.M.).

   3. Employees are on the job when necessary to get the job done. And where the Agency determines that operating needs require hours of coverage other than those covered by core time, the employee will be required to work them.

d. Employees will not be required to adjust their present work schedule to hours which will be inconvenient or cause a hardship as long as they work an 80-hour pay period and meet the requirements of (c) above.

   Lunch breaks will be one-half hour minimum, with two hours maximum.

   Two paid breaks per day, not to exceed one-quarter hour in duration each, will be taken at times established by the Agency.

Credit, equal to the hours worked, will be granted for work before 7:00 A.M. and after 6:00 P.M. when it is undertaken at the request of the employee and with the permission of the immediate supervisor.

No debit or credit of time may be carried forward to the next time period.

On arrival and departure, employees are not to disturb other employees already or still at work.

Work away from the office will be credited as the number of hours appropriate to the individual circumstance and should be reported to the immediate supervisor.

Time off during core times in excess of the work breaks must be approved by the immediate supervisor.

Source: *Memorandum of Understanding*, International Federation of Professional and Technical Engineers, Local 21, and County of Alameda, 1979–1981.

DOCUMENT A-3. OVERTIME DEFINITION IN THE AGREEMENT BETWEEN COUNTY OF ALAMEDA AND LOCAL 21, INTERNATIONAL FEDERATION OF PROFESSIONAL AND TECHNICAL ENGINEERS

SECTION 7. OVERTIME

a. OVERTIME WORK DEFINED. Overtime work is all work performed pursuant to Section 6, paragraph a, in excess of the pay period set forth in Section 6, paragraph b. Holidays and paid time off shall count toward the accumulation of the pay period.

b. OVERTIME WORK IN FLEXTIME SCHEDULE DEFINED. Time worked will only be classified as overtime in a flexible schedule where:

1. It is authorized by the supervisor.

2. It is in excess of 80 hours in any pay period.

3. It involves the employee in arriving before or staying after the times at which he would normally start or finish work. For purposes of establishing normal starting and finishing time for overtime determination, an employee may be required by his immediate supervisor to submit a tentative schedule of his weekly attendance. The tentative schedule is only an understanding between the employee and his supervisor and does not bind the employee to adhere to it.

c. HOW OVERTIME IS AUTHORIZED. Work for the County by an employee at times other than those so scheduled shall be approved in advance by the department head or the department head's designated representative or, in cases of unanticipated emergency, shall be approved by the department head or the department head's designated representative after such emergency work is performed. No employee shall receive compensation for overtime in cash, in time off, or a combination thereof unless such overtime work has been approved in writing by the department head or the department head's designated representative, as set forth herein.

d. OVERTIME COMPENSATION. All employees shall receive overtime compensation in cash, in compensating time off, or a combination thereof at the option of the department head.

e. RATE OF OVERTIME COMPENSATION. All employees shall receive overtime compensation at a premium rate of one and one-half times the regular straight-time hourly rate. Compensation will be made pursuant to paragraph c above. For the purpose of overtime, compensation shall include the certification rate. If overtime compensation is compensating time off, compensating time off will be accumulated at the rate of one and one-half hours for each hour worked.

Source: *Memorandum of Understanding*, International Federation of Professional and Technical Engineers, Local 21, and County of Alameda, 1979–1981.

DOCUMENT A-4. EMPLOYEE FLEXITIME AGREEMENT AT GROUP HEALTH COOPERATIVE

EMPLOYEE AGREEMENT

As an employee of Group Health Cooperative working under the flextime scheduling system, I understand and agree with the following:

The Office and Professional Employees Union Local 8 has given approval to waive the eight (8) hours per day contract stipulation for those employees participating in flextime scheduling.

My paycheck will be calculated on the total number of hours worked in a seven (7) day work period (from Saturday through the following Friday) regardless of the number of hours worked in any one day. I will be expected to work forty (40) hours (which includes two 15-minute rest periods per day) during this period. Overtime payment for hours in excess of forty (40) in any one-week period must have prior supervisor authorization.

My responsibility will be to account for and record on my timecard at least a total of forty (40) hours for each work period. For the hours worked, I have the personal option either to record the exact number of hours worked each day or the daily average number of hours worked during the week (i.e., eight hours a day). If the total hours worked during the week period are less than forty, the remaining hours must be accounted for on the timecard as either sick leave, vacation, or leave without pay. If I take sick leave or vacation time off, then I may work only the number of hours remaining in the week period, which brings the total number of hours to forty (40). Reporting over forty (40) hours per week period must have prior supervisor authorization.

If my supervisor has approved overtime (over 40 hours in the week period) then I will be responsible for accounting for and recording on my timecard the total number of overtime hours worked in the week period.

As I will be paid only for the total hours worked (including sick leave and vacation) each week, my supervisor will only be responsible for verifying on my timecard this total number of hours worked each week.

Signed _____   Date _____

Signature of this Agreement indicates that I am a participant in the Flextime Program and that I have read and understood the above provisions.

Source: Group Health Cooperative internal documents

DOCUMENT A-5. LABOR AGREEMENT ON PART-TIME EMPLOYMENT BETWEEN THE COUNTY OF SANTA CLARA AND LOCAL 715, SERVICE EMPLOYEES INTERNATIONAL UNION

Section 7.4–Part-Time Salaries

a) *Salary Ranges*
The salary ranges provided in the attached appendices are for full-time service in full-time positions, and are expressed in dollars per the number of working days in a biweekly pay period. If any position is established on any other time basis, the compensation for such position shall be adjusted proportionately.

b) *Benefits*
Workers filling part-time positions of half time or more shall receive all other benefits of this Agreement.

c) *Split Codes*
The County shall provide a minimum of two hundred (200) full-time codes to be filled on a half-time basis at any one time. The location and choice of these codes will be determined on a departmental basis. Requests for split codes shall not unreasonably be denied. Reasonable denial shall include, but not be limited to, demonstration that the work is not divisible, demonstration that qualified partners, if needed, are not available, or that the two hundred (200) available codes are filled. Workers shall make a written request for a split code to their immediate supervisor. If the request is denied, it shall be reviewed by their department head and they shall receive a written response. If the worker is not satisfied with the decision of the department head, the worker, through the Union, may proceed in the manner listed in Article 8.3 of this Agreement.

Source: Agreement between County of Santa Clara and Local 715, Service Employees International Union, AFL–CIO, July 1979–June 1981.

DOCUMENT A-6. EXAMPLES OF CONTRACT LANGUAGE FOR TRAINING PROGRAMS, SANTA CLARA COUNTY

General Maintenance Mechanic Training

A maximum of eight (8) General Maintenance Mechanic II's shall be alternately staffed with General Maintenance Mechanic I's at a salary range ten percent (10%) below the Maintenance Mechanic II rate. The Maintenance Mechanic I classification shall be an entry-level classification in this series with demonstrated mechanical aptitude required.

The County shall provide on-the-job work-related training to enrollees. Workers participating in this program will, in addition to the on-the-job training, enroll in and successfully complete a series of educational courses designated by GSA-Building Operations Division Management. . . .

Park Maintenance Worker Training

During the term of this Agreement ten (10) County workers, determined by application review and interview, shall be selected to work in Park Maintenance Worker trainee positions. The salary for these positions shall be five percent (5%) below the first step of Park Maintenance Worker I. Participants shall be assigned to a work location on the basis of seniority preference within the group. Assignment to the positions shall be for four (4) pay periods at one (1) of two (2) park locations to be determined by Management. Following an initial sign-up period, the scheduling of assignments shall be made with due consideration to worker preference and department needs. Temporary work location pay (Section 8.11) shall not apply to work at that location. Such workers shall not schedule vacations during this period. Workers shall consider this a regular work assignment except where a return to their former assignment is required because of an emergency or unsatisfactory progress.

Source: Agreement between County of Santa Clara and Local 715, Service Employees International Union, AFL–CIO, July 1979–June 1981, pp. 106–108.

DOCUMENT A-7. SEPTEMBER–DECEMBER 1980 PARTNERSHIP AGREEMENT UNITED AIRLINES PARTNERSHIP TIME OFF PROGRAM

We have read the information explaining the Partnership Time Off Program. We agree to be Partners. As Partners, we will be responsible for our awarded schedule subject to the contractual provisions of the 1980–82 Flight Attendant Agreement.

We understand that the Company is responsible for the administration of the program. We also understand that so long as the Company distributes our pay in accordance with our instructions (or 50% to each if no instructions are given), and that so long as the Company properly administers other aspects of the program, the Company shall have no liability for any disputes that arise between us.

By the 12th of each month, we will tell the Company how our pay will be allocated, e.g., 50/50, 40/60, and, if necessary, whose sick-leave bank will be used. If we fail to notify the Company concerning the above, the pay will be issued 50/50 to each partner; however, the senior partner's sick-leave bank will be used.

If there is time loss during the month due to an occupational illness or injury, it will be paid to the partner who is ill or injured.

_____   _____

Signature—Senior Partner   Signature—Junior Partner

_____   _____

File No.   File No.

DOCUMENT A-8. ILLUSTRATION OF HUMAN-RESOURCE PLANNING PROCESS FOR CONTROL DATA CORPORATION

Macro-issue	Company Goals	Strategic Objectives	Programs
Job security for employees	Guarantee employment to workers who give sustained satisfactory performance	Spread the impact of economic downturn before it centers on permanent employees	Use employment buffers: –work sharing –temporary employees –overtime before new hiring –contracted outside work –variable hours for permanent part-timers
		Build assessments of risk to the work force into the business plan	Establish an early warning system for changes in company employment levels Retrain workers whose skills become obsolete instead of laying them off
Effective use of human resources	Achieve human resource needs via: –planning –recruiting –development –balancing	Use creative nontraditional means of staffing	Use job sharing to increase the quality of the work force Change managers' stereotypes about job sharing and part-time employment

Effects of energy costs and shortages	Minimize the negative effects of energy costs on the company and its employees	Determine the effects of reduced use and increased costs of energy on the organization and jobs	Establish a placement program for displaced, outplaced, and misplaced workers
			Use performance appraisals as a communications vehicle
			Adopt homework (work performed by employees without offices who work at home)
	Provide opportunities to significantly reduce energy usage		Develop managers who can manage dispersed organizations (including homework and project teams not located together)
			Encourage use of car and van pools and mass transit
			Expand use of alternative work schedules

Source: Control Data Corporation internal document

DOCUMENT A-9. GENERAL MOTORS CORPORATION

Date: March 19, 1979

Subject: Flextime Administrative Guidelines

To: General Managers of Divisions
   Presidents of Subsidiaries
   Personnel Directors
   Central Office Staff Heads

"Flextime" within General Motors may be defined as any program in which employes work a five-day schedule but have a measure of choice in determining the schedule of their daily working hours. . . .

In the implementation of a flextime program, it is necessary that productivity, work flow, and required levels of service be maintained. The experience of units with established programs indicates that flextime can be expected to have a positive impact on employe morale and job satisfaction, which, in turn, may reduce absenteeism, tardiness, and overtime.

The most effective programs have been designed to improve the quality of work life of salaried employes by providing them with greater latitude and flexibility in the establishment of their work schedules. The most significant impact on employe attitudes has been noted in those instances in which the employes themselves are included in the design of the flextime schedule. For a program to be successful, it is essential that an atmosphere of trust and cooperation exist among employes as well as between employes and their supervisors.

It is generally appropriate to initiate a program on a trial basis for several months in order to provide management and the employes involved with an opportunity to evaluate its design and effectiveness. . . .

Departments desiring to initiate flextime programs must submit them in writing to the divisional personnel department for approval. In order to assure that consistent application is present within a division, it is recommended that a personnel representative be responsible for monitoring the development and implementation of flextime programs.

Source: General Motors Corporation internal document

DOCUMENT A-10.   FLEXITIME POLICY GUIDELINES

Based on experience with successful flextime programs in General Motors, the following provisions should be included in any such program being developed. Provision 12 is an option which can be considered when implementing or modifying an existing flextime program.

PROVISION	EXPLANATION
1. Terms and conditions of the flextime program should be printed and made available to all employes affected by the program.	In order to avoid confusion on the part of employes and inconsistent application on the part of supervisors, the provisions of any flextime program, after being approved by the divisional personnel deparment, should be clearly communicated to those employes covered by the program.
2. Flextime must be prescheduled.	Individual employes and their supervisors must mutually agree on the work schedule in advance of it being placed into effect. The period of time covered by the schedule should normally be one week; however, this may vary depending on the needs of the activity involved. Deviations from the established schedule must be approved by the employe's supervisor.
3. Participating employes should be scheduled for an 8-hour day, 5 days per week (Monday through Friday) unless a banking-of-hours provision is adopted. Specific starting and stopping times are to be determined by the operating location.	The resulting effect of this provision is that the shift hours within a workday may be staggered to accommodate the needs of individual employes. Holiday, vacation, and supplemental time-off days should be considered as 8 hours. One-half day for vacation or supplemental time off should be considered as four hours. Participating employes are required to sign a waiver ... in those instances when flextime scheduling results in starting times which under GM Policy would require the payment of night-shift premiums. The completed waiver forms should be retained by the unit's Salary Payroll Department.
4. Hours worked in excess of 8 hours per day or 40 hours per week at the request of management are considered as overtime hours.	Affected employes will be compensated in accordance with the provisions of Section 1600 of the Salaried Policy and Procedure Manual.
5. Employes must take at least a 30-minute lunch period when working more than five hours per day.	These flextime guidelines are not intended to establish paid lunch periods.

PROVISION	*EXPLANATION*
	Extended lunch periods are permissible in accordance with locally established procedures.
6. Supervisors are responsible for departmental coverage.	Supervisors must have control over and responsibility for flextime schedules of individuals under their jurisdiction. In addition, supervisors should be responsible for assuring that adequate departmental coverage exists during normal working hours in order to preclude any deterioration of service.
7. A core time must be established.	In order to assure that adequate job coverage exists during prime working hours, a mandatory period of time during the workday (core time) must be established. Divisions which have more than one flextime program are not required to have the same core time for each program. All employes scheduled for work are expected to be available during whatever period is designated. For example, all employes could be scheduled to work between the hours of 10 A.M. and 2 P.M., or for any other designated period required by the needs of the organization.
8. Employe participation should be strictly voluntary.	Consistent with the quality-of-work-life concept, employes desiring not to avail themselves of nontraditional starting and stopping times should not be required to do so.
9. Opportunity to participate should be consistently applied.	To the extent possible, all employes within a work group should be afforded the same opportunity to participate.
10. Personal time off should be administered in accordance with existing policy.	Employes who need personal time off (excused absence with pay) which is not accommodated through flextime scheduling, may be permitted the time off with pay based upon individual circumstances and prior supervisory approval.
11. Flextime programs should be reviewed periodically to determine their effectiveness.	If productivity, work flow, and required levels of service are not maintained, it may be necessary to modify the programs or resume traditional schedules.

PROVISION   *EXPLANATION*

In addition, participation in the flex-
time program may be withdrawn from
an individual employe for misuse of the
program.

Participating employes desiring to with-
draw from the program should advise
their supervisors and be allowed to
work the regularly scheduled hours
established by management.

12. Banking of hours within the workweek   Banking of hours permits participating
    is permissible.   employes to carry over hours from
                                            one day to the next within a work-
                                            week (Monday through Friday).
                                            Employes may draw on hours only
                                            after they have been accumulated in
                                            the bank.

These guidelines are not intended to permit employes utilizing a banking of
hours provision to carry over hours
from one week to the next.

Since GM Salaried Policy provides for
the payment of overtime for hours
worked beyond 8 in a day and 40 in a
week, a waiver (see Attachment B)
must be secured from participating
employes involved in a banking provision. Once executed, this form should
be retained by the unit's Salary Payroll
Department.

Hours worked at the request of management in excess of those scheduled as
part of the flextime program are considered as overtime hours. In lieu of
pay, employes may be permitted to
bank these hours unless they occur on
Friday in which case overtime pay will
be required.

When a banking provision is used,
employes should not be permitted to
work in excess of 12 hours on any given
day in order to accumulate hours. Conversely, employes must work a minimum number of hours (the established
core hours) on Monday through Friday
of each week.

PROVISION	*EXPLANATION*
	If a banking provision is implemented, management should assure that scheduling does not conflict with the core time.

P.A.D. Staff, Detroit
March 1979

Source: General Motors Corporation internal document

DOCUMENT A-11. GENERAL MOTORS CORPORATION
FLEXTIME WAIVER OF ELIGIBILITY

As a General Motors employe participating in an approved flextime program on a voluntary basis, I certify that I understand and agree with the following provisions:

1. Night-shift premium will not be applied to hours I have elected to work under an approved flextime program.

2. Overtime compensation will not be applied to hours I have elected to work in excess of eight hours per day in order to utilize flextime.

3. This waiver will remain in effect until terminated at my request.

_____
Date

_____
Signature of Participating Employe

_____
Date

_____
Signature of Supervisor

Source: General Motors Corporation internal document

DOCUMENT A-12. FLEXITIME PROPOSAL, ABC CORPORATION

ASSUMPTIONS: 1. 5-day, 40-hour workweek
2. 45-minute lunch

POPULATION: All exempt and nonexempt employees at Headquarters.

GENERAL RULE: Flexitime will apply to all Divisions and General Corporate Departments except for Building Services, where some services must be supplied continually, as for example, security.

Any other exceptions require review and approval.

Each work unit will establish individual work schedules to meet the needs of the respective businesses.

Flexible Starting Time	Core Time (45 min. lunch)	Flexible Quitting Time
7:00 A.M. 9:00 A.M.		3:45 P.M. 5:45 P.M.

Flexible starting time spans the hours of 7:00 A.M. to 9:00 A.M. As depicted, the 9:00 A.M. to 3:45 P.M. period is the time when all employees are to be at work (excluding a 45-minute lunch break), and flexible quitting time spans the hours of 3:45 P.M. to 5:45 P.M. Quitting time is determined by starting time. For example, employees starting at 7:00 A.M. can leave at 3:45 P.M. Employees starting at 9:00 A.M. can leave at 5:45 P.M.

The proposal does not offer the following options, although they are alternatives:

1. Midday flexibility options (flexible lunch).

2. Working more or less than the normal workday for the purpose of crediting or debiting work hours.

Recordkeeping:

• Nonexempts will complete a wage-and-hour sheet to comply with the Fair Labor Standards Act (existing practice).

• Exempts honor system (existing practice).

All employees are required to give one-week prior notice of reporting time.

Source: ABC Corporation internal document

DOCUMENT A-13. PERSONNEL DEPARTMENT PRESENTATION OF FLEXITIME TO TOP MANAGEMENT, CORNING GLASS WORKS, SULLIVAN PARK RESEARCH AND DEVELOPMENT FACILITY

Our mission is to help bring about improvement in productivity—a lofty but difficult goal to measure. . . . We have to make sure that we are organized in such a way that we make best use of our resources. People are a resource. How can people contribute best? How can they be most productive? There is no easy recipe to apply to all people across all situations. Look at some of the things we do.

• People need to know what is expected of them. So we give them direction by defining objectives, tasks, responsibilities, and results needed.

- We need to know whether the job is getting done. So we review performance; we look at results and compare them to assignments.

- People need to know what they can expect from the company. So we review people's salary and promotional status and we review career and training possibilities and make plans. . . .

These are part of the nuts and bolts of managing. We are accustomed to juggling variables that affect the contributions that people can make—variables important to productivity.

There's another variable about which we have so far done very little. That's time—the time over which human energy is applied. We know a lot about the dynamics of heat and therefore can use it effectively. We have a whole discipline called thermodynamics but we are nowhere close to anything similar for human energy . . . We seem to be stuck with following a calendar of 8 A.M. to 5 P.M., five days a week. Is that the best way to use human energy? . . . We do it for historical reasons, by habit. That may be just fine. On the other hand, maybe we can do better. What we are proposing is that we try being flexible about the time over which we apply human energy. There appear to be positive effects on productivity for these reasons:

- More hours of actual work—because of the actual reduction in paid absences (personal time, doctor's visits, and even idle time).

- Improvement in the organization of work—we can concentrate telephone work and interaction times to core periods, leaving the front and back of the day for thinking time.

- There is a biological clock—some people work better earlier, and others later.

- We can accommodate a better relationship between personal time and interests and time at work.

- This encourages employees to take responsibility for themselves; it helps the manager to spend his time facilitating rather than controlling.

But there are some effects that could go either way, that is, contribute or detract:

- Communications—if everybody is not present at all times, you might not be here when you are needed by somebody else. Then again, work organization may be improved.

- Overhead costs—longer hours of operation may create higher utility costs. But if you end up getting more done, these costs could be offset.

- There may be inequity—some people, e.g., a receptionist, might have to be at work regular hours and could not be eligible for a flexible schedule.

- Supervisors' time—you may think you have to spend more time because you have to control. On the other hand, it may be that you just have to spend your time differently, not spend more of it.

Source: Corning Glass Works internal document

DOCUMENT A-14. FLEXITIME GUIDELINES FOR SALARIED EMPLOYEES CORNING GLASS WORKS, SULLIVAN PARK RESEARCH AND DEVELOPMENT FACILITY

The laboratory is initiating a test of the applicability of Flex-Time in three Sullivan Park departments. A test period of 120 days will begin in July 1980, after which an assessment will be made to determine the future of the program.

In brief, Flex-Time allows the employee to vary his/her working hours, within certain limitations, to better accommodate personal needs and desires.

The "key" to having Flex-Time work successfully is an environment of trust, integrity, and honesty on the part of all employees. It is felt that such an environment exists here at Sullivan Park and thus permits the adoption of this plan.

It should be emphasized that the election to use Flex-Time is a voluntary personal decision for each eligible employee. However, it should also be understood that there are certain jobs where Flex-Time cannot be applied due to the particular nature and requirements of that task. Each Department Manager will establish such additional departmental ground rules as are necessary to assure employee safety as well as continued efficient and effective departmental operations.

The general guidelines for the operation of Flex-Time are as follows:

Normal Lab Hours. The "normal" Sullivan Park workday will remain 8 A.M.–5 P.M. All Lab activities must be operational during these hours.

Work Days. The normal work days are Monday–Friday.

Core Hours. All employees must be present during the "core hours" of 10 A.M.–12:00 noon, Monday through Friday.

Starting and Quitting Time. This will vary according to your schedule, but you must be here during core hours—so your starting time won't be later than 10:00 A.M.

Lunch Period. The minimum unpaid lunch period is one-half hour every day that you work at least 6 hours.

Length of Workday. Because you must be at work during core hours, your shortest day can be 2 hours. The policy will also be that you cannot work more than 12 hours per day.

Length of Workweek. The workweek is 40 hours. Employees may borrow up to six (6) hours any one day. However, hours accumulated or owed must be zeroed by the end of the week.

Overtime. Overtime will be paid to eligible employees for hours in excess of 40 hours per week and requires prior approval of supervision in accordance with past practice.

Scheduling. Flex-Time weekly schedules must be submitted by each employee to the supervisor at least two (2) full days prior to the scheduled period. Deviations from the schedule are permitted with the approval of the supervisor.

Personal Time Off. It is not intended that previously granted privileges for necessary excused absences be withdrawn with the adoption of Flex-Time. However, the purpose of Flex-Time is to permit each employee to adjust his/her working schedule to accommodate personal needs and wishes. Thus, in the spirit of this program, employees are expected to utilize excused absences in a reasonable and fair manner.

Holidays, Vacation Days, and Absences. Holidays, vacations, and absences may not exceed eight (8) hours per day.

Department Activities. Flex-Time shall be adjusted by the employee to ensure attendance at scheduled meetings and other activities when requested by Departmental management.

Program Participation. The privileges of a flexible schedule may be withdrawn from those who fail to adhere to the guidelines and principles that have been established.

Source: Corning Glass Works Consumer Products Development Department

Index

Index

cc

HD   Nollen, Stanley D.
5109
.N64   New work schedules
       in practice

DATE			